KV-144-468

Crime and Punishment in Contemporary Culture

Today, questions about how and why societies punish are deeply emotive and hotly contested. In *Crime and Punishment in Contemporary Culture*, Claire Valier argues that criminal justice is a key site for the negotiation of identities and modes of belonging. Exploring both popular cultural forms and changes in crime policies and criminal law, Valier elaborates new forms of critical engagement with the politics of crime and punishment. In doing so, the book discusses:

- Teletechnologies, punishment and new collectivities.
- The cultural politics of victims rights.
- Discourses on foreigners, crime and diaspora.
- Terror, the death penalty and the spectacle of violence.

Crime and Punishment in Contemporary Culture makes a timely and important contribution to debate on the possibilities of justice in the media age.

Claire Valier is Lecturer in Law at the University of London and a graduate of Queens' College, Cambridge. Her other works include *Theories of Crime and Punishment* (2001).

International Library of Sociology
Founded by Karl Mannheim
Editor: John Urry
Lancaster University

Crime and Punishment in Contemporary Culture

Claire Valier

Routledge
Taylor & Francis Group

LONDON AND NEW YORK

First published 2004
by Routledge
2 Park Square, Milton Park, Abingdon, Oxon, OX14 4RN

Simultaneously published in the USA and Canada
by Routledge
270 Madison Ave, New York, NY 10016

Transferred to Digital Printing 2004

Routledge is an imprint of the Taylor & Francis Group

© 2004 Claire Valier

Typeset in Times New Roman by
Keystroke, Jacaranda Lodge, Wolverhampton
Printed and bound in Great Britain by
TJI Digital, Padstow, Cornwall

All rights reserved. No part of this book may be reprinted or
reproduced or utilised in any form or by any electronic,
mechanical, or other means, now known or hereafter
invented, including photocopying and recording, or in any
information storage or retrieval system, without permission in
writing from the publishers.

British Library Cataloguing in Publication Data
A catalogue record for this book is available from the British Library

Library of Congress Cataloging in Publication Data
A catalog record for this book has been requested

ISBN 0–415–28175–X

BLACKBURN COLLEGE
LIBRARY
Acc.No. BB01313
HSC ClassNo. 364 VAL
Date. Feb '05

Contents

Acknowledgements

This book arises from discussions with colleagues, students and friends, as much as from the reading of texts. I owe a debt of gratitude to a number of individuals who have read and commented upon my work, and opened up spaces in which to speak and write. In particular these have included Ronnie Lippens, John Urry, Derek McGhee, Elena Loizidou, Les Moran, David Garland, Alison Young, Tony Jefferson, Richard Sparks, Beverley Brown, Geoff Pearson, Keith Hayward, Wayne Morrison, Robert Reiner, Richard Jones and Simon Hallsworth.

My work has benefited immeasurably from the hospitality of a number of institutions. I would particularly like to thank some people in Cambridge for providing an exceptionally convivial milieu for scholarship. Queens' College, Cambridge, was home for many years. I would like to express my gratitude to the President and Fellows for the award of my Munro Scholarships, which provided great rooms and tuck, as well as the company of kindly colleagues like Stewart Sage, Jackie Scott, Peter Spufford, John Eatwell, Stuart Bridge, and Brendan Bradshaw. The Institute of Criminology was the locus of my doctoral research and my first ventures in lecturing. I would like to thank all there, and in particular Loraine Gelsthorpe and Anthony Bottoms, who have offered considerable support and inspiration over the years. The Radzinowicz Library and Helen Krarup continue to provide a welcoming place of study, for which I am truly grateful.

A number of institutions have generously awarded me scholarships, research grants, and bursaries. I would like to thank the committees and administrators of the following bodies: the University of Cambridge, the Economic and Social Research Council, the British Academy, the British Society of Criminology, the Leverhulme Trust, and the Law Society. Earlier versions of chapters 1, 3 and 6 were published in the *British Journal of Criminology* and *Theoretical Criminology*. I would like to thank the publishers of these journals, their editors and reviewers.

My friends and family have been a constant source of pleasure and support over the years. I would like to thank and to salute: Teddy McCollom, Kat Astley, Harriet Neuberger, David Hugh-Jones, Alexander Wedderburn, Lavinia Mitton, Orlando Sayer, Elizabeth Kendal, Bryony Worthington, Louise Watson, Gabrielle Hinsliff, Rupert Thompson, Clare Hayward, Guillaume Metayer, and Kit McCormick. The greatest thanks are due to my family, and to Annabel.

Introduction
Punishment, culture and communication

> He stands, staring down the curve of closed doors, while a fear he knows to be irrational begins to nibble at his belly. A few months ago a fourteen-year-old girl was thrown from a train by some yob who hadn't got anywhere when he tried to chat her up. Miranda's thirteen. This is all rubbish, he knows that. But then, like everybody else, he lives in the shadow of monstrosities. Peter Sutcliffe's bearded face, the number plate of a house in Cromwell Street, three figures smudged on a video surveillance screen, an older boy taking a toddler by the hand while his companion strides ahead, eager for the atrocity to come.
>
> (Barker 1998: 3)

The crime control and penal practices of today unfold in the shadow of monstrosities. On the television, computer or cinema screen, staring out from the cover of the newspaper, and from shelf upon shelf of true crime books and magazines, there they are, the face of the Yorkshire Ripper, the 'House of Horrors' where at least nine young women were killed, the CCTV footage of James Bulger's abduction from a busy shopping mall. These shadowy and macabre images menace a man late to collect his daughter from a railway station. Fearful for her safety, he imagines the horrors of injury and murder evoked by certain remembered images. Images connected with notorious crimes, it seems, become inseparable from the attributed meanings of crime and punishment, and central to their symbolic power. Pictures like these include the faces of murdered children like Megan Kanka, Polly Klaas and Sarah Payne, smiling out from family album snapshots. They live on in memorial legislation, with over fifty US laws in recent years named for children who were victims of violence. Other images bring into the home within minutes, or in real time, the scenes of grave bodily trauma, mental anguish and devastation from the distant site of a terrorist attack. These big news crimes become image events.

Above and beyond their documentary worth as evidence, the CCTV footage and amateur video that, we are told, increasingly reconstitutes public space as a technologized scanscape, strikes us with a deep resonance. One might mention here the tape of the Rodney King beating, the live footage of OJ fleeing in his Bronco, pursued by both police and television helicopters, or the videoed 'execution' of Daniel Pearl. Hours of footage from inside the courtroom can now be watched, confronting viewers with scenes like those of Louise Woodward crying when her murder verdict was read. Then there are the mug-shots, the plaintive faces of the 'Bulger killers', terrified young boys subjected to the ultimate in vengeful fury. Who can forget the face of Myra Hindley, dubbed by the tabloids, 'the icon of evil'? Images connected with some crimes are circulated globally. As I write this text, the snapshot of Holly and Jessica wearing matching Manchester United shirts, taken hours before their abduction, is shown on televisions and published in the newspapers. The *Sun*'s headline reads 'WORLD WEEPS WITH SOHAM.' The article tells readers that thousands across the globe have been leaving messages of shock and grief on the town's website. The *Mirror*'s headline reads, 'WORLD WIDE TEARS', and reports that within days 16,500 people from all over the world had posted messages on an internet book of condolence set up by the County Council. There is, the article informs, no country untouched by the Soham tragedy (*Sun*, 19 August 2002, *Daily Mirror*, 21 August 2002). Both newspapers demand the return of the death penalty.

Each of the images described above, in its own way, dramatizes a connection between penal practices and mediated visibility. Furthermore, these striking and repeatedly displayed images demonstrate the importance of studying the relations between punishment, culture and communication. It is the object of this book to tease out some connections between the teletechnologies, those technologies of the afar, and the passions of punishment. The need to undertake work of this kind is rendered all the more pressing given the major trans-formations in communication technologies that have transpired over the last two centuries. It is time to look into the changing textual, rhetorical and pictorial practices through which penal practices draw the imaginative engagement of multiple viewing and reading publics. We now inhabit societies called 'pictophagic' and 'iconocentric'. This calls for scrutiny of what Peter Goodrich (2001) terms 'law in the videosphere', addressing the increasing prominence of visual media within crimino-legal practices. We need to survey the images, the at times global televisual and cyberspatial enactments within which punishment is carried out. In addition to charting the visual culture with which penality is tied up, this book addresses the impact of changes to the modes of information. Communication takes on new and distinctive forms in a time when large volumes of superficial information are rapidly and continuously circulated. Furthermore, technologies like mobile phones and the internet make imagined co-presence more possible with people who are thousands of miles away. These changing communicational practices have far-reaching implications for the pro-cesses through which collectivities are engaged. They hence have ramifications in terms of how the passions of punishment are to be understood.

Crime and Punishment in Contemporary Culture outlines a vocabulary and approach through which we might be able to comprehend the changing forms taken by punitive cultures. The point is not to produce a fully comprehensive and authoritative description of all facets of the contemporary scene, nor to present another general explanation of punishment. Instead, I develop a set of theoretical tools which may facilitate critical analysis of the striking features of punitive cultures, elucidating practices which I consider inadequately addressed in the extant literature. Although a range of punitive practices are seen in many countries at present, this book argues that distinctive punitive cultures emerge in different countries at specific historical moments. The chapters examine in some detail several of these national and historically specific punitive cultures, most notably in the USA, Canada, the UK, France and Australia. However, the analysis also addresses the significance of transnational flows of images and ideas. These make crime debate and penal practices increasingly matters that develop both within and beyond the traditional confines of the nation-state.

A punitive culture is a historically and geographically specific set of practices through which a retributive and vengeful penality is performed. This is a matter of performance because modern republics, unions and constitutional monarchies are democratic states which punish in the name of their people. Different modes of display are employed, which seek to recruit individuals as subjects of the punitive state. However, a punitive culture does not produce a singular and univocal viewing and reading public. The analysis in this book notes both the dominant aesthetic of mainstream public culture and a range of counter-aesthetics, which emerge through critical interventions of various kinds. Let us pause for a moment to consider what I mean by the dominant aesthetic of mainstream public culture. One feature of this aesthetic is the rhetoric of spin, with its catchy soundbites, and the associated prominence in public discourse of dramatic and memorable images. Crime talk is a staple of spin, which is ill understood as a matter of ideological distortion, for it is constitutive of a new political style. It indexes the changing nature of both politics and public life more generally brought by mediated visibility (Thompson 2000). Having said that over the last few decades crime and punishment have become politicized, scholars must now go further to describe the visual culture within which the penal and electoral politics are entwined.

Reflecting upon manifesto images of parlimantary candidates, Roland Barthes (1957/1993: 91) wrote 'photography has a power to convert which must be analysed'. The use of images of crime victims and their relatives in political campaigning is one key instance of this 'power to convert'. The father of Polly Klaas appeared in Bill Clinton's electoral television adverts. Polly was a twelve-year-old girl, kidnapped and murdered in California, and named by the press 'America's Child'. Her father became widely known as an anti-crime activist and took a vocal place in the securing of draconian 'three strikes and you're out' sentencing for repeat violent offenders. Klaas made frequent appearances on talk shows, held high-profile meetings with politicians, and gave testimony to a House of Representatives committee on crime. In the Clinton campaign adverts he appeared saying,

> My daughter Polly was only twelve years old. She had her whole life in front of her. But a criminal who shouldn't have been out on parole

kidnapped her and took it all away. President Clinton forced Congress to pass his tough crime bill: life in prison for dangerous repeat offenders and an expanded death penalty. I hear people question the President's character and integrity. It's just politics. When it came to protecting children the President had the courage to make a difference.

Images in the advert juxtapose a photograph of Polly in which she seems to have a pose of vulnerability with footage of cell doors slamming and gavels being banged. This is followed by scenes showing the President marching down the granite steps of an official building, flanked by uniformed police officers. The aesthetic of dominant culture simultaneously recruits punitive subjects and constructs privileged viewing positions through which individuals are addressed as vengeful victim-citizens. In the advert, images and phrases that evoke harsh crime measures secure an image of worthy personal qualities. Masculine leadership is associated with protecting the familial through excluding and killing. Barthes (1957/1993: 91–2) writes that

> the use of electoral photography presupposes a kind of complicity: a photograph is a mirror, what we are asked to read is the familiar, the known . . . the voter is at once expressed and heroized, he is invited to elect himself, to weigh the mandate which he is about to give with a veritable physical transference.

The images in the Clinton advertisement are addressed to the vengeful and familial constituency upon whom the victim's rights discourses of mainstream public culture are premised.

Various modes of counter-aesthetic question the hegemony of the dominant discourses. For decades there have been regular editorial cartoons in daily newspapers, which satirize punitive crime measures. One of the most controversial counter-discursive productions of recent years is Benetton's *We, On Death Row*. This was a series of photographs of, and interviews with, condemned inmates in US prisons, distributed as a supplement to a gossip magazine. A heated debate ensued, over what it means to humanize somebody, and over whether only crime victims should benefit from this kind of sympathetic treatment. A new medium is oppositional internet communications, like the Lee Davis execution images (Lynch 2002). There has been a diverse body of counter-aesthetic artworks, including for instance Van Gogh's *La Ronde des Prisonniers* (Valier 2000), Warhol's electric chair series and his *Thirteen Most Wanted Men*. More recent artworks of this kind include Lucinda Devlin's *Omega Suites* and Marcus Harvey's *Myra* (Young 2000). The cinema has provided a forum for alternative visions of crime and punishment, including *Kiss of the Spider Woman, Aileen Wuornos: The Selling of a Serial Killer* and *Natural Born Killers*. Literary works too have provided a counter-aesthetic space, including poems like Wilde's 'The Ballad of Reading Gaol', Millay's 'Justice Denied in Massachusetts', and Lowell's 'Memories of West Street and Lepke', and novels like Genet's books, Mailer's *The Executioner's Song*, and Pat Barker's *Border Crossing*, a text which is discussed in Chapter 7. These counter-aesthetics challenge the dominant public culture in a number of different ways. Typically, they resist and subvert simple binaries between criminal and non-criminal, illegal and legal, victim and offender. Additionally, they work to expose the viewing relations of spectatorship through which audiences are addressed in vengeful citizenship.

Andy Warhol's *Thirteen Most Wanted Men* is a counter-aesthetic par excellence. It exploits fully the ambiguity of the penal displays that recruit individuals as subjects of the punitive state. Warhol's mural is a space in which the dominant aesthetic of mainstream public culture is shown shot through with a subversive counter-aesthetic. Commissioned to produce an artwork for the façade of the New York State Pavilion at the World's Fair of 1964, Warhol manufactured a silkscreen mural of mugshots taken from FBI 'Wanted' posters. When the state authorities ordered it removed and requested an alternative submission, Warhol instead had the portraits covered over with a layer of silver paint. The installation was only in situ for forty-eight hours. Rather than censoring them, the silvering left a trace of the images as a silent reminder of their prohibition. The silvered screen blankly showed the ruling's paradox, that the 'most wanted' were not wanted there, on the wall of the state's exhibition-hall. The mural had sent up the fair promoters' public relations work, with Warhol choosing to represent the state by displaying a grid of criminal mugshots. *Most Wanted Men* turns inside out the didacticism of the Rogue's Gallery. Instead of the salutary communicational work of exposing malefactors and thereby teaching both us and them the lesson that crime does not pay, the idea of 'most wanted' figures on a number of different levels as a double entendre. FBI 'Wanted' posters circulate images of fugitive 'public enemies'. However, Warhol's mural is celebratory and openly sexual, with all the allure of the Krays' images produced by Francis Bacon and David Bailey.

The deadpan presentational portraiture of the mugshots resembles the mode adopted by Warhol for his celebrity portraits. Popstar, 'personality' and notorious criminal are all, in Gordon Burn's words, 'corpsing it'. *Most Wanted Men* is a comment on the nature of spectacle, showing that it is not produced by or contained within an image, but instead arises from the viewing relations of spectatorship. Guy Debord (1967: 4) put this matter slightly differently when he wrote, 'the spectacle is not a collection of images, but a social relation among people, mediated by images'. In photographs of *Thirteen Most Wanted Men*, as in *White Burning Car III* (1963), there is somebody walking past, who does not pause to look at the spectacle, but who is nevertheless important to the staging of the scene. These passers-by index the ubiquitousness of the dramatic images circulated in the daily news, which make spectacle no longer a matter of the extraordinary. As Hal Foster (1996) has noted, in this mural Warhol evokes the subject of mass culture through the figure of notoriety, the fame of fifteen minutes. The mural trades on a complex and fascinating set of relationships pertaining between celebrity culture, crime and punishment. Most of all,

Warhol's mural exposes to scrutiny the intimacy effect produced within modern media, bringing to our attention the mechanisms through which imagined relations of reciprocity, participation, dialogue and nearness are produced.

Crime and Punishment in Contemporary Culture underlines the extent to which national and transnational punitive cultures arise in and through contestation. The analysis demonstrates that the mediated spectacles that typify punitive cultures are ambiguous, reversible and open to critique. The chapters emphasize the ways in which penal practices mark gender, sexuality, race and religious difference. While enacting rites of belonging and exclusion, penal practices give rise to a diverse set of imagined collectivities. They have contributed powerfully to the imagination and memory central to diaspora, and to the production of the subaltern through both resistance and subordination. The notion of the cultural adopted in this book hence does not specify 'shared meaning' or 'common feelings and sensibilities', but rather envisages culture as a site of contestation.

The analysis of punitive cultures must start by rewriting the scholarly image of penal modernity. In several of the chapters of this book, important features excluded from the established account are discussed. Without analysis of these important aspects of modern penality and social order, the contours of the present cannot be outlined, and an effective critical intervention is forestalled. The task of rewriting the memory of penal modernity involves a substantial critique of some classic theories of punishment and society. Foucault's claim that we inhabit societies of surveillance and not societies of the spectacle is rejected by this book. During modernity, we see the development of communicational forms of many kinds, including for instance the novel, the telephone, the mass press and the photograph. Each of these became a site for the mediated spectacle of crime and punishment. Let's take the example of the photograph, first introduced in 1840. Within a few years, police forces had begun to take and circulate mugshots of convicted criminals, and rogues' gallery displays were organized. Sometimes photographs were taken of executions conducted behind prison walls, and reproduced as woodcut illustrations in magazines. In high-profile trials, photographs of the defendant were a lucrative commodity – for instance six images of Lewis Payne, one of the Lincoln conspirators, were copyrighted in 1865. A fascinated public eagerly consumed pictures like this. The work of Doré and Dickens supplied pictorial and literary images of punishment for the middle classes, and the mass press produced sensational narratives and pictures for a broader audience. Photography in courtrooms was eventually banned in England by the Criminal Justice Act 1925, after the judges were scandalized by the use of flash to capture notorious offenders like Dr Crippen in the dock. Courtroom sketches in the mass circulation dailies drew readers into the dramas of the trial (Nead 2002). In terms of punishment, a range of regulations have surrounded the circulation of audio-visual representations. For instance, soon after the electric chair was introduced in 1890, death chamber images of electric executions were banned. An illicit image of Ruth Snyder in the chair, the femme fatale depicted in *The Postman*

Always Rings Twice and *Double Indemnity*, raised the circulation of the *New York Daily News* by 750,000 in 1928. These images circulated a penality that was retributive, and in varying degrees stigmatizing, exclusionary and eliminatory.

For both Foucault and Durkheim, modernity was centred on reintegrative penal practices, whether these were construed as correctional disciplinary technologies, or forms of restitutive law based in ideals of tolerance and humanity. Foucault constructed several schematic discontinuities, using these to characterise the movement from the *ancien régime* to penal modernity and the modern order of subjectivity and subjection. *Discipline and Punish* emphasized a decisive break, with the replacement of retributive 'armed power' by an insidiously 'gentle', correctional disciplinary power. Turning to Durkheim, his theory of punishment and communication envisaged a simple shift from hostile sentiments and severe, exclusionary penalties to tolerant ideals and lenient, reintegrative legal regulation. Drawing upon aspects of Durkheim and Foucault to paint a picture of modern penality as part of a humane trend, today's punitive practices are being depicted by some influential voices as a striking 'reversal', as 'archaic', 'anti-modern' or 'non-modern' phenomena.[1] This book adopts an alternative approach, discarding the logic of discontinuity and exploring features of penal modernity excluded from these accounts, before going on to describe their subsequent reconfiguration within the contemporary scene. The task of rewriting the scholarly image of penal modernity begins in the first half of the book. This is followed by a detailed study of some recent events and debates, which begin to restructure in important ways the outlines of modern penality, rather than reversing them.

Chapter 1 opens the account by addressing the extensive discourses surrounding 'undiscovered crimes' and criminal detection, which remain a notable absence from scholarship on crime and punishment despite the huge cultural weight of cases like that of O.J. Simpson. These practices have played an important part in the mediated spectacle of modern penality. Detective work contributed to a profusion of images of criminality, policing and punishment. These circulated from the nineteenth century and produced a mediated relation with crime and punishment. Criminal detection technologies, as part of a modern 'war on crime', have played a substantial part in the emotionality of policing and penal practices. They are not a feature of the compassionate correctionalism drawn by some scholars as the core of modern penality. Furthermore, these technologies and the images and stories circulated about them produced images of the city as dark and labyrinthine, peopled by shadowy, inscrutable suspects and malevolent elusive criminals. Foucault's account abruptly moved from the spectacular display and 'blind' power of the *ancien régime* to the subtle surveillance and *pan*opticism of modernity. My account, however, discusses the ways in which the mediated spectacle of criminal detection and punishment engaged onlookers as audiences of fearful victims and enraged avengers.

The chapters that follow inquire further into the importance of mediated spectacle within modern and contemporary penality. These spectacles have included those of the degradation and exile of a traitor in France, the federal government's execution of a terrorist in the USA, and the lifelong imprisonment of a notorious English murderess. These practices mediate an ambiguous spectacle of suffering, reconfigured as a dissemination of images and ideas about the pain and injury of the condemned criminal or lifer. In Chapter 2, a culture of retributive punishment in turn-of-the-century France is related to the constitution of the national political space of the imagined community. I show how the spectacle of the harsh punishment of Dreyfus, a Jewish army officer convicted of treason, brought furious contestation of the boundaries of the nation. It was at this *fin de siècle* moment that an influential theory of punishment and communication emerged in the work of Emile Durkheim, who also wrote two essays on the Dreyfus case. My analysis shows how his vision of social and penal change entailed a republican assimilationist politics based in the disappearance of ethnic and religious conflict *and* difference. Durkheim hence obscured the part played by modern penal practices in the marking and repudiation of the alien, in the contested location of boundaries. Linking punishment and communication, he did not convey the import of the triadic relationship of punishment, *nation* and communication. His work, and later that of Foucault, overlooked the transformation of the monarchical spectacle of punishment into a modern form of *mediated armed justice*, which marked out and expelled enemies. The Dreyfus affair combined elements of both direct and mediated armed justice, and the chapter analyses both modes of spectacle. These forms of penal display depart greatly from Foucault's theory, within which disciplinary power produces a docile and productive body. My analysis explains how print culture textualized the body of Dreyfus, mediating a spectacle of the body in pain. In this unforgettably dramatic instance of armed power, the contested boundaries of the nation were imagined and performed. In sum, the chapter describes the practices through which the punishment of Dreyfus engaged onlookers in the negotiation of the limits of the nation-state.

Chapter 3 takes further questions about the penal politics of assimilation and the marking of foreigners as aliens and enemies to be assimilated, expelled or eliminated. Debates about communication in the early twentieth century encompassed both the movements of images and ideas, and those of people. An influential discourse on changing mobilities, cultural identities and crime emerged within work published by members of the Chicago school of sociology. Chicagoan scholars inherited Durkheim's politics of assimilation and applied them to elucidate crime in America. Their concepts were grounded within a particular set of ideas about mobilities, identities and forms of belonging. The chapter shows how their discourse on mobilities and crime was part of the colonial and national histories of the United States of America, implicated in the processes by which the USA demarcated its nationals from 'foreigners'. My analysis demonstrates that the Chicagoan notion of cosmopolitan solidarity envisaged a purified nation of individuals. Once again, crimino-legal discourses were involved in the contestation of the boundaries of the nation.

The final four chapters of the book move on to address aspects of the relationship between punishment, culture and communication in contemporary western societies. Chapters 4 and 5 both address the relations between the internet and contemporary penality. Punishment has been an important locus for the development and publicization of changes in communicational practices. For instance, the name and reputation of Reuters, the international news agency, was made in 1865 when the company was the first to bring news of the assassination of Lincoln to Europe. In this event, the reporting 'scoop', and the rapid and international transmission of news, was linked to the occasion of a high-profile murder and the new practices of public mourning that followed upon it. The internet brings new forms of instantaneous, global and interactive mass communication. The cases discussed in Chapters 4 and 5 look into some of the defining cyber-events and debates of the early internet culture.

Chapter 4 presents an analysis of the Timothy McVeigh execution webcast case. Like Chapter 3, this chapter has an eye to the formation of new collectivities which are both national and postnational. The chapter argues that the punitive subjects of the USA are at present convoked through emotive images of national trauma, within which victim-citizenship is premised on membership of a certain national-familial collectivity. Additionally, with the global circulation of images and information about serious crimes, the collectivity addressed as traumatic subjects transcends that of national citizenship. Marshall McLuhan's account of the shift from print to electronic culture is critiqued, which associated the latter with global empathetic engagement and the obsolescence of punitive detention. My reading of the mediated spectacle of punishment in the cases discussed in this book suggests a critical focus on their reversibility, instead of the resigned conclusion that media neutralize meaning and wholly emasculate political intervention. I argue that spaces of irony, in this case editorial cartoons on the McVeigh execution, provoke effective critique of the ways in which individuals are interpellated as subjects of the killing state.

In Chapter 5, the debate about the internet's impact upon contemporary penality is taken further through analysis of the extensive online communications around several murder cases. I argue that internet communications about crimes and punishments performatively construct new collectivities in a process which begins to reconstitute the modern outlines of penality. The internet traffic on three cases was analysed, with an eye to its invocations of group membership and exclusion. In Durkheim's theory, outraged expressions, severe punishment and a rigid collective morality were emblematic of 'primitive' premodern societies. Late modernity departs radically from the mechanical solidarity linked by Durkheim to angry talk and severe punishment. The time–space compression and disembedding wrought by contemporary technologies brings new proximities, and forms of affiliation and exclusion. I argue that the construction and reconstruction of collective identities and dominant cultural values involves active strategies of inclusion and exclusion, to which online communications about murders are a contributor. The chapter discusses the notions of sociality and identity advanced by two persuasive theories of internet and society, namely

Howard Rheingold's vision of altruistic virtual community, and Manuel Castells' alternative claim that the internet is a medium of networked individualism. Contra Castells' theory, online communications are, according to my research, an important site for the contestation of group values. Indeed, it is through this very contestation that new forms of collectivity are imagined and performed. However, I also show that online talk about murders does not typically demonstrate the compassionate practices of Rheingold's 'virtual community'. Some speculative links are postulated between the complex connectivity of internet and the penal escalation seen in many western countries. Additionally, cyber-communications about murders are seen as practices through which various forms of national and transnational identities are both displayed and moulded.

Chapter 6 explores another set of textual practices through which the mediated spectacle of punishment in contemporary culture engages riveted yet fearful publics. It addresses the iconic images and dramatic soundbites characteristic of communicational flows in high-profile cases like the killing of James Bulger. The chapter describes and critiques the gothicity of true crime fiction, media reporting, penal policy and case law. These employ gruesome images of injury and frightening tales of victimization at the hands of 'faceless killers'. The chapter delves into the significance of the oft-observed emotionality of contemporary penality, and examines just how raw emotions are implicated in appeals to retributive punishment and the fearful agenda of 'public protection'. The visceral passions aroused by both the murder of James Bulger and its punishment are discussed through a reading of Pat Barker's fascinating novel *Border Crossing* (2001), a counter-aesthetic text that, in effect, reopens the Bulger case. I argue that to fathom the depth of emotion surrounding cases like this, we need to move on from the concept of moral panic. The chapter hence takes up the concept of abjection, to relate the powers of horror invoked through popular cultural representations, case law, and penal practices, to the horror of that which breaches borders. The aesthetics of retributive punishment in contemporary culture, I argue, is an aesthetics of abjection, both invoking gut feelings and dramatizing the remaking of distinctions between legal and extra-legal, public and private.

In Chapter 7, I argue that for more than a century, British penality has been haunted by the shadow of the death penalty. The analysis traces the outlines of this shadow in the juridico-political rituals of modern and contemporary severe punishment. The chapter rejects the notion of penal leniency inherent in the idea of abolition, showing that the death penalty for murder has been superseded by a *dead time*, a life-cancelling penalty. A reconfiguration of the spectacle of the ultimate penalty and the state's power of life and death, in which death is written into the law and communicated to audiences in changing ways, is discussed. As in the case of Dreyfus discussed in Chapter 2, penality involves a mediated spectacle of suffering. Chapter 7 focuses on the case of Myra Hindley, the notorious English 'Moors murderess'. My analysis shows how her punishment is communicated through a visceral immediacy, in which readers/viewers are invited to relish the spectacle of her pain and suffering. In this way, the force of law is coercively and violently inscribed upon and into the body, communicating forms of state power that incorporate populist punitiveness. Marshall McLuhan wrote in the 1960s that with the advent of electronic media we had entered the age of the icon, an inclusive image which generates communal, deep participation, fostering an immediacy of participation in the experience of others. McLuhan theorized the icon as the medium of a sensuous embrace, through which the viewer of the image reaches out compassionately. The iconic images that are mass produced and rapidly circulated through contemporary communications technologies do emotively engage viewers. However, the sensuous global embrace of compassionate concern and empathetic involvement anticipated by McLuhan has not resulted. In the chapter, the gendered character of the mediated spectacle of retributive punishment is explored. A connection between the spectacle of severe legal punishment and that of femininity is traced. This demonstrates how in some prominent displays of exemplary retributive punishment, a potent relationship between violence, spectacle and femininity pertains. However, I also argue that displays like this of severe punishment repeatedly show the law passing beyond itself.

Taken as a whole, the book asks some searching questions about the possibilities of justice in the media age. It also opens up a space for critical scholarship that aspires to be theoretically sophisticated and properly reflexive. The stakes of this form of critique are considered in the postscript to the text, which looks into the idea of 'addressing the contemporary'. My best hope is that you take as much pleasure from reading these pages as I have had in writing them.

1 Murder will out

There is no den in the wide world to hide a rogue.
Commit a crime and the earth is made of glass.

(Ralph Waldo Emerson, *Essays*)

Once upon a time, a storyteller named Geoffrey Chaucer had one of his pilgrims proclaim, 'Murder will out, certain, it will not fail.'[1] In this tale of his, the Prioress asserts that God will not suffer a crime to remain forever concealed. Later in the story divine intervention, a miracle of the Virgin, produces the discovery of the corpse and provides a narrative of its violent death. Chaucer's tale locates the oft-repeated maxim, murder will out, within a medieval and ecclesiastical view of justice and morality. In modern and secular times, this 'certain' moral maxim began to turn into an intriguing and dramatic plot device, central to a new specialist genre of detective fiction. 'Undiscovered crimes', the problem of impunity and criminal detection practices were an important feature of the modern mediated spectacle of punishment, and they remain so to this day. Nevertheless, their significance has been overlooked by scholars of penality. The first chapter of this book argues that the history of criminal detection technologies, with which there has always been great popular fascination, does not accord with the established account of penal modernity. The conventional account has scant interest in matters of mediated spectacle. In it, modern penality is depicted as centred on correctional technologies, on a disciplinary form of punishment working through surveillance practices and normative judgement. The picture of disciplinary penal modernity is based in a reading of the work of Michel Foucault. This chapter looks at the story told by Foucault in *Discipline and Punish*, and shows that another story is equally persuasive, that of spectacle, retributive penality, and juridical forms of power.

Discipline and Punish stands among the most striking and beautiful of academic texts. Its power does not emanate from the promise of a fully comprehensive and authoritative account of historical reality. On the contrary, the effect of this book comes about through its construction as a dissident fiction.[2] It achieved a superb political intervention, published at a moment when Foucault distributed a manifesto warning, 'police control is tightening on our everyday life . . . we live in a state of custody' (Eribon 1992: 224). The impact of the text lay in its eloquent depiction of the condition of modernity as, 'a prison house of technical knowledge' (Beck 1998: 11). Relatedly, it has been remarked that Foucault privileged metaphors of imprisonment in outlining the process of subjectivization, depicting the soul as 'an imprisoning effect' (Butler 1997: 85). His claim that modern society had a carceral texture was complemented by this textual strategy. On several occasions, Foucault stated that capitalist societies were confinement societies, in the sense of the dispersion throughout the social body from the nineteenth century of networks of surveillance and punishment. He named the closing chapter of *Discipline and Punish* 'The carceral', and in it presented the picture of a carceral continuum, 'a subtle graduated carceral net, with compact institutions, but also separate and diffused methods' (Foucault 1975/1991: 297). Overall, he contended that society itself could be seen as carceral, writing that 'the carceral texture of society assures both the real capture of the body and its perpetual observation' (ibid.: 304). Foucault claimed that the person conscious of being watched would come to exercise control over themselves, writing that 'he who is subjected to a field of visibility, *and who knows it* . . . becomes the principle of his own subjection' (ibid.: 202–3; my emphasis). He famously alluded to the dissident literature of Aleksandr Solzhenitsyn when he used the phrase, 'the carceral archipelago'. In interview, Foucault (1980a: 168) explained that he had alluded to the Soviet writer's novel to express 'the way in which a punitive system is physically dispersed yet at the same time covers the entirety of a society'. Solzhenitsyn had written his novel, which was repressed by the authorities, in prison, and in the early 1970s defected to the USA. *The Gulag Archipelago* opened with a depiction of how in Russia the network of penal institutions and police machinery was all around, yet invisible. Systematically, and out of sight, it eliminated and purged society of all that might be considered subversive. Arrests were sudden and could occur anywhere, and people disappeared for years or forever, leading Solzhenitsyn (1974: 614) to reflect, 'the cell was constricted, but wasn't freedom even more constricted'. Foucault's allusion to this carceral archipelago protested against the constitution of western societies as societies of surveillance, through a regime which embedded the power to punish more deeply within the social body than ever before. The political strategy by which he sought to transgress the carceral logic of modernity required a shift from traditional history to an 'effective history'. In this mode of critique, the scholar sets aside teleological narratives of progress, tolerance and humanity, and works to produce an 'insurrection of subjugated knowledges' (Foucault 1980a: 81). *Discipline and Punish* was a brilliant and timely strategic intervention published at a specific socio-historical conjuncture. It was crafted to induce specific political effects through a practice of 'fictioning' history. The book's power arises through a re-telling of the past as a certain kind of story, by exploiting the constitutive link between history and story in the term *l'histoire*.

An integral part of this dissident textual strategy was Foucault's construction of several schematic discontinuities, and his painting of a number of associated memorable scenes. He used these to characterize the movement from the *ancien régime* to penal modernity and the modern order of subjectivity and subjection. Most strikingly, *Discipline and Punish* emphasized a decisive break, with a shift from spectacle to surveillance. Foucault associated this break with the replacement of retributive 'armed power' by an insidiously 'gentle', correctional disciplinary power. He illustrated the distance between the two punitive styles by drawing contrasting images of the dramatic public execution of a regicide and the banal institutional timetable of a penitentiary. Accompanying the narrative of this story of penal change and new modes of rule was an elevation of the power of the norm over the power of law. *Crime and Punishment in Contemporary Culture* tells the story differently, moving away from the Foucauldian strategy of schematic discontinuities.[3] In several of the chapters of the present book, the transformation of spectacle with the reconfiguration of retributive penality and armed power in mediated forms is discussed.

Criminal detection and the war on crime

Detective work contributed to a profusion of images of criminality, policing and punishment that were circulated throughout western societies from the nineteenth century. These images produced a mediated relation with punishment, a relation that is not directly experienced but arises from imaginative engagement. While the spectacular regime of the public display of execution declined, this decline was accompanied by a massive proliferation of narratives and images of crime and punishment in both popular and official texts (Hutchings 2001). Foucault spoke boldly of a shift from the juridical to the normalizing. However, in the process of diffusion, in which law's spectacle was transformed from the public performance of the scaffold towards an imaginative practice, law did not lose the visceral and potent, yet also lacunary, power of its force. The force of law, in its hold upon the imagination, does not simply operate as an abstract set of principles, but rather through specific textual practices. As will be shown in this chapter, the juridical represents and reconstructs events in certain ways, disseminating persuasive yet ambiguous narratives of injury and victimization.

Criminal detection technologies have played a substantial part in the emotionality of policing and penal practices. They are not a feature of the compassionate correctionalism drawn by some scholars as the core of modern penality.[4] In *Police!*, Clarkson and Richardson (1889: vii) wrote, 'civil power is constantly at war with crime'. Criminal detection practices were described in both official and popular discourses as part of an aggressive war on crime centred on deterrence and retribution. The rationale, design and efficacy of criminal detection and its technologies has repeatedly been linked to control through the fearful example of certain punishment. For instance, in *War With Crime*, Baker (1889: 46) wrote, 'to be deterrent the punishment must be certain'. The notion of 'war' against crime figured criminals as formidable adversaries, as enemies within, constantly upping the ante by the use of new tactics and tools: 'In the constant state of warfare between the lawmaker and the lawbreaker . . . every new invention or practical application of scientific discovery has supplied each side with new weapons frequently of much greater precision' (Mitchell 1911: 1). The importance of criminal detection in the war on crime was highly publicized in the USA during the period of the rise of the Federal Bureau of Investigation under Hoover. At this time, the Bureau undertook elaborate public relations and publicity campaigns. Hoover made regular announcements vilifying gangsters as public enemies, deadly wanton killers and mercenaries, whom he readily described as depraved and ruthless evil monsters that must be 'eliminated'. A similarly hostile, combative and repressive discourse is found in other official reports and announcements concerning criminal detection.

As I outline below, Foucault drew an image of modern penality and disciplinary power as discreet, preventative and automatic. The term detection (derived from the Latin, *tego, -tect*, cover), means, literally rendered, 'to uncover'. Its temporal orientation is retrospective, and at the close of the twentieth century, the use of scientific methods in criminal investigation remained primarily reactive rather than proactive (Tilley and Ford 1996). Criminal detection methods try to take us back to crimes which have already been committed, in this gesture recalling unacceptable events about which very little may be known. Through both systematic and scientific methods, as well as chance discoveries, the crime event must be 'painstakingly' reconstructed in detail, producing an image of a suspect and a proposed narrative of their actions. With their retro-active impetus, criminal detection practices seek to reconstruct an authoritative narrative of what really happened, to produce a singular truth of the crime event. However, over the years considerable anxiety has been evident about the general efficacy of criminal detection practices, as well as their implication in miscarriages of justice. To this day, new scientific technologies are described by professional and government bodies as part of a 'techno-police revolution'.[5] This rhetoric echoes the disciplinary history of the forensic sciences, replete as it is with celebratory acclamations. For instance, 'since 1837, the Microscope, strengthening notably anatomy as well as toxicology, has repeatedly released the innocent from the jailor's clutch and delivered the culprit the hangman' (Chaillé 1876: 403). However, with the expansion of the mass media and the proliferation of popular cultural representations, the failures of vision and the contested character of reconstruction were widely publicized. High public expectations, and plenty of stern criticism, have accompanied the use of modern criminal detection practices. Despite their objectivist rhetoric and the regular claims to 'absolute certainty' made by the practitioners of scientific methods, criminal detection practices differ markedly from those of surveillance. Circumstantial evidence, to which scientific criminal detection methods contribute in court, is precisely 'the evidence of things *unseen*'. The visualizing practices of criminal detection hence do not have the structure of watching over involved in this term '*sur*veillance'. Instead of the inspection theorized within the notion of panopticism, they reconstruct and re-write things in certain ways, and the images and narratives that they produce must be read (Pugliese 1999).

Traces must be looked for after the crime event, which may be indistinct, incomplete, and are very likely to be challenged in court.

The place of interpretation and opinion in criminal detection was already hotly disputed by the mid-nineteenth century. One instance of this contestation was the Road murder of 1860. The case, which was extensively publicized, began when an infant boy was found murdered in a middle-class residence in Wiltshire. The magistrates soon called for a Scotland Yard detective, who focused his investigation on members of the family, and especially on the boy's step-sister, Constance.[6] A year passed by and the crime remained unsolved, despite the detective charging Constance with murder, and bringing committal proceedings against her. Great public clamour ensued when he gave evidence that Constance was a violently jealous child who had previously ran away disguised as a boy, and that her father had affairs with the family servants. At this point, an incensed surgeon who had assisted at the post-mortem examination published a monograph, aiming to dissipate popular suspicions and to refute press inaccuracies and distortions. In his text, Stapleton (1861) rejected the proposition that the killer was a family member as 'revolting and unnatural', deploring the damage done to the reputation of the pater familias, the privacy of his home invaded, his daughter suspected. He told his readers that he would examine the 'silent witnesses' collected by the police, observing that much of the material evidence pertaining to various bloodied items had been disregarded or misused by the police (Stapleton 1861: 105). Stapleton firmly believed that clarity could be brought by the adoption of a scientific perspective, and depicted the press as progressively obscuring the truth. For him, scientific methods were a means of access to new facts able to point out the culprit and exonerate the innocent. However, he admitted that conflicting explanations could be made of the same facts, undermining somewhat his claim that 'murder will out' as scientific methods end all speculation and dispute. His narrative produced fearful images of injury, for instance, 'these cuts upon the left finger proclaim the consciousness of the child to the first sharp pang which waked him from his happy dreams, to look one moment at the treacherous murderer, and then to die' (ibid.: 63). The monograph portrayed a multitude of possible suspects, including the violent inhabitants of the nearby cottages, vengeful ex-servants, escaped lunatics, and ferocious homicidal children. Commenting on the continuing mystery of the Road murder, *The Times* (11 December 1860) stated, 'if great crimes remain undetected, they are neither undiscussed nor forgotten', and aspects of the murder and its detection featured in both Wilkie Collins' *The Moonstone* (1868) and Dickens' *The Mystery of Edwin Drood*.

Discourses about undiscovered crimes and criminal detection technologies have been significant to the engagement of fascinated and fearful audiences in the mediated spectacle of crime and punishment. Criminal detection produced images of the city as dark and labyrinthine, of shadowy, inscrutable suspects and predatorial elusive criminals. A rising demand for sensational crime reporting and fictional literature has been related to urban fears about anonymous strangers (Goldberg 1998). The urban itself came to suggest the inscrutable in

Poe's *The Man Of The Crowd* (1840/1984). The tale follows an image of the satisfactions of surveillant observation with the story of a frustrating pursuit of an elusive and ultimately unknowable criminal. The narrator of the story sits at the window of a London coffee-house, looking out from this vantage-point onto a busy thoroughfare. The street becomes more crowded as evening sets in, and the narrator passes the time in picking out the traits of the passers-by in relation to their kind of occupation. Observing the passers-by, he feels that he can tell their history from a brief glance at them. At this moment of confident mastery, the face of an old man strikes him, its curious expression attracting his whole interest, bringing to mind 'ideas of vast mental power . . . of excessive terror, of intense- of extreme despair' (Poe 1840/1984: 243). The narrator follows this man with difficulty through the dense crowd, shadowing him in a determination to find out more. Through the fog and darkness, the old man crosses and re-crosses the street, doubles back upon himself, and repeats the same route several times. Poe closes his tale by informing the reader that the darkest of hearts cannot be read. This intriguing tale epitomizes the potency with which the mediated spectacle of criminal detection engages audiences, but as fearful and fascinated consumers and not as masterful surveillant viewers.

Defects of power and knowledge

In *Discipline and Punish* (1975), Foucault asserted that the choice of imprisonment as the predominant mode of punishment was a matter of the elaboration of techniques, 'to locate people, to fix them in precise places . . . a whole technique of human dressage by location, confinement, surveillance' (Foucault 1984/1990: 104–5). In *Discipline and Punish*, this claim was supported by an analysis of treatises, plans and reports, which demonstrated the emergence of a prolonged reflection on how the techniques for conditioning individuals could be improved. On the rare occasions when he wrote about policing, this was construed as a form of surveillance rather than as a detective kind of investigative practice. Foucault contended that the organization of a centralized police force was one of three modalities by which norms were extended throughout the social body. He claimed that this was a police force occupied upon the task of exercising a 'permanent, exhaustive, omnipresent surveillance, capable of making all visible' (Foucault 1975/1991: 214). Despite his talk of techniques to fix and locate people, and of the emergence of modern police forces, Foucault did not discuss criminal detection. According to him, the period beginning in the late eighteenth century saw a reversal of the axis of visibility. He charted a schematic discontinuity between the spectacular display of monarchical power and the emergence of a micro-power through which each person could be seen and known in their individuality. Foucault reasoned that the power of the old regime was, while not chaotic when in action, so intermittent in operation that it was highly inefficient. Monarchical power, he claimed, had a 'weak capacity for "resolution", as one might say in photographic terms' (Foucault 1996: 230). According to his story, with social and political change, sovereign power became obsolete, and was superseded by a new modality of control which implied 'an uninterrupted, constant coercion' (Foucault 1975/1991: 137). This account of the surveillant visual culture of modernity accorded with his theory of penal change and modern disciplinary power. Foucault (ibid.: 9) described another schematic discontinuity, noting a shift in the exemplary mechanics of punishment from penal severity to certainty. He suggested that publicity shifted from the punishment to the trial and sentence, but he did not problematize the changing relationship between the spectacle, the severity and the certainty of punishment. Foucault linked leniency in modern punishment to the effectively continuous character of the power to punish:

> It seems to me that, even in eighteenth-century society, the number of people who actually escaped the laws under which they normally would have fallen was enormous. The penal power, the power to punish, was discontinuous, full of holes. This explains why, when they actually got hold of a criminal, the punishment was all the more formidable. . . . They sought a punitive power, which could be more lenient precisely because it was more continuous and in principle nobody escaped it.
>
> (Foucault 1996: 140)

The panoptic pressure theorized by Foucault is constant, and acts before any offence is committed. It is also noiseless, of low visibility, discreet. However, criminal detection practices have for two centuries made visible blindspots. They have highlighted failures of vision, and vision's partiality, noted for instance by the government's forensic chemist, 'In how few cases is it possible to produce the man who can say "I saw the deed done," and even in such cases, what errors of identification may occur' (Mitchell 1911: 11). Lacunae of this kind cannot be simply ignored, or written off as insignificant relics of the *ancien régime*. In answer to criticism, Foucault objected that:

> Power is not omnipotent or omniscient – quite the contrary! If power relationships have produced forms of investigation, of analysis, of models of knowledge, etc., it is precisely not because power was omniscient, but because it was blind, because it was in a state of impasse.
>
> (Foucault 1996: 258)

This claim that modern power-knowledge relations not only emerged from the 'weak resolution' of monarchical power, but that obscurities persist today, was not developed in Foucault's work. His account abruptly moves from the 'blind' power of the *ancien régime* to the *pan*opticism of modernity. However, from the late eighteenth century, a proliferation of practices and images brought the problem of impunity powerfully to the public view. Contemporary with the theses outlining disciplinary training methods described by Foucault, we see the circulation of philosophical treatises, and works on the police, reflecting upon the problem of the certainty of punishment.

Let's begin with Foucault's reading of Jeremy Bentham's 'Panopticon Plan' (1791), which has commonly been taken as a persuasive illustration, or even a proof, of disciplinary modern penality. The status of this depiction as a reading of Bentham's text, which should be counterposed against other readings, is seldom recognised. In *An Introduction to the Principles of Morals and Legislation* (1789), he postulated that the individual's perception of the likelihood of their 'obnoxious act' being detected by others was essential to the deterrent force of self-interest as a restraint upon illegal conduct. Two years later, he presented his 'Panopticon Plan', which proposed a particular arrangement of architecture that he hoped would put into practice an 'inspection principle'. This principle required both that inmates conceived themselves to be potentially visible at any moment and that they actually were under the view of an inspector for as long as possible. The greater the chance of actually being under inspection, the more intense the feeling that one might be so. Bentham noted that the inmate soon discovered the existence of a lax inspection, testing the omniscience of the overseer by committing various minor infractions. The desired overall effect of the inspection principle was that the inmate be assured that all their actions were known and hence would believe that, 'in this house transgression never can be safe' (Bentham 1791/1995: 105). He introduced several modifications to the original Plan, which addressed both the difficulty of rendering the presence or absence of the inspector unverifiable, and the problem of producing a maximal 'real presence' of the inspector. His suggestion for the latter difficulty was to dupe inmates by recording for a whole day every infraction committed by one very refractory prisoner, and then communicate each one, which would impress on all the inmates the effectiveness of monitoring. In Bentham's apparatus there was hence a subtle and important relationship between the real and the apparent. The 'Panopticon Plan' foregrounds the rational calculability of law and the importance of the constancy of demonstration. It included no provisions for rehabilitative techniques, and Bentham characterized the institution as one designed to show the individual his miscalculation in choosing to commit crime rather than obeying the law. Foucault, however, did not address these juridical features of Bentham's design.

Many of the leading legal and philosophical writers of the eighteenth century discussed the problem of the certainty of punishment. Chaucer's moral maxim, murder will out, began to be problematized at this time, with the beginnings of systematic criminal detection efforts. Henry Fielding's extravagantly didactic text *Examples of the Interposition of Providence in the Detection and Punishment of Murder* (1752) attributed a recent increase in murders to a general neglect of religion, seeking to convince the reader of the immediate and terrible intervention of the Almighty in pointing out the culprit. The text concluded with a warning of the rigours of divine wrath, even for those who succeeded in avoiding punishment during their earthly life: 'what are the terrors of earthly judgement compared to this tremendous tribunal' (Fielding 1752: 72). Fielding's text shows that adherence to the authority of an absolute unexplained could no longer be assumed. The adage 'circumstances cannot lie' has been most associated with William Paley, who, in *The Principles of Moral and Political Philosophy* (1785: 551), argued for the potency of circumstantial evidence. While the Deity was omniscient and punishment in his hands was a surety, humans possessed imperfect faculties, hence their 'authority over their fellow creatures is limited by defects of power and knowledge' (Paley 1785: 531). For Paley, this meant that the uncertainty of punishment must be compensated for by its severity.

In the nineteenth-century novel, the maxim 'murder will out' worked as an entertaining rhetorical device. In fact, one can note its presence there at the birth of the criminal detection genre of literary works. Wilkie Collins' story *The Woman in White* (1861/1994) was so popular that when it first appeared in serialized form long queues of people waited to buy the next instalment. At one point in the tale, the dark villain Count Fosco ridicules the rather credulous and naïve ladies:

> how easily society can console itself for the worst of its shortcomings with a little bit of clap-trap. The machinery it has set up for the detection of crime is miserably ineffective – and yet only invent a moral epigram, saying that it works well, and you blind everybody to its blunders from that moment. Crimes cause their own detection, do they? And murder will out (another moral epigram), will it? Ask Coroners who sit at inquests in large towns if that is true, Lady Glyde. Ask secretaries of life assurance companies if that is true, Miss Halcombe. Read your own public journals. In the few cases that get into the newspapers, are there not instances of slain bodies found, and no murderers ever discovered? Multiply the cases that are reported by the cases that are not reported, and the bodies that are found by the bodies that are not found . . . on this tottering foundation you build up your comfortable moral maxim that crime causes its own detection!
>
> (Collins 1861/1994: 207)

Fosco presents the ladies with an alarming glimpse into the dark figure, the shadowy mass of undetected crimes. In Collins' story, Fosco's crime is eventually exposed. However, the detection is not done by the authorities, and anyway it is too late for the woman in white, who has been murdered. In detective stories, what was once a moral maxim becomes the occasion for fiction.

Detection was also an important concern of nineteenth-century works on the new police force. Mainwaring's *Observations on the Present State of the Police of the Metropolis* (1821) contrasted the activity of the old watchman with the vision of a more effective police. The watchman had a prescribed course of duty, carried a lantern, and made half-hourly cries, so in effect, 'he acts as a moving light-house to warn off all advances till it disappear' (Mainwaring 1821: 50–2). Mainwaring appealed instead for 'a police of *unseen* and unconfined action', writing that 'Officers, I know, cannot be everywhere, but they may be expected *any*where' (ibid.: 53 and 69). Three decades later, Charles Dickens described a tour of the London rookeries, guided by a detective well known to the local criminals. According to his story, in every public house or lodgings, 'coiners and smashers droop before him; pickpockets defer to him' (Dickens 1851: 267). Instead of the medium of inefficient warning complained of by Mainwaring, the constable's lamp is represented as symbolic of a relentless and inescapable scrutiny. The party picked up constables in different areas to guide them, each bearing his 'flaming eye.' They entered a crowded tramps' lodging house, and wherever the constable directed his lamp, 'there is a spectral figure rising, unshrouded, from a grave of rags' (ibid.). An inscription on the sheets of one lodging-house, intended to deter theft, 'STOP THIEF', caused Dickens to indulge his imagination in a reverie:

> To lie at night, wrapped in the legend of my slinking life; to take the cry that pursues me, waking, to my breast in sleep; to have it staring at me, as soon as my consciousness returns; STOP THIEF! . . . And to know that I must be stopped, come what will. To know that I am no match for this individual energy and keenness, or this organised and steady system.
>
> (ibid.: 268)

To construct a persuasive representation of certain detection in this tale, Dickens wrote about visible policemen at large in criminal regions. He also drew on this image in *Bleak House* (1852), depicting Inspector Bucket with his bulls-eye lantern searching the squalid city streets for a suspect. His tale did not portray the police of 'unseen action' sought by Mainwaring; the policemen in Dickens' tale are known to the criminals. Similarly, Thomas Archer described a street scene in which youthful pickpockets were watched by their 'Nemesis', a detective officer 'known, it would seem, to every man, woman, and child, in that neighbourhood, and with a power of "dropping on" anybody who "is wanted"' (Archer 1863: 123). These promotional activities undertaken by the police, and the tales told about them, show the difficulty with which ever-present surveillance and efficacious detection could be represented.

Wanted! Publicity and detection

At the same time as systematic detection methods were being introduced, we see the proliferation of new kinds of texts seeking to recruit the public in the work of detection. Despite the technologization of the hue and cry in the nineteenth century, the involvement of the public in the search for the criminal was retained. Indeed, their assistance was solicited through an expanding variety of means, in which a constant slippage between detection as real social activity and as fictional entertainment can be discerned. In *Dei delitti e delle pene* (1764), Cesare Beccaria criticized the system of rewards for the apprehension of criminals as one proof of the weakness of a government. Distribution agencies still included private prosecution agencies in the first half of the nineteenth century.[7] Reward notices were issued from the public office at Bow Street, county constabulary offices, the Criminal Investigation Department at Scotland Yard, and the detective department of city police forces. Some notices offered a free pardon to any guilty parties who supplied evidence leading to the conviction of their accomplices. Rewards relied principally on the existence of informers acting from a pecuniary interest rather than from altruism. Yet it was also recognized that rewards brought in an avenue for mistaken, or deliberate, incrimination of the wrong person. Half of the 1812 *Report Of the Select Committee on the Police of the Metropolis* dealt with the propriety of giving rewards, and by 1884 they had been officially discontinued.

From the late eighteenth century, reward notices were supplemented by a range of mass circulation weekly police gazettes on sale to the public, which mixed civic duty, fear and pleasure. In 1786, the publication of the *Weekly Hue and Cry* was commenced from Bow Street, issued twice weekly, and changing its name to *The Police Gazette* in 1829. In the early-nineteenth-century series of the *Hue and Cry and Police Gazette* there were notices of escaped prisoners, military deserters and lunatics, offenders to be apprehended, the occasional runaway apprentice, items stolen, and rewards offered. Notices of persons sentenced and executions conducted were regularly published. However, series of notices seeking the same person can be found over numerous issues, which finally petered out without supplying any resolution to the question of a missing or escaped person's location. By the second decade of the nineteenth century, the central significance of the *Police Gazette* in the institution of a new and more effective police force had been recognized by several writers. These commentators urged that the circulation of information and its publicizing be made both swift and broad (Radzinowicz 1956). The anonymous 'Plan For Improving The Police And For Preventing Desertion In The Army' of 1828 stated that 'the principal defect in the Police Regulations of this Country is a deficiency in the means of communication and publicity' (cited in Radzinowicz 1956: 523). The plan proposed a twice-weekly circulation of the *Police Gazette* to constables, magistrates and licensed houses, commenting that:

> With such means of universal, and almost instantaneous publicity, it would be next to impossible that offenders should escape. A criminal could not enter a village, or seek refreshment in a public house, without the risk, nay, the almost certainty of being recognised and apprehended.
> (cited in Radzinowicz 1956: 525)

The author stated that the public would be encouraged to check on suspicious strangers if there was the supporting incentive of a system of rewards.

A whole range of other 'police' newspapers were published, mingling the work of detection with that of entertainment, and disseminating alarming images of the violent and the professional criminal. These demonstrate the repetition of a certain formula or theme over the nineteenth century, that predatorial criminals were among us yet invisible to us. When *The London Policeman* first appeared in 1833, its editorial referred to the 'thousands of miserable wretches' who prowled the streets preying on their 'industrious fellow-citizens'. Similarly, the *National Police Gazette* began its circulation in 1845 in New York, selling itself through the imaginative creation of an internal danger. According to the author, the whole country swarmed with thieves, burglars, pick-pockets, and swindlers. The press was not being used to protect the community against the criminal:

> until a system be adopted which will effectively hold him up to public shame and irrevocable exposure, the public will still remain at the mercy of his depredations, and nine-tenths of his fraternity go scot-free of any punishment. . . . It will be our object, therefore, to strip them of the advantages of a professional incognito, by publishing a minute description of their names, aliases, and persons; a succinct history of their previous career, their place of residence at the time of writing, and a current account of their movements from time to time.
>
> (*National Police Gazette*, 16 October 1845: 56)

The first edition carried a story that was in effect a marketing device, titled 'The Invisible Pursuer'. This told the story of a brutal murder in London, made doubly awful because no clue could be obtained as to the perpetrator of the deed. Public horror was at its utmost, and every effort was made to solve the crime. At length, a day labourer who had absconded a few days after the commission of the crime was suspected. The *London Police Gazette* immediately distributed a description of his person. Three days after publication, and ten after the murder, an aged magistrate of Ireland was sitting before his door in the evening, and looking over the papers from London. In the *Police Gazette* he noticed the account of the London murder and read the description of the suspect:

> While thus engaged, a shadow glanced across the sheet, caused by the figure of a man passing between him and the sun. He raised his eyes carelessly, as one will in cases of casual interruption, but was suddenly paralyzed by the appearance of the figure before him. It appeared as if the monster of his imagination had been suddenly conjured into life, and had slipped from the columns of the journal to glare upon him as a hideous reality. In the next moment, alarmed at the old man's stare, the object slipped away. It was too late – the silent spirit of the press had performed its object.
>
> (*National Police Gazette*, 16 October 1845: 53)

The alarm was raised, the fugitive captured, and the following day saw him on his way back to London to stand trial. This tale imagined the supreme potency of publicity in detection, the spotting of a wanted criminal, a 'shadow', while engaged in the act of reading his description. The plausibility of the account is strained, containing as it does, so many elements of the ideal scene. The observer is an official agent of the law, who while at leisure spots the criminal. The image of the criminal is constructed spectrally in the act of looking; he is a figure, a monster, a shadow.

While the assistance of the public continued to be actively sought, concerns about the poor reliability of 'eye-memory' were increasingly voiced. Dickens gave the following example of sharply discordant eye-witness testimony in a murder case, 'The suspected man was tall; he was not tall; he was of middle stature; he was fair; he had light whiskers; he had a long beard. He appeared, at last, to have none of these characteristics, to be non-existent altogether, mythical' (Dickens 1868: 575). By the late nineteenth century, a systematic critique of testimony was underway, which developed into the specialist field of legal psychology. The subjective feeling of certainty was thoroughly criticized, ironically producing axiomatic statements like, 'witnesses do not know what they know' (Gross 1911: 8). This critique of testimony, reported in both academic publications and popular journals and magazines, analysed the ways in which the subject's knowledge was not only limited, partial, but also unclear and confused, their vision fuzzy and awry, their utterances opaque and tangled. Experimental data showed that even when witnesses spoke in good faith, their testimony was riddled with error. Cattell (1895), working in a laboratory at Columbia University, insisted that science should establish the reliability and significance of witness testimony, writing that unscrupulous attorneys could readily discredit the statements of truthful witnesses, so the court needed to know the normal range of errors in recollection. The aptitude of witnesses to tell the truth could no longer be simply equated with their perceived moral integrity, and the sincerity of an individual was no guarantee of the truth of his deposition.

Experiments demonstrated that in the memory of objects seen, truth and falsehood were interwoven, a finding wholly at variance with commonplace and legal notions that witnesses were either worthy of credence or altogether without value. Details escaped attention, and the memory was subject to forgetting. The effect of memory was seen as both simplifying and lacunary. Memories tended to become schematic and abstract, and the progressive simplification obliged subjects to intervene with an increasing activity to fill in the gaps. William Stern of Breslau University was a prominent figure in the field, establishing a specialist journal on the subject. Stern (1902) demonstrated that error was the rule in testimony rather than the exception. Yet this discipline systematically erased the significance of interpretation and did not support a view of the relativity of knowledge. Legal psychology simply presumed that an objective singular version of events could be recovered and given authoritative force. Claparède (1907: 143) of Geneva University wrote in the *Strand Magazine* that 'nothing, indeed, is more difficult than to tell the truth'. He stated that the confidence of many witnesses was erroneously legitimized by the existence of heavy penalties for perjury and the special status conveyed in court by speaking under oath. This was an opinion shared by Hugo Munsterberg of Harvard, the most prominent popularizer of the findings of legal psychology. Munsterberg's experiments led him to write that pure sensory perception never occurred, with associations, judgements and suggestions entering into every apparent observation, 'we never know from the material in itself whether we remember, perceive, or imagine, and in the borderland regions there must result plenty of confusion which cannot always remain without dangerous consequences in the courtroom' (Munsterberg 1909: 61). The failings of testimony were regularly emphasized in order to argue for the pre-eminent reliability of the 'silent witnesses' of crime scene traces.

The scene of the crime

Crime scene analysis traces the vestiges, after they have left the scene, of elusive criminals, rather than constructing legible disciplinary spaces that produce docile, knowable bodies. In *Discipline and Punish*, the production of knowledge and the exercise of power do not work through exclusion but rather spatial distribution. The mechanism of partitioning is one such practice, within which 'each individual has his own place; and each place its individual', aiming to eliminate 'the uncontrolled disappearance of individuals' to establish an order of 'presences and absences, to know where and how to locate individuals' (Foucault 1991: 143). For Foucault, spaces of constructed visibility constituted the subject (Rajchman 1988). The concept of disciplinary power specified legible spaces that through a spatialization of the personality made possible a subjection by illumination, both literal and figurative. This notion of legible spaces, produced through the banishing of gothicity, and constitutive of both individualized personalities and subjection to disciplinary power, can be challenged. Rather than being produced as legible spaces, crime scenes are highly cathected. They are made knowable by virtue of a reconstruction of injurious events. Despite objectivist claims, the sentiments of Stapleton about the postmortem in the Road murder discussed above reveal it to have produced a traumatizing reconstruction rather than a simple process of codification, 'to translate into science the records of pain and wasting, of weariness and woe, from the hieroglyphics graven in the human flesh' (Stapleton 1861: 58). Crime scenes are spaces that become invested with meanings, both collective and individual, and are used to ground contestation about the 'truth' of past events. Despite the use of an objectivist aesthetics in some of the discourses of criminal detection, which seeks to translate the blinding force of trauma into incontro-vertible knowledge, their actual use and publicization does not eliminate uncertainty or readily produce singular truths purged of affect. While crime scene trace analysis may be depicted as an 'impersonal, technological' procedure, it tells highly intimate stories of sex, murder and human relationships (Joseph and Winter 1996).

It is worth looking a little closer into scientific detection's objectivist rhetoric of interpretation and authentication. Circumstantial evidence, the evidence of things unseen, came to increasing prominence from the late eighteenth century. Its rhetorical effects were potent, inviting readers to participate in the work of drawing inferences (Welsh 1992: x). The clue was depicted, both among forensic scientists, and in advocacy before the courts, as a thread leading the detective out of the labyrinth, a signature and a silent witness, 'mute, severe, incorruptible', yielding 'valuable, silent testimony' (Caussé 1854: 177, Garson 1906: 115). There was also a rhetoric of tiny particles, of the incredible power of scientific methods to detect the tiniest of traces. However, the effects of this rhetoric were marked by ambivalence, repeatedly counterposing the potency of scientific detection to the helplessness of the crime victim. This is seen, for instance, after the murder of a sleeping victim, a situation in which, as (Webster 1851: 61) put it, 'midnight assassins take no witnesses'. Writing on bloodstain analysis, Fleming made this typical contrast between scientific detection and the vulnerability and passivity of the victim:

> it is a high tribute to science to know that she can by her powers aid in fastening the guilt on him who, under covert of darkness and in the stillness of the night, steals upon his victim while in calm and peaceful slumber and for sordid lucre or revenge commits the crime of murder.
>
> (Fleming 1859: 85)

Despite the laudatory tone, the criminal event has already taken place, and in this case the victim is already dead. The vulnerability of the victim is not eliminated by conjuring up images of the potency of scientific method.

The claim that scientific methods could yield certainty was often made, but also undermined or denied in various ways. Francis Galton told the Troup committee that the probability of an erroneous match, a false positive, was 'enormously greater than what in popular language begins to rank as certainty' (Troup 1894: 57). In *Finger Prints* (1892), he attested to the marvellous persistence in both minutiae and the general character of the pattern. He stated that while proportions might change, details and overall form did not. The ridges, he explained, were fully formed by the sixth month of foetal life, and persisted after death until they were destroyed by decomposition. This kind of notion was typically the focus of popular representations of fingerprinting, for instance in *Puddn'head Wilson*, Mark Twain presented a courtroom fingerprint scene and wrote, 'Every human being carries with him from his cradle to his grave certain physical marks which do not change their character, and by which he can always be identified – and that without shade of doubt or question' (Twain 1894/1969: 215–16). This episode did not portray legal reasoning, instead dramatizing the way in which fingerprint evidence converted the jury to Wilson's way of thinking by evoking and arousing the imagination (Joseph and Winter 1996). The notion that 'the evidence speaks for itself' as regards fingerprinting took the form that operators were technicians rather than experts. The Troup (1894: 29) committee described fingerprints as 'an absolute impression taken directly from the body itself'. However, despite the repeated rhetoric of certainty, absolute impressions and freedom from all error, fingerprinting systems were actually based on probabilities, and the question of interpreting partial or unclear prints was debated from early times. Probabilities expressed the likelihood of a match between suspect and crime scene prints matching in mathematical terms, based upon calculating the distribution of characteristics. However, there have from the outset been concerns over the police's use of scientific detection evidence. This has included questions about planted material, about the reliability of the chain of evidence being correctly maintained to avoid incorrect provenance and contamination, and the failure to collect or realize the significance of trace evidence. The possibility of police and/or scientists using faked or planted scientific evidence to 'frame' suspects is seen in the question of forged finger-prints. This matter was dramatized in Conan Doyle's story 'The Adventure of the Norwood Builder' (1905) and was also the subject of disgreement between experts.

During the nineteenth century, disputes over the reliability of tests, and questions of contamination, bias and incompetence, were widely publicized. The problems of partisan and erroneous scientific evidence, and disagreement among expert witnesses, were hotly debated. Huge popular interest and alarm surrounded a series of 'secret murder' (poisoning) cases. In the Palmer strych-nine trial of 1856, Taylor clashed with the Bristol chemist William Herapeth and characterized his rival as one of a class of 'traffickers in evidence' (Taylor 1873: 38). Three years later, in the Smethurst poisoning trial, a man was tried for the murder of a woman with whom he had been living. She had died follow-ing an illness involving continuous vomiting and diarrhoea. Taylor for the prosecution was forced to admit in cross-examination that arsenic alleged to have come from the body could have actually come from copper gauze used in his test procedures.[8] Nevertheless, the defendant was convicted, and an outcry ensued in the press. The Home Secretary asked another scientist to review the trial papers, and later pardoned Smethurst. The disputes in court led the forensic chemist Letheby to write in indignation:

> the apparent contradictions of science, the seeming uncertainty of its results, and the conflicting testimony of its alumni, are such as to deprive it of that value which it ought to have in the estimation of the public, as the most powerful and certain of all modern means for the detection of secret murder.
>
> (*The Times*, 28 August 1859: 8)

By the 1870s, Taylor readily stated that with good pay the witnesses needed on either side of any medico-legal issue could always be found. He added that, 'all that is requisite for future murderers by poison to do, is to use small doses, combine the use of various drugs, and subpoena the proper medical witnesses for the defence' (Taylor 1873: 196). The 1890s saw alarm about a 'poisoning epidemic' in the USA. This widespread fear of, and fascination with, poison murder, relates to its status as the emblematic undiscovered crime (Essig 2002). Each case that made it to trial publicized the uncertainty of symptoms and diagnosis, raising the spectre of scores that had gone undetected.

Criminal detection does not produce a disciplinary codification of legible spaces. Instead, it yields highly contested narratives of the crime event, and proliferates fearful images of vulnerability and injury. Furthermore, both crime scene trace analysis and identification technologies seek to coercively translate involuntary residues and unconscious acts into narratives that 'solve' crimes (Joseph and Winter 1996). Rather than snaring them in a carceral net, detection practices track a mobile and duplicitous criminal, 'a protean being who constantly changes his skin', cleverly eluding detection through alibis, aliases and disguises (Aylmer 1897: 91). These technologies are not correctional. They were introduced as an inherent part of a modern retributive and deterrent force of law, warring with the habitual criminal 'who wilfully and persistently breaks the law' (Clarkson and Richardson 1889: 356).

Criminal identification, penality and the body

Foucault argued that the transformative effect of disciplinary techniques was produced by the incorporation of a norm, and hence an argument concerning the relationship between subjectivity and embodiment was advanced. Subjectivity was construed as the product of the direct exercise of disciplinary power upon the body (Foucault 1975/1991: 29). He argued that in studying disciplinary power, there was no need to consider the question of its mediation through the subject's consciousness because this form of power directly took hold of the body. John Tagg depicted the criminal identification photograph (mugshot) as a disciplinary technology, that shows, 'the body made object; divided and studied . . . made docile and forced to yield up its truth; separated and individuated; subjected and made subject' (Tagg 1988: 76). However, the visual practices of criminal identification do not function automatically and mechanically. Like the scientific analysis of crime scene traces described above, identificatory acts of looking, however technologized, are not processes of codification. Both their operation and their publication have produced dimensions of penality, power and embodiment that depart considerably from a Foucauldian framework. They coercively transfer the body's signs into a text (Sekula 1986: 33).

Systematic study of the physical signs of uniqueness and their reliability was well underway by the middle of the nineteenth century. The indelibility of tattoos was studied in terms of fading and deliberate effacement, and alterations like callouses and discolouring caused by occupational tasks were noted. Others wrote on scars, and methods for dyeing and bleaching the hair. Mugshots were taken by the police from at least 1841, and attempts were made to measure dimensions of the body for criminal identification purposes from mid century. Bertillon's system was practised in Paris from 1882 and generalized throughout France from 1885.[9] This involved bodily measurements, a mugshot and a record of distinctive bodily marks. Bertillon saw the old descriptions on criminal record cards as hopelessly vague and random. They were too easily thrown by criminals, who gave aliases. For instance, in 1892, the names Martin, Bernard and Duval had piles of cards measuring 5–600m high (Bonhomme 1892). Bertillon hence calculated the signaletic value of each characteristic, and standardized both the technique of making observations and the conventions used for notation (Bertillon 1881). Herbette, director of the French prison system, lauded the potential of bertillonage, praising its capacity, 'to fix the human personality, to give to each human being an individuality, that is certain, lasting, unchangeable, always recognisable and easily demonstrable' (cited in Bertillon 1883: 223). Bertillonage could produce 'a recognisable sign, indubitable, fixing his physical personality, his identity in a certain way' (De Ryckere 1893: 361). Edmund Spearman, arguing for the introduction of bertillonage in England, stated that the police should, 'trust nothing to the eye' and rely upon, 'the inflexible laws of mathematics', which would render mistakes of identity obsolete (Spearman 1890: 366).

Systematic criminal identification methods were introduced during the second half of the nineteenth century, and their rationale and design were premised on deterrent punishment rather than correctionalism. In England under Carnarvon and du Cane a system of amoral scientific punishment was put into place based in notions of individual responsibility, penal austerity, and harsh prison labour. Carnarvon was incensed by the figure of the habitual offender, whom he construed as a professional criminal. He advanced the Security from Violence Act of 1863, which legislated for bouts of flogging in the early stages of a sentence of penal servitude. Harsh, painful measures like this were designed to impress upon 'persons of such low and base spirit . . . a fear of punishment' (Carnarvon cited in McConville 1995: 62). His successor, du Cane, built upon this deterrent penality, and stated that the certainty of detecting and apprehending the criminal was vital to the deterrent effect of punishment (ibid.: 179). Modern criminal identification technologies were aimed at the professional criminal, directed at the offender who typically saw judicial punishment as an 'ordinary mishap incidental to a criminal career' (Anderson 1896). The criminal for whom identification technologies were designed was figured as mobile, duplicitous and refractory. Bertillon explained that there were thousands of simulations, writing, 'in the pick-pocket, in the travelling wheeler-dealer, everything is calculated to maintain the incognito' (Bertillon 1883: 92). Note the use of the phrase 'travelling wheeler-dealer' here; criminal identification technologies were directed at criminals quite prepared to move around the country and across national borders in pursuit of their nefarious career. Seeking to have bertillonage introduced into Britain during the time of du Cane's deterrent penality, Spearman attested to the fear of this certain identification:

> there is more wholesome terror to the accused in that terrible *mauvais quart d'heure* in the identification bureau than in all the rest of the experience at the Depot and the Judicial Palace. They know that all secrets will be revealed before that anthropometric judgement seat.
>
> (Spearman 1893: 71)

As well as using all manner of tricks, criminals were also refractory. Whatever their fear, they often struggled, contorting their bodies and faces under the measuring instruments and before the camera. Sometimes they had to be held down by the hair and beard by several policemen for these identificatory practices. In 1885, the Home Office made the refusal to be photographed a punishable breach of prison discipline.

The historical record of criminal identification technologies hence departs considerably from the Foucauldian idea of a meticulous control of operations producing an obedient and docile body, a body 'that may be subjected, used, transformed and improved' (Foucault 1975/1991: 136). Disciplinary power involved the internalization of a norm. Criminal detection technologies were designed to strike deterrent fear into incorrigible rogues, as well as to make them an example to keep others law-abiding. Unlike criminal anthropology, which as Guarnieri (1991) shows was rejected by the courts, criminal detection technologies were developed and designed in an interface between scientific and legal evidentiary discourses. As juridical technologies, they seek to arrest the perpetrator of an act and not an abnormal person, directed at the legal subject and not at the anthropological figure of *homo criminalis*. Mugshots, as we will see in Chapters 2 and 5, were also sometimes part of the mediated spectacle of suffering imposed upon criminals, producing stigmatizing images and textualizing a degraded body. Furthermore, both mugshots and 'Wanted' reward notices have been a point of condensation in the changing connections between punishment, notoriety and celebrity.

Everywhere and nowhere

At mid century, Hepworth Dixon described crime as 'sporadic' and 'migratory', writing of the criminal, 'sometimes he is one thing, sometimes another' (Dixon 1850: 225). Foucault wrote of disciplinary power, 'everywhere and always alert . . . it leaves no zone of shade' (Foucault 1991: 177); yet this puissant optics was denied by crime fiction stories that imagined spectral figures who were at once 'everywhere and nowhere'. The illegibility of criminality was publicized by a whole range of nineteenth-century texts. Gaston Leroux's *The Phantom Of The Opera* (1910) played with the materiality of its ghostly villain. The author stated openly to readers that 'the Opera Ghost really existed . . . he existed in flesh and blood, though he assumed all the outward characteristics of a real phantom, that is to say, of a shade' (Leroux 1985: 26). The managers of the theatre disbelieved stories of the ghost, and Richard commented that 'if he is everywhere I cannot have people telling me that he is nowhere'. A year later, Marcel Allain and Pierre Souvestre published the first of their many *Fantômas* novels, depicting a ruthless master criminal who killed without leaving any trace and seemed able to be in two places at once. The series presented a spectral master criminal, one of the 'enigmatical beings who are difficult to trace and too clever or intelligent to let themselves be caught (Allain and Souvestre 1987: 13). The magistrate Bonnet told his fellow diners that even if the police were more effective than ever before, science could also be used by criminals, making the work of the police still more difficult. He then set out to describe Fantômas:

It is impossible to say exactly what or to know precisely who Fantômas is. He often assumes the form and personality of some particular and even well-known individual; sometimes he assumes the forms of two human beings at the same time. . . . That he is a living person is certain and cannot be denied, yet he is impossible to catch or to identify. He is nowhere and everywhere at once, his shadow hovers above the strangest mysteries.

(ibid.: 14)

In the course of the novel, Fantômas assumes the identities of two separate individuals, and the reader never 'knows' who Fantômas has been until he is no longer that person. Inspector Juve employs the latest scientific detection technologies, including bertillonage, the dynamometer, and the analysis of clues like a drop of blood, a fragment of a map, footprints, and spots of dirt. However, despite these advanced techniques, Fantômas dramatically eludes punishment, escaping from prison and substituting an actor for himself, who is executed in his place. The drop of the guillotine secures neither capture nor justice.

A multitude of cases during the course of the nineteenth and early twentieth centuries gave considerable publicity to missing persons and cases of mistaken and disputed identity. These cases asked the question 'in just what did identity reside?' Was it simply observable from one's external physical appearance? Could it be read off the surface of the body? If many indicators were changeable, in quite what did the essence of identity reside? How then could one keep track of it? The difficulties of identifying unknown cadavers were widely publicized. Missing persons cases were dramatized in a large number of novels during the mid nineteenth century, and combined with newspaper coverage the problem was publicized to a broad audience.[10] The lengthy and broadly known Tichborne case is probable the most infamous of these trials. It seemed to confuse together the confidence man and the mistakenly accused individual, the imposter and the victim of a miscarriage of justice. Roger Tichborne, heir to a baronetcy and great estates, was thought to have perished at sea in 1854. Eleven years later, on the death of the baronet, a man living under the name of Thomas Castro in Wagga Wagga, Australia proclaimed himself to be Roger Tichborne. The Dowager was from the outset convinced that this man was her son, but other family members disagreed, and a dispute over title ensued. The legal proceedings spanned seven years.[11] As well as the questioning of a large number of witnesses for both sides, the focus of the trials was on the minute interrogation of the claimant. In the course of the criminal trial, the prosecution asserted that the claimant was one Arthur Orton, a butcher of Wapping. Yet how could a butcher pass himself off successfully as a peer educated at Stonyhurst? In what, then, did the mark of aristocracy reside? Proceedings in the Tichborne case received massive publicity. The volume and range of mementoes for sale, which both disputed and commemorated aspects of the trials, was vast, and included street ballads, poems and specialist newspapers.[12] While on bail, the claimant addressed meetings the length and breadth of the country, becoming a popular anti-Establishment figure celebrated by the working classes. The verdict seemed dubious to many. Troublingly, one witness had declared of the claimant, 'I am as certain of him as of my own identity' (*The Times*, 20 May 1871: 11). The penal politics of space and embodiment theorized by Foucault was premised on panopticism and, as Stuart Hall (1996:12) has remarked, 'there is no account of how or why bodies should not always-for-ever turn up, in place, at the right time'.

The city in a nightmare

A case that seems to exemplify the ideas rehearsed in this chapter, and which has important resonances with features of the contemporary scene, is that of Jack the Ripper. Looking back on the Ripper affair gives us important clues about detective work and its engagement of fearful onlookers. Between 1888 and 1891 there were eleven gruesome murders of women in the East End of London, which were attributed to an elusive killer who called himself Jack the Ripper. The Whitechapel murders, as the series of crimes came to be known, produced the figure of a monstrous dual personality. Both press depictions and the official psychological profile produced for the police imagined an outwardly respectable gentleman living a double life. Journalists and social commentators alike referred to gothic and detective fiction, to the shadowy figures of Poe and Stevenson and the clever killers of detective stories (Walkowitz 1992). Stevenson's highly popular *The Strange Case of Dr Jekyll and Mr Hyde* drew the reader into a web of fears and confusions in a city shown as labyrinthine. The story depicted a murderer with a divided personality, and alluded to a latent barbarity in everyone, with the idea that 'man is not truly one but truly two' (1886/1979: 82). Jekyll the respectable medical scientist is doubled with Hyde, a being 'hardly human', a fiend about whom there is 'something troglodytic', some unnameable deformity' (ibid.: 40). Hyde tramples a child and clubs an MP to death. He is barely described in the police handbills, the authorities have no photographic record of this vicious repeat offender, and nobody knows or can describe him clearly despite the 'hitherto unknown disgust, loathing and fear' that he elicits from them (ibid.: 42). Hyde is depicted as a phantasmatic figure, the stuff of nightmares, indistinct yet terrible, and despite thousands of pounds in reward and extensive efforts by the police, it seems that the fiend 'disappeared out of the ken of the police as though he had never existed' (ibid.: 56). Utterson, who is Jekyll's lawyer, searches with a Scotland Yard inspector through the dark, foggy, labyrinthine city, the 'city in a nightmare' (ibid.: 48). Stevenson chooses this moment in the narrative to evoke the force of law, writing that sitting next to the detective, Utterson 'was conscious of some touch of that terror of the law and the law's officers which may at times assail the honest' (ibid.: 48). But Hyde cannot be found, and Utterson only discovers what has taken place after Hyde–Jekyll has killed himself.

Stevenson's story, showing as a play in the West End at the time of the murders, was often referenced by journalists reporting on the Ripper murders. The inquest on the death of Mary Nichols heard that both police constables on their beat and night watchmen had been close to the crime scene but had heard and seen nothing suspicious (*The Times*, 3 September 1888: 12). Despite the nightly deployment of hundreds of plain-clothes police officers in Whitechapel, the police failed both to detect the culprit and to prevent further murders. Senior police officers and local figures wrote to the press complaining of the poor lighting and gloomy squalor of the locality. Reverend Samuels warned that 'dark passages lend themselves to evil deeds' and the Commisioner of the Metropolitan Police Force stated that 'darkness is an important assistant to crime' (*The Times*, 19 September 1888 and 4 October 1888). Petitions from local residents protested that the government could no longer ensure security of life and property in East London and demanded extra police.

Criticism of the government's failure to announce a large reward for information leading to the conviction of the killer was made repeatedly and vociferously. Sir Charles Warren, Chief Commissioner of the Metropolitan Police Force, advised the Home Office that a reward would probably not secure the capture of the Ripper but that one should be offered to 'allay the public feeling', warning that 'if other murders of a similar nature take place shortly ... the omission of the offer of a reward on the part of the Government may exercise a very serious effect upon the stability of the Government itself'.[13] The Home Secretary noted this suggestion of a reward as a 'politic step' which might satisfy the public, but no official reward was offered, although after the horrific murder and mutilation of Mary Kelly a free pardon was announced for information from accomplices. Both government and police found themselves under harsh criticism, and a telegram from the Queen at Balmoral insisted that the courts be lit. However, the government ignored demands for a reward and for lighting of the dark, labyrinthine East End.

This profusion of images engaged a fascinated and fearful public. The Ripper narrative produced terrible images of gruesome injury and the proliferation of menacing suspects. The city was portrayed as dark and labyrinthine, peopled by elusive and dangerous strangers, indeed the theory that the killer was a foreigner was well publicized and thoroughly investigated (Gilman 1990). The authorities' unsuccessful efforts to apprehend 'Jack' or to assuage anxieties brought severe criticism of their ability to maintain law and order. In sum, the Jack the Ripper affair illustrates powerfully the importance of discourses about undiscovered crimes and criminal detection to the mediated spectacle of crime and punishment.

'Commit a crime and the earth is made of glass'

Beside the words of Emerson, which stand as the epigraph to this chapter, we can place those of Carpenter (1905: 37) when he wrote, 'the giant apparatus fails to detect or to punish a hundredth part of the criminal actions it is in search of'. Foucault (1996: 232) described the imaginary spaces of the gothic novel of the Revolutionary period as 'like the negative of the transparency and visibility that the new order hoped to establish'. He stated that these literary and fictional spaces were the opposite of the 'space of exact legibility' represented in the Panopticon Plan. In reversing the principle of the dungeon, he argued, both a new penality and a new politics of space was initiated that made possible a 'subjection by illumination' (ibid.: 232). The narratives and images of criminal detection do not depict a transparent order of legible and locatable individuals, positioned and controlled through an omniscient, impersonal eye of power. The gothic is not banished from modern and contemporary penality, which have remained, albeit in changing ways, suffused with tropes of the dark, the shadowy and the monstrous.

Foucault's dissident fiction rejected the narratives of penal leniency and humanity underlying accounts of the rise of imprisonment, and replaced these with a story about the dispersion of a new and subtle modality of power. The tales told by *Crime and Punishment in Contemporary Culture* also discard these liberal notions. Nevertheless, it is a premise of this book that if we are to comprehend penal change, and the connections between penal practices and power relations in contemporary western societies, we need to fiction a different history to that written by Foucault. In particular, the changing ways in which the mediated spectacle of criminal detection and punishment has engaged onlookers as fearful victims and enraged avengers require scrutiny. This task is begun in the chapters that follow, starting with two that explore the relations between penal practices, national collectivities and the marking, exclusion or elimination of foreigners. When Chaucer's Prioress exclaimed 'murder will out', she was retelling the old story of blood libel, the story of Jews murdering Christian children. As ever with the blood libel, the narrative of the crime serves as the pretext for violent persecution. In 'The Prioress's Tale', all of the 'accursed people' are judged guilty and killed. Devotional reverence and the certainty of detection stand out against a medieval order of justice and morality premised on violent and exclusionary anti-Semitism (the Jews had been expelled from England in 1290). The next two chapters of the book explore some instances in which the spectacle of modern criminal detection and punishment became a question of revealing the dangerous 'passing' Jew or the subversive immigrant.

2 Punishment, print culture and the nation

This chapter connects the mediated spectacle of punishment with a penal politics of assimilation. The analysis presented explores the place of exemplary punishment within the constitution of the modern nation as an imagined community. In addition to constituting a specific geographical territory, the nation is constructed through the political arrangement of boundaries. The location and maintenance of these boundaries fosters both national sovereignty and a sense of belonging. According to Benedict Anderson's book *Imagined Communities*, the members of a nation never meet the majority of their fellows, but nevertheless retain a mental image of collective belonging. He linked the constitution of the modern nation to the political unification of populations brought by vernacular print culture. The printed word, according to him, constructed homogenized national and political spaces. A similar argument had earlier been advanced by Marshall McLuhan (1964/2002: 193), when he wrote, 'nationalism itself came as an intense new visual image of group destiny and status, and depended on a speed of information movement unknown before printing'. He explained that novels and newspapers appealed to and constituted national reading publics by condensing various symbols into vivid and readily identifiable images. Anderson emphasized that the modern nation was imagined as limited, as contained within 'finite, if elastic boundaries'. In this chapter, a culture of retributive punishment in turn-of-the-century France is related to the constitution of the national political space of the imagined community. The spectacle, both witnessed and mediated, of the harsh punishment of a Jewish army officer convicted of treason, brought contestation of the boundaries of the modern nation.

Anderson's idea of the nation as imagined political community emphasized the constitutive role of print culture. It was at this *fin de siècle* moment that an influential theory of punishment and communication emerged in the work of Emile Durkheim, who also wrote two essays on the treason case addressed in this chapter. Durkheim correlated the move from primitive to advanced societies with a shift from severe to lenient penalties. It is less often remarked that his theories of social and penal change entailed a politics of the assimilation of foreigners, of those marked by ethnic and religious differences. As a person from elsewhere, a foreigner is one who has crossed a border, one who is out of place. Foreigners are people who figure as 'in' the social body, but also in some sense not 'of' it. For centuries, the notion has carried connotations of stranger-hood, and been used to identify certain people as different from oneself in some significant way. In earlier usage, a foreigner could be somebody from another county or parish, who was thereby an outsider to one's immediate locality. By the late nineteenth century, 'foreigners' were more likely those who hailed from another nation. They included those born beyond the frontiers of the national territory, as well as the native-born barred from full national belonging because of 'alien' parentage, or linguistic or corporeal features. Either way, 'foreigners' called up an elaborate and often exoticizing imagination of what lay beyond the national boundaries. Durkheim related the communication of hostile, vengeful and retributive sentiments to the rigid mechanical solidarity of primitive societies, which he associated with harsh punishment and practices of exclusion. He believed that the communication of a new set of tolerant sentiments based in ideals of humanity and rights would temper the severity of penal practices. His vision of organic solidarity employed a rhetoric of universal human rights, but entailed a republican assimilationist politics. This involved the disappear-ance of ethnic and religious conflict *and* difference. Durkheim maintained this vision of republican nationhood throughout his prominent involvement with the Dreyfus affair. His work obscured the part played by modern penal practices in the marking and repudiation of the alien from within the national body, in the contested location of boundaries. Durkheim's theses linked punishment with communication, but obscured the significance of the triadic relationship of punishment, *nation* and communication. His work, and later that of Foucault, overlooked the transformation of the monarchical spectacle of punishment into a modern form of *mediated armed justice*, which marked out and expelled enemies.

Penality and mediated armed justice

The notion of penality as a mode of *mediated armed justice* describes the recon-figuration of the monarchical armed power that Michel Foucault associated with the *ancien régime*. Foucault argued that the executions of that time were important ceremonies by which power was manifested and reactivated. He depicted these executions as explicitly militarial performances. Not only was this penal style part of the sovereign's power of life and death, it was an aspect of the monarch's right to make war on enemies. Foucault wrote that 'the sword that punished the guilty was also the sword that destroyed enemies', hence the spectacle of the scaffold was one of 'armed justice', 'a ritual of armed law' (Foucault 1975/1991: 50). In this performance of capital punishment, injured sovereignty was reconstituted through the display of disproportionate power as penal excess. Foucault tells us that these punitive ceremonies were exercises of terror, in which the vengeance of the sovereign against enemies manifested the superiority of monarchical force. This vanquishing power, this invincible force, was enacted through dire corporeal punishments, not only upon regicides or treasonous plotters, but also upon common murderers and thieves. The vengeance of the sovereign rained down in tortures and violent, painful deaths upon the bodies of the condemned, the atrocity of this penal practice ritually annihilating infamy by omnipotence.

Foucault pointed out that monarchical armed power solicited the assistance of its subjects. As onlookers at the foot of the scaffold the crowd participated in the sovereign's vengeance against enemies, and especially when these enemies were to be found among them. Yet he also emphasized that these terroristic rituals were ambiguous and equivocal, writing of public execution, 'that uncertain festival in which violence was instantaneously reversible' (Foucault 1975/1991: 63). He associated armed justice with insurgency, writing of the unstable intersection of 'the excess of armed justice and the anger of the people' (ibid.: 73). Foucault described a shift from the terror of armed law to a gentle disciplinary power, from spectacle to surveillance in penality. He depicted disciplinary power as in a sense militarial, deploying tactics and training practices to shape docile, productive bodies. His vision of modernity as a carceral archipelago mentioned its genealogical descent from 'a military dream of society', producing through the coercive control of bodies obedient and useful individuals (ibid.: 169). The militarial motif of modernity in Foucault is hence emblematic of the replacement of spectacle by normalizing judgement.

However, during modernity the spectacle of armed power continued, becoming reconfigured as a mediated mode. Unlike in the era of monarchical power, modern armed justice was primarily witnessed and consumed in mediated form, assuming an important place within the terrain of infotainment. Print culture, and especially newspapers, played a crucial role in the elaboration of modern penality. The Dreyfus affair, a case explored in this chapter, combined elements of both direct and mediated armed justice. A public, punitive spectacle of degradation was staged, attended by large crowds. The event was widely reported in the press, yielding numerous striking and memorable images. With the intervention of the celebrity writer Emile Zola, the affair became hotly contested, and the spectacle of Dreyfus' severe punishment was reported internationally. A huge volume of cartoons, caricatures and commentary proliferated images and ideas about the case. In this unforgettably dramatic instance of direct and mediated armed power, a range of textual practices through which the modern nation was imagined as limited and contained within 'finite, if elastic boundaries' is visible. In sum, the punishment of Dreyfus engaged onlookers in the negotiation of the boundaries of the nation-state.

In 1894, Captain Alfred Dreyfus was accused of authorizing a treasonous memo, which delivered certain military secrets to the Germans. Dreyfus came from a family of prosperous Jewish industrialists, and was a highly successful officer. He was tried by a court martial, in which the criminal identification expert Alphonse Bertillon, whose system was discussed in Chapter 1, gave evidence. Bertillon was a notorious anti-Semite and admirer of the military, and advanced an elaborate theory of 'self-forgery'.[1] When Dreyfus was found guilty of high treason, a furious dispute arose over what might constitute an appropriately condign punishment. A law of 1848 had prohibited the penalty of death for political crimes. Angry debate raged in the Chamber of Deputies over the reintroduction of the guillotine for the 'treasonous' convict. While Dreyfus was not put to death, his penalty was particularly severe. He was sentenced to military degradation, followed by deportation for life in a fortified place. His punishment began with a humiliating ceremony held on the Jewish Sabbath, in which he was literally stripped of his rank in front of troops, new recruits, journalists, and the general public at the Ecole Militaire. With angry gestures a warrant officer tore the epaulettes, braid and buttons from Dreyfus' uniform, striking off the insignia of rank and throwing them in the mud. He then broke a sword over his knee. The scene, with its dramatic theatricality, provided for numerous graphic images and vivid commentary.

The ceremony was intended to be a cruel one, 'a didactic ritual designed to instill the fear of humiliation' (Burns 1993: 151). Dreyfus protested, shouting out his innocence, while the crowd beyond the courtyard gates chanted, 'Death to the Jews, Death to the Traitor, Death to Judas!' He was forced to undergo a prolonged parade before the troops and public, during which ordeal an officer's wife spat in his face and journalists yelled 'filthy Jew' at him. Dispatched in a prison wagon in his torn and stripped uniform, his memoirs record the stigmatizing and coercive identification procedures to which he was subjected on arrival at prison, 'dragged from hall to hall, searched, photographed and measured' (Dreyfus 1977). His identification photograph recorded the image of him attired in his tattered uniform, displaying both a man not fit to be a soldier, and a traitorous Jew exposed.

While Dreyfus was in custody awaiting transportation, the French parliament passed a law reinstating the Iles du Salut off Guiana as an official locus for 'deportation in a fortified place'. Between 1852 and 1946, 74,000 convicts were transported to the forced labour camps of Guiana. During debate for the establishment of penal colonies one member of parliament stated, 'the goals of transportation are intimidation, the preservation of society and the correction of the wrongdoer' (cited in Merle 1996: 23). Deportation was intended to cleanse the body politic by exiling malefactors (social defence) and by creating the fear of a harsh law (deterrence). Whereas in Britain convicts could return at the expiration of their sentences, French law introduced a notion of perpetuity. Prisoners who received a sentence of more than eight years' hard labour were exiled for life. All others must remain overseas after their release for a period equivalent to the duration of their sentence. Given that the minimum term of transportation was five years, this system of *doublage* imposed an exile of at least a decade. The French penal colony was hence a place of perpetual or long-term exile, and whereas the terms of rehabilitation were included in the discourses surrounding transportation, in practice this was allowed only far away from the mainland. Guiana had a particularly terrifying reputation as an intemperate and disease-ridden 'hell'. Four years after France opened another penal colony in Nouvelle Caledonie, it ordered that all 'European' convicts be sent there, and only 'coloured' prisoners who could purportedly stand the climate would remain in Guiana. Sending Dreyfus into permanent exile in this particular destination was hence an emphatically punitive gesture.

Dreyfus was sent into life imprisonment on the Ile du Diable, the smallest and most uninhabitable of the islands, at the time used to house a leper colony. The lepers were relocated and Dreyfus became the island's sole inmate. On this tiny barren island he was housed in a small stone hut guarded by a watchtower equipped with a machine gun. He was subjected to constant surveillance, and absolutely forbidden any conversation with the guards. Before long he was forced to wear irons at night, inflicting upon him an unbearably uncomfortable posture. The irons were attached to his bed, forming what the prisoner called a 'torture machine', the rings lacerating his ankles and becoming caked in blood. He suffered chronic dysentery and malarial fever, and was not allowed to be treated in the penal colony's hospital. His punishment, a 'superhuman torture', was legitimated both in terms of preventing an escape purportedly planned by a 'menacing international Jewry' and for the purpose of maximizing his punishment (Paul de Cassagnac *L'Autorité*, 13 September 1895). By the time he was exonerated in 1906 the formerly trim soldier had undergone great physical deterioration. Emaciation and premature ageing had rendered him virtually unrecognizable. This penal practice of incarceration in exile departs greatly from Foucault's story, in which disciplinary power produces a docile body that is useful. A volume containing Dreyfus' letters and autobiography, first published in 1901, was an immediate bestseller, translated into most European languages. This book textualized the suffering of the body of Dreyfus, a spectacle of the body in pain, the pain of mental and physical degradation and torture.

Assimilation, passing and punishment

Images and commentary on the Dreyfus affair in the anti-Semitic press conveyed to the reading public notions of the alien concealed beneath the surface of the 'passing' Jewish officer. Many eyewitness accounts of the degradation ceremony claimed that the foreign physiognomy of Dreyfus had revolted spectators, for instance:

> His was the color of treason. His face was ashen, without relief, base, without appearance of remorse, foreign, to be sure, debris of the ghetto. . . . This wretch is not French. We have all understood as much from his act, his demeanour, his physiognomy.
>
> (Daudet cited in Gilman 1995: 75)

Franco-Judaism as an ideology was constructed upon the foundational act of emancipation of the Jews by France in 1790/1. France was the first European country to end legal discrimination, but this came in return for 'regeneration', the rapid divestment of all external manifestations of particularism. Additionally, Third Republic France saw a resurgent new right, aggressively resistant to the presence of Jews, however 'Frenchified'. In 1890, Edouard Drumont founded the *Ligue Anti-sémitique de France*, and in 1892 he launched *La Libre Parole*, its subtitle 'France for the French'. His *La France Juive* was the biggest best-seller in late-nineteenth-century France. The book made a defence of 'traditional France' and an attack on modern greed and materialism, as typified by Jews. Military defeat in the Franco-Prussian war had aroused alarm and those on the political right were able to manipulate anxieties about the threat of foreign agents. Dreyfus had moved to Paris when the Germans annexed Alsace in 1871, but his brothers had chosen to remain there and become German citizens. Not only was Dreyfus the first Jew on the army's General Staff, through family ties he was close to the enemy.

One of the most vocal pressure groups was the *Ligue des Patriotes*, number-ing 30,000 members, a violent body which worshipped the army. It drew on a volatile mix of authoritarianism and wounded nationalism. The militant daily *La Croix*, with a circulation of 180,000 was the biggest selling Catholic publication. In vehement rhetoric, it blamed the decline of Catholic influence on the Jews. *La Croix* depicted the Dreyfus affair as a 'race war', orchestrating outrage against those intellectuals who spoke up for Dreyfus. Three years before the arrest of Dreyfus, Jules Simon had warned of the rise of extreme anti-Semitism in France, observing that people who were usually non-violent now:

> eagerly welcome the calumnies heaped on the Jews, for whom they have neither justice nor pity. They do not ask for proofs. . . . If they have not resorted to open cruelty and violence against them, it is simply because the police prevent them.
>
> (Simon 1891 cited in Conybeare 1898: 7)

Yet the affair cannot be reduced to a simple polarization between an extreme anti-republican and anti-Semitic group and a Dreyfusard camp espousing truth, justice and the republican principles of 1789. Extremism was the tendency of the minority, whereas moderate anti-Dreyfusism was quite widespread (Cahm 2001). This response to the case emphasized the imperative of respect for repub-lican legality, seeing truth and justice as emanating from institutions like courts and governments, and seeking to quieten criticism by adherence to the authority of *la chose jugée*, the court's decision. This anti-Dreyfus stance hence imagined legal process as devoid of the practices of alien inscription and repudiation that were promulgated more overtly by anti-Semitic organizations and publications.

The Dreyfus case 'provides a model for the decline of the healthy body of the acculturated, westernised, male Jew into the sick, decaying body of the essen-tial Jew he is concealing, the *exemplum* of racial predestination' (Gilman 1995: 70). Illustrators and caricaturists embellished the details of the degradation and punishment into a series of highly focused and crude images, exposing the passing and treasonous Jew. This proliferation of images made spectacle of the dangerous alien hidden within the undetectable bodies of assimilated Jews, reinscribing sinister traits upon a man who could almost pass for gentile.

Corresponding with this 'exposure' of the deceptive traitorous Jew hiding in a military uniform was the repeated figure of a powerful conspiracy or syndicate of international Jewry. Drumont wrote, 'in order for a man to betray his country, it is necessary first of all that he has a country, and that country cannot be acquired by an act of naturalization' (cited in Snyder 1973: 95). He termed the Jews 'cosmopolitans', who because they had no homeland could not serve any country faithfully. Drumont employed over and over again the rhetoric of 'strangers within' and 'enemies within', calling the Jews 'a nation within a nation'. He villified the 'hooknosed tribe' of foreigners. These crude physiognomical images were circulated broadly in anti-Dreyfusard cartoons, which contrasted the scheming Semite and the chivalrous Aryan.

Republican nationhood, assimilation and the Dreyfus affair

Durkheim was one of the intellectuals who opposed the dramatic and harsh punishment of Dreyfus, and he published two articles intervening in the affair. These used the case to illustrate and elaborate upon his theory of punishment and communication. The two essays associated a lenient modern punishment with abstract notions of universal human rights and ideals of tolerance, and hence depicted the ordeal inflicted upon Dreyfus as archaic, premodern and passé. Ultimately, Durkheim's theory obscured the contested relations between modern punishment, *nation* and communication.

Durkheim stated that pre-industrial societies had been composed of small groups, in which solidarity was attained through the sharing of an all-encompassing set of norms and values. The cohesion of these groups was based on the similarity and likeness of the individuals within them. Within these societies of 'mechanical solidarity', reactions to nonconformity had been harsh. Durkheim characterized the communication of hostile, angered sentiments against criminals, and what he called 'the passion of punishment', as features of the old societies of mechanical solidarity. In *The Division of Labour in Society* he depicted punishment in those societies as an intense collective phenomenon driven by irrational forces. Its practices were seen simply as rituals expressing the furious moral outrage of the group against those who had violated its sacred moral order. In response all 'healthy consciences' came together to reaffirm powerfully the shared beliefs. This ireful public wrath was depicted by him as the expression of dutiful moral outrage. Durkheim equated mechanical solidarity with the communication of hostile sentiments and harsh punishment, which condemned the wrongdoer and marked him or her as an outsider to be cast aside. According to him, the values suited to industrial societies constituted a 'religion of humanity' focused on the civic values of individual dignity, reason and tolerance. In the incendiary climate of the Third Republic, he appealed for a new kind of *amour patrie*, resting in the fundamentally sacred character of the individual. Durkheim condemned physical punishment as a degrading affront to the dignity and sacredness of humanity. He declared his opposition to oppressive appeals to punishment, seeing these as distractions from the urgent need for fundamental reforms (Miller 1996: 269). The organic solidarity of advanced societies was associated by Durkheim with restitutive law, which acted to restore the status quo. However, as Cotterell (1999) notes, Durkheim readily recognized social complexity and differentiation in considering the conditions of organic solidarity and restitutive law, but refused to do so in considering repressive law and punishment. The result is that in Durkheim's work the very idea of punishment is tied to the concept of an homogeneous, all-embracing collective consciousness.

Durkheim's thesis on punishment, communication and solidarity was further outlined in 'Two Laws of Penal Evolution' (1901/1992). In this essay, he portrayed the replacement of brutal bodily punishment by imprisonment as a sign that collective values increasingly hallowed human dignity, bringing changing sensibilities towards physical punishments. Durkheim reiterated the tenet that penal severity declines with increasing social differentiation. He argued that protection/vindication of the victim via harsh punishment also violated the sacred humanity of the criminal, a problem managed by a moderation in the severity of punishment. He wrote that in modern advanced societies with collective values centred on the sanctity of the individual, the distance between the offender and the offended is reduced, 'they are more nearly on the same level' (Durkheim 1900/1992: 42). This situation pertained all the more, he claimed, to the extent that the crime victim 'offers himself in the guise of a particular individuality, in all respects identical to that of the transgressor' (ibid.: 42). He hence portrayed modern punishment as, 'that calmer and more reflective emotion provoked by offences which take place between equals' (ibid.: 46). Durkheim added that penal severity varies not only with changing sensibilities, but also with shifts in political organization. Specifically, he argued that instances in which the trend towards milder punishment was moderated or reversed coincided with times in which central power was absolute. He wrote that centralized and absolute power is not counter-balanced or limited by other social functions and hence is subject to no restraints. In such a society legal relations are not bilateral and reciprocal and the centralized absolute power enjoys a monopoly over rights, exercising what Durkheim terms 'dominance' over the rest of society (ibid.: 23).

Durkheim called the periods of penal severity that he associated with absolutism of power 'perturbations' (ibid.: 38). His association of severe punishment during modernity with absolutism involved no recognition of the complex relations between the democratic state and populist engagement in the spectacle of punishment. Furthermore, his argument about political organization and the severity of punishment took no account of the politics of assimilation central to his notion of organic solidarity. His continued insistence upon a correlation between the move from primitive to advanced societies with the shift from severe to lenient penalties involved a number of problematic arguments about assimilation. He asserted that in modern societies the distance between the offender and the offended is reduced, as each appears in his individuality.

However, this claim wholly disregarded the immersion of the penal practices of his day within a culture of the penal marking of essentialized foreigners. In terms of the Dreyfus case, the mediated spectacle of penality as armed justice figured the Jew as a dangerous alien, and repudiated the enemy so marked from within the body of the nation.

Durkheim's writings on the affair espoused a similar position to the group at *La Revue Blanche*, a journal which became a leading *centre dreyfusard*. This group were assimilated and non-practising Jewish intellectuals, anxious to demonstrate that their support for Dreyfus was based not on religious solidarity but on secular values and beliefs linked to the defence of the Republic (Datta 1995). Durkheim was active in the *Ligue pour la Défense des Droits de l'Homme*, acting as secretary to its Bordeaux branch. Both Dreyfus and Durkheim rejected religious traditionalism and orthodoxy in favour of faith in a secular and all-inclusive society. Durkheim came from a rabbinical family, but after arriving in Paris, he put his Judaism aside. The surviving documents seem to support Ivan Strenski's (1997: 4) assertion that Durkheim 'actively tried to dissolve his sense of ethnic and religious identity in French national identity'. In addition to his involvement with the Drefyus affair, questions of ethnic and religious identification and conflict were a matter of personal significance to Durkheim. He was the subject of anti-Semitic hostilities in connection with his promotion to eminence within French academia (Hanna 1998). In fact, in 1916 *La Libre Parole* went so far as to make the accusation that Durkheim himself was a German agent.[2]

Durkheim's first intervention in the affair was published as a response to Ferdinand Brunetière, who had defended the army as crucial to security, prosperity and democracy. He had depicted these as threatened by a malign individualism, particularly found in intellectuals, whom he claimed were defending Dreyfus out of wounded vanity. This article provoked Durkheim to publish a spirited defence of his vision of organic solidarity. He began with an appeal to the sacredness of the human condition, which he thought must induce respect for others, 'The human person, whose definition serves as the touchstone according to which good must be distinguished from evil, is considered as sacred' (Durkheim 1898/1969: 21). This sacred quality, according to Durkheim, generated a protective space around the human being, hence, 'Whoever makes an attempt on a man's life, on a man's liberty, on a man's honour inspires us with a feeling of horror, in every way analogous to that which the believer experiences when he sees his idol profaned' (ibid.: 22). He wrote that because the religion of humanity rose far above individual concerns, it served as a rallying point, producing social cohesion by uniting people in pursuit of a common end. For him, the religion of humanity was a historically specific form particularly suited to the France of his day. He asserted that as societies became more populated, they admitted more variation, and the division of labour operated as a further force of differentation and discord. Society was moving, he warned, towards conditions in which the only thing that members of a social group had in common was their humanity, 'there remains nothing that men may love and honour in common, apart from man himself' (ibid.: 26). By cruelly punishing Dreyfus, French society renounced all that constituted the worth and dignity of living for the sake of a public institution, the army.

In this essay there is no mention of race or anti-Semitism, which Durkheim turned into an abstract issue of individualism and collectivism. Though he appealed to abstract universal principles as the source of social solidarity, his intervention in the affair was partisan, and specifically republican. Furthermore, his notion of organic solidarity involved an explicit politics of assimilation. In his account of the transformation from primitive to modern societies, Durkheim argued that the category of race became obliterated as a result of the emergence of differentiated individuals. Overall, he saw neither race nor religious differences as divisive forces within the system of social relations. Lehmann (1994) argued that Durkheim silenced the perpetual and severe conflict between races, classes and sexes that was characteristic of the period within which he was writing, suppressing from his historical narrative the sounds of protest, demonstration, riot and war. He unconvincingly resolved questions of race, class and sex conflict in the terms of organicism, dissolving confrontational social groups into individuals confronting society.

Durkheim's second article on the Dreyfus case did address the issue of anti-Semitism, but only to depict this as an error or illusion. In this essay, he (1899) figured anti-Semitism not as a racial problem but as a symptom of the 'crisis of transition' between mechanical and organic solidarities. He described anti-Semitism as a misplaced symptom of social suffering, an error in that it projected racial essentialism onto social assimilation. It was an old-fashioned error, ascribing distinctive qualities to a group, where no such entity existed, 'The Jews are losing their ethnic character with an extreme rapidity. In two generations the process will be complete' (Durkheim 1899: 346).[3] By contrast, Hannah Arendt's writings on the Dreyfus case, first published in the early 1940s, gave a compelling analysis of the contradictions of assimilation. Arendt had escaped from Nazi Germany to live in France for eight years, before fleeing the collaborationist Vichy regime and going to the USA as a refugee. Her work emphasized the connections and continuities between the anti-Jewish Vichy legislation and the mobilization against Dreyfus, with its persecution of every Jew, its 'passion-driven hunt of the "Jew in general", the "Jew everywhere and nowhere"' (Arendt 1951: 87). The Jew, Arendt argued, was caught between the status of pariah and parvenu. Jews were, she explained, only granted assimilation if they presented themselves as distinct exceptions from the 'ordinary Jew' from 'the mass of the Jews', from 'the Jew in general'. Under this assimilative logic, they occupied an ambiguous and precarious position; as Arendt put it, they must try 'to be and yet not to be Jews' (ibid.: 56). She depicted Dreyfus as a parvenu, experiencing hostility when he tried to enter the upper echelon of the army:

> The case of the unfortunate Captain Dreyfus had shown the world that in
> every Jewish nobleman and multimillionaire there still remained something

of the old-time pariah, who has no country, for whom human rights do not exist, and whom society would gladly exclude from its privileges.

(ibid.: 117)

Instead of Durkheim's idea of penal severity and absolutism, totalitarianism involves populist forms of engagement, one of the classic questions being of course, 'how were the masses won over to fascism?' Arendt closely linked the ideology supporting the 'death factories', the 'horror machine', and the 'passionless efficiency' of the holocaust, to the Dreyfus affair, which she saw as a precursor, a 'foregleam' of Hitler's ideology. My research found contestatory populist forms of engagement through iconic images and emotive rhetoric, used to legitimate and to oppose the penal politics of assimilationism.

The *affaire*, print culture and the imagined limits of nation

Anderson's idea of the nation as imagined political community emphasized the constitutive role of print culture. He explained that novels and newspapers appealed to and constituted national reading publics by condensing various symbols into vivid and readily identifiable images. Print, according to Anderson, constructed homogenized national and political spaces through which the modern nation was imagined as limited, as contained within 'finite, if elastic boundaries'. The print culture of turn-of-the-century France produced a mediated spectacle of punishment which brought contestation of the boundaries of the modern nation. The trial of Dreyfus and the campaign for revision of his treason conviction were much more than a court case, they were an *affaire*. The case became a hotly disputed criminal *cause célèbre*, an exceptionally divisive major political controversy. Issues far beyond the legal question of the guilt or innocence of the accused are involved in an *affaire*, which has the power to engage powerful emotions in large numbers of people over a lengthy period. It attracts the involvement of prominent individuals as well as mobilizing large numbers of ordinary people. The furies of the Dreyfus affair were amusingly depicted by Caran D'Ache in his cartoon of a family dinner erupting into a brawl when the diners failed to avoid discussing the affair.

An *affaire* is both reported and debated internationally. The Dreyfus *affaire* became known throughout the west, and even remote regions of Europe were drawn into vicarious participation (Brennan 1998). Technologies also facilitated the inexpensive and rapid transmitting of news of the case to US readers (Feldman 1981). The discourse of an *affaire* is often marked by sensationalist journalism and lurid details of scandal and taboo. It gives rise to striking images, for instance those of the breaking of Dreyfus' sword, or the snapshots of the dangling body of the lynched Frank, which were reproduced in mass and sold for many years (Lindemann 1993). Specialist newspapers and a range of mementoes are often produced, for instance those involved with the Tichborne case discussed in Chapter 1. In France, an anti-Dreyfusard satirical magazine,

Psst, and the Dreyfusard *Le Sifflet*, were sold. The cultural afterlife of an *affaire* is also a weighty and complex one, for instance the trial and punishment of Dreyfus found echoes and reflections in novels and stories by writers like Proust, Mirabeau and Kafka (Wilkinson 1992, Gilman 1995).

The most well-known moment in the mediated spectacle of the Dreyfus affair must be Emile Zola's famous intervention of 1898, which produced a sensation. Zola published a letter to the President of the Republic in the newspaper *L'Aurore*. Its headline was simply, 'J'ACCUSE' and it denounced the army's cover-up, selling 200,000 copies within two hours. This was a masterpiece of polemic, and provoked massive public debate and commentary. People literally fought for copies. Zola accused senior French officers of perjury and challenged them to sue him. His article, which stated that 'it is a crime to play on patriotism to further the aims of hatred', sparked off anti-Semitic rioting in sixty towns, which continued sporadically for eighteen months (Zola 1898/1996, Wilson 1973). Editorials expressed violent hatred and a range of negative pseudo-scientific representations of Jews were promulgated. Hostile marches and demonstrations were staged, and synagogues were desecrated. Beatings in the street and the destruction of businesses took place, in some instances with the complicity of the police. Zola was charged with criminal libel, and hundreds of reporters from across the world covered his trial. The military and clerical newspapers put the names and addresses of the jurors on their front pages and made grave threats if a guilty verdict was not reached. Convicted by the jury, he received the maximum sentence, and fled to England.[4] This conviction was proclaimed by the right as a vindication of the 1894 treason verdict. Dreyfus underwent a retrial in 1899, during which his lawyer was shot in the back on the way to court. When this hearing confirmed the 1894 verdict, it was widely seen as a farce. Dreyfus was not vindicated until 1906, when he was honoured by a rehabilitation ceremony at the Ecole Militaire. In 1908 the ashes of Zola, who had died in 1902, were transferred to the Pantheon. Right-wing groups like Action Française released incendiary announcements about the expression of legitimate national anger against the 'Jewish traitor' and his 'protector'. Louis Gregori, a right-wing journalist, fired two revolver shots at Dreyfus, wounding him in the arm. Put on trial for attempted murder, his plea in court was that he had merely intended a 'demonstration'. He was acquitted by the jury and the right-wing press praised the shooting as an echo of the people's anger, the symbolic act of a patriot. Each of these events during the *affaire* were covered extensively by the press.

The mediated spectacle of armed justice that constituted the punishment of Dreyfus involved both national and colonial constructions of the imagined political community. For instance, Robert Tombs (1998) presented an analysis of the kind of Dreyfusard position taken up by the British establishment, and of the reasons for people whose values included patriotism, militarism and deference to traditional authority to express sympathy for the 'martyr'. He described the vocabulary of horror and indignation used by English diplomats, publications like *The Times* and even Queen Victoria. Tombs depicted this

Dreyfusard position of the Victorian establishment as a means of confirming their own prejudices, as an important reassurance as to the rightness of their own beliefs and practices at a time of economic and political challenges. He noted that severe criticism of the French judicial system was prominent, and, counterposed to the notion of the impartial British rule of law, used as an index of civilization and central support of a national myth. Comment in *The Times* stated that the affair had brought, 'a hideous recrudescence of medieval passions', which demonstrated alarmingly that the forces of progress had not yet triumphed. On the other hand, French nationalists drew on the old Anglophobic theme of 'perfidious Albion' to denounce what they depicted as English support for a 'syndicate of treason' (Cornick 1996).

The dramatic mediated spectacle of an *affaire* was exceptionally pronounced in the Dreyfus case, but similar punitive displays on a smaller scale can be seen in other countries at this time. In addition to the case of Beilis in Russia and that of Frank in the USA, two early-twentieth-century criminal *causes célèbres* in England merit a mention. These also featured a celebrity writer and the harsh punishment of an 'alien'. The cases were those of George Edalji and Oscar Slater, with which the detective writer Arthur Conan Doyle was involved. In 1909 at the High Court of Justiciary in Edinburgh, 'an alien German Jew who bore the pseudonym of Oscar Slater' was convicted of the murder of an elderly woman, Marion Gilchrist.[5] She had been subjected to a frenzied attack in her Glasgow apartment, and a valuable brooch was missing from her jewellery collection. Slater had left for the USA under an assumed name, and was arrested when he landed in New York. The prosecution asserted that the burglar, about to be interrupted by the maid, had silenced his victim brutally, employing the emotive phrase, 'dead men (and women) tell no tales' (Roughhead 1910: lxv). Reporting on the trial promulgated a range of mysterious, confusing and frightening images of the crime. For instance, the *Scotsman* (4 May 1909) told its readers that numerous witnesses had seen a man watching the Gilchrist residence, a man 'after no good'. The trial occasioned extensive speculation and bitter indignation and hostility. One journalist wrote that 'the circumstantial evidence seems to fade into the shadowland of abstract speculation' (*Glasgow Herald*, 7 May 1909). When Slater was convicted of the murder and sentenced to death, a petition claiming that there had been insufficient evidence was signed by over twenty thousand people and sent to the Scottish Secretary. A reprieve commuted his sentence to penal servitude for life. A number of known figures took up Slater's case, including Conan Doyle (1912), who wrote indignantly of the 'martyrdom' of Slater (Doyle 1927: 5). In 1926, the Scottish Criminal Appeal Court was established, and a year later government passed a special Act to enable Slater to present an appeal. Slater, who became known as the 'Scottish Dreyfus' served eighteen years in prison, before being released in 1927 and awarded £6,000 compensation.

A similar case was that of George Edalji, an Anglo-Indian solicitor, whose father had married an English woman, and lived as an Anglican vicar in Staffordshire for thirty years. The Edaljis were the butt of local hostility and anonymous threatening letters, which Conan Doyle attributed to the villagers' refusal to accept an Indian as a man of the cloth. The Chief Constable of Staffordshire decided that George had been the author of these offensive missives, and when in 1903 an outbreak of savage attacks on horses and cattle took place, the police immediately focused on him as the culprit. Holding to the opinion that George had sacrificed horses to his alien gods, they set out to find evidence against him. When he appeared before the magistrates, a crowd attacked the cab bringing him to court and tore the door from its hinges. He was convicted under the Malicious Damage Act 1861, and given the severe sentence of seven years' penal servitude. 10,000 Edalji supporters signed a protest petition and the Home Office formed a committee to look into the various allegations. This body severely condemned the hostility directed at Edalji, criticized the police for framing him, and stated that his conviction was unsatisfactory. The inquiry committee stated that he had probably written the menacing letters, stating that he had 'to some extent brought his troubles upon himself' and he was denied compensation (Edalji report 1907: 407). George was hence released from prison in 1906, but remained under police supervision as a discharged convict. Despite public indignation, Conan Doyle made his own investigation of the case, denouncing it in the *Daily Telegraph* and sending his report to the Home Office (Conan Doyle 1907/1985). This was copied and sold as a pamphlet for a penny on street corners. Doyle (1907/1985: 35, 42) characterized Edalji as a 'scapegoat' and the police as 'zealous'. He denounced the 'prejudice' of the Chief Constable, a 'dislike' that had, he asserted, filtered into the whole force (ibid.: 75). Doyle argued that they had planted hairs from one of the maimed animals on his coat, and depicted the whole affair as 'a kind of squalid Dreyfus case' (ibid.: 75). This case demonstrates the significance of the mediated spectacle of criminal detection and punishment to the politics of assmililation, within which 'the existence of an upright and talented Indian in England represented a confusion of category' (Lahiri 1998: 31).

Maintaining his emphasis upon assimilation, Durkheim did not address the respects in which violent and schismatic conflicts like the Dreyfus affair contributed to the constitution of diasporic identities. The notion of diaspora foregrounds the maintenance of ties to the homeland, and attends to the history of collective trauma. Even those who pronounced their Frenchness rather than their Franco-Jewish identity were made strikingly aware of barriers to assimilation, and their communication through the practices of modern penality.[6] Theodor Herzl, a Jewish journalist from Vienna who witnessed the Dreyfus degradation ceremony, concluded that assimilation furnished no protection from anti-Semitism. He argued in his book *The Jewish State* (1896) that Jews would remain strangers in their country of residence and must build a country of their own, writing, 'In the lands we have lived in for centuries we continue to be called strangers.' The punishment of Dreyfus was emblematic of the illusory emancipation of Jews everywhere, the only solution to which was the re-establishment of a homeland in Palestine. The precedence of assimilation over diasporic attachments and identities is a prominent feature of the criminological discourse of the Chicago school of sociology described in Chapter 3, as seen for instance in Louis Wirth's essay 'The Ghetto' (1927). Wirth argued that in countries which had seen several generations of contact between Jew and Gentile, and had undergone no recent waves of Jewish immigration, both the institution of the ghetto, and any distinct Jewish identity, disappeared. He stated that through social intercourse and interbreeding, the cultural values of the world at large replaced those of the ghetto. For him, exodus from the ghetto was closely linked to both national belonging and self-identity:

> If you would know what kind of a Jew a man is, ask him where he lives; for no single factor indicates as much about the character of the Jew as the area in which he lives. It is an index not only to his economic status, his occupation, his religion, but to his politics and his outlook on life, and the stage in the assimilative process that he has reached.
>
> (Wirth 1927: 68)

Wirth wrote that those Jews who moved out from the ghetto established new areas less distinguished by external signs of their faith. He also made comments about the individual's personal appearance, mentioning the telling length of beards and coats. As we shall see in Chapter 3, the Chicagoan discourse on mobilities, cultural identities and crime, like the writings of Durkheim, sited crime and punishment within a penal politics of assimilation.

Punishment/communication, the national and the postnational

This chapter has explored some modes in which the modern nation as an imagined political community arose through mediated relations. A culture of retributive punishment centred on the Dreyfus affair has been linked to the constitution of this imagined national space. The rituals and textual practices through which the spectacle of the treasonous Jew brought contestation of the modern nation's boundaries have been described. The significance of penality as a mode of mediated armed justice, marking and expelling enemies, has been emphasized. It has been argued that Durkheim's theses linked punishment with communication, but obscured the significance of the triadic relationship of punishment, *nation* and communication. He assumed that new values of humanity would collapse the exclusionary distance between victim and offender, which had created hostility, stigmatization, harsh punishment and repudiation. The chapter has demonstrated how juridical, penal and media productions formed a powerful communicational nexus, working to mark and expel criminals as enemies of the nation. I have shown how the spectacle of Dreyfus' punishment embodied, quite literally, the paradoxical logic of assimilation, within which the normative injunction to invisibility is coupled with the stigmatizing reinscription of difference as pariah-hood. The contestatory communicational flows that mediated the affair displayed different ways of imagining and performing the national body. Durkheim's idea that periods of severe punishment during modernity were associated with regimes of absolute power has been criticized. My analysis replaces this highly simple political philosophy with an emphasis upon the way in which the communicational practices of modern punishment engaged combative audiences. I have conveyed the extent to which the Dreyfus affair shows in bold relief the polysemic character of images and the divergent reading publics produced by print culture.

A theory of punishment and communication for today must engage with the shift from print to electronic media, as well as transnational flows of images and ideas. Scott Lash (2002) writes that communications are so central to the contemporary postsocietal framework of images and flows that we can speak of a communications culture. He argues that the paradigmatic unit of this culture is the message, a byte-like medium characterised by its brevity, speed and ephemerality, and contrasts this to the narrative and discourse of older media like painting, cinema and the novel. The message is highly abbreviated, coming to you increasingly in real time. This type of communication is not an enduring form, rather it is throwaway, its value limited to the brief moment in which it is news and quickly declining in value once transmitted. The imperative to circulate short segments of information rapidly and continuously permits no time for reflection in the production of contemporary communications. Neither is there time for reflection in the user of the media, consuming not through a concentrated gaze or relaxed contemplation, but under conditions of distraction. Whereas narrative took the linear form of beginning, middle and end, information compresses these into an immediacy and simultaneity of the now. Lash writes that the imagined community of the modern nation was already discontinuous, stretched out to a certain extent, but contemporary technological forms of life are so stretched out that spatial links and social bonds sever and are reconstituted as the links of networks. He writes of a 'mosaic of networked communities' (Lash 2002: 21), with which one has plural identifications. Lash writes that social and cultural life is pervaded by the media and theorises a 'disinformed information society', in which the deep meaning of older media is replaced by a relentless non-stop flow of real-time circulation. Lash argues that the transient, rapidly circulated, superficial and anti-mediatory form of the message was already being diffused through newspaper journalism. The Dreyfus affair took place at a moment when this communications culture was coming into being, when the message was beginning to replace the older form of the narrative. The affair demonstrates the event-like character that Lash associated with the communicational practices of news.

The final four chapters of this book address debates around the movement from print to electronic culture. They explore the consequences for penality of the shift from the printed page to the space of the screen, bringing new forms of mediated visibility and imagined copresence. These new modes of communication can be related to changing penal practices and the invocation of novel forms of punitive collectivities. Before embarking upon the task of delineating these transformations, the place of criminological discourses within modern punitive cultures merits discussion. The next chapter of this book takes further questions about communication and the penal politics of assimilation. The argument explores the Chicagoan discourse on mobilities, cultural identities and crime, and relates this to the processes by which the USA demarcated its nationals from foreigners.

3   Travelling cultures

When two Italian anarchists, Sacco and Vanzetti, were sentenced to death in America in 1920, the case occasioned international protest:

> A hurricane of protest swept through the world after the decision of Governor Fuller to electrocute Sacco and Vanzetti was flashed to every corner of the earth. Resentment and dismay broke in furious floods. . . . Such an international demonstration would have been utterly impossible a generation ago. Cables, radio, improved news-gathering facilities, the development of the press, made the events in Boston known to the rest of the globe. Every meeting, every demonstration was intimately aware of similar meetings and demonstrations elsewhere. The protest thus attained a force and dimension never before equaled.
>
> (Lyons 1927/1970: 169)

In the international protest around this execution, flows of information and those of people came together in the mediated spectacle of punishment. Communication is a matter of movement. Debates about communication in the early twentieth century encompassed both the movements of images and ideas, and those of people. A discourse on changing mobilities, cultural identities and crime emerged within work published by members of the Chicago school of sociology during the 1920s and 1930s. Their concepts were grounded within a particular set of ideas about mobilities, identities and forms of belonging. Chicago school scholars inherited Durkheim's politics of assimilation and applied them to elucidate crime in early-twentieth-century America. The Chicagoan discourse on mobilities and crime is part of the colonial and national histories of the USA. I argue that these concepts are implicated in the processes by which the USA demarcated its nationals from 'foreigners'.

Spatial mobility or 'locomotion', the movement of people and things from place to place, has served as a distinct root metaphor for the contemporary situation for over a century (Matthews 1977: 124). During the nineteenth century, locomotion began to be transformed by artificial means of transportation, and contemporaries pondered the likely consequences for their society. The historian Macaulay (1849: iii, I, 370) confidently asserted that 'every improvement of the means of locomotion benefits mankind morally and intellectually'. Chicagoans were less sure that increasing locomotility necessarily brought progress. The early twentieth century brought new technologies which accelerated and made more complex the movements of people and things. The term 'communication' referred to transportation as well as the movement of ideas and images. Chicago school scholars wrote about radio and the press as well as the aeroplane and the automobile. They thought that the mobilities of their day were central to both social organization and personal identity. They saw new transportation and communication technologies as breaking down old kinds of ties and bonds, but also wondered whether they might not bring new forms of social integration.

One set of transformative mobilities particularly noted by Chicagoans was national and international flows of people. Chicago, sited at the hub of the American railroad network, was the American city that received the highest proportion of immigrants at this time. The newcomers included immigrant labourers, colloquially known as 'birds of passage', who undertook a seasonal or short-lived migration to earn money, as well as more permanent settlers. At this time there were also significant developments in internal migration. In the 'Great Migration' during and immediately after the First World War, over 450,000 southern blacks moved north, and Chicago's black population doubled in less than three years. Debates around foreigners and crime in the first decades of the twentieth century took place within an inflammatory context, with the recrudescence of the Ku Klux Klan marking a more generalized hostile nativism. At this time, Chicago was commonly thought of as the crime capital of the world. It was associated by many with organized crime syndicates peopled by lawless immigrants; indeed by 1925 'the symbol of Chicago for most outsiders was no longer the stockyards but the gangster' (Matthews 1977: 127). Foreigners were often depicted as possessing criminal tendencies crudely associated with their 'alien' cultural differences. For instance, fighting was seen as a national habit of the Irish, to the extent that bricks were popularly known as 'Irish confetti' (Thrasher 1927/1936: 212). As well as being thought of as predisposed to criminality, some foreigners were considered dangerous subversives, determined to destroy the American nation on account of their purportedly extreme anarchist or communist beliefs (Higham 1974). Chicago school scholars urged assimilation rather than exclusion, and sought to dispel malign stereotypes of blacks and immigrants. They valorized the notion of the cosmopolitan, a person freed from nationally based hostilities by their experience of encounters with foreign people and places. Chicagoans believed that a number of processes would have a cosmopolitizing effect, fostering a stance of openness towards different cultures. They accordingly associated xenophobia and ethnocentrism with conservatism. However, their theories of crime relied upon a number of questionable beliefs about ethnic and national identities, forms of belonging, and spatial mobilities.

Mobilities, orientalism and the city man

The conceptual importance of mobilities to Chicago school scholars cannot be emphasized enough. Indeed, Robert Park (1925/1967c) went so far as to claim that mentality and sociality were themselves products of locomotion. Fascinated by 'how life moves' (Burgess and Bogue 1964: 9), Chicagoans sensed that they were writing at a time of profound transformation in the nature and frequency of mobilities of various kinds. They wrote about the seasonal movements of migratory labourers, the annual movements back and forth across the ocean of immigrant workers, the travels of pleasure-seekers and tourists, the transient population of hotels and rooming houses, and the daily tide of commuters. Chicagoans were also interested in flows of images and ideas through radio, the press, and the movies, as well as the circulation of consumer products through both national and international commerce.

The Chicagoan vision of modernity was premised upon a number of historical and orientalist narratives about mobilities. Park (1928) described a historical mutation from the time of the migration of whole tribes, through the period in which classes like knights and merchants travelled, to the mid twentieth century, which he characterized by the increasing mobility of private individuals. He (1931/1950) argued that the multiplication of new means of transportation brought about a more rapid dispersion of individuals than ever before, noting a trend away from centrifugal movements (away from centres of population) and towards centripetal flows (towards cities). For Park, mobilities were characteristic of modern occidental societies, and especially of the rapid pace and tempo of American cities, which he described as, 'notoriously the products of the steamship, the locomotive and the automobile' (Park 1931/1950: 11). He explained that in the 'immobile' society, habits were fixed, activities were controlled by custom, and the individual was born into an established tradition. In contrast, mobile societies were characterized by flexible social forms, personal relations were shortlived, and the individual had a keen sense of inner insecurity. His depiction of modern, fast-paced society, of which the city of Chicago was taken to be emblematic, was based in an imagination of the rigidity of social and cultural life in both past times and foreign places. This perspective framed immigrants as backward peasants who required assistance in making a swift transition to the accelerated pace and flexible mores of the American city.

Chicagoans linked mobilities to personal, social and cultural change, and gave them centrality within a narrative of detraditionalization. In his programmatic essay 'The City', Park (1925/1967a) argued that developments in transportation and communication technologies had brought about the 'mobilization of the individual man'. These technologies which put people into circulation with others had a disembedding effect, weakening ties to the local and breaking the stifling hold of tradition. Park thought that modern movements multiplied opportunities for contact and association with others, but also made interactions transitory and less stable. Similarly, Ernest Burgess (1929) wrote that the automobile, the motion picture, the aeroplane and the radio enlarged the freedom of the individual, undermining the social control exercised by their immediate locale. Chicagoans depicted a distinctive kind of mobile individual as the increasingly typical inhabitant of the western city, a cosmopolitan who benefited from both a broader horizon and a more detached and rational viewpoint. To this end, Park drew on Georg Simmel's notion of the stranger, an 'outsider within' who took a less prejudiced view of others, an individual bearing 'the characteristics of the city man, the man who ranges widely, lives preferably in a hotel' (Park 1928: 892). For Chicagoans, cosmopolitanism stood in contra-distinction to ethnocentrism and xenophobia. They adopted W.G. Sumner's (1906: 13) description of ethnocentrism as 'this view of things in which one's group is the center of everything, and all others are scaled and rated with reference to it'. For Ellsworth Faris (1926/1971: 30), ethnocentrism meant narrowness, and he described it as 'enthusiasm for our own due to ignorance of others. It is an appreciation of what we have and a depreciation of what differs.' Park (1931/1950) associated ethnocentrism with primitive and isolated social groups, and considered it an ill-fitting hangover of the past in the present.

Chicagoans did not approach cosmopolitanism as a distant ideal, but rather comprehended it as an observable socio-historical process. Louis Wirth (1938) related the tolerant cosmopolitanism of the city to the functional interdependency brought by an increasingly specialized division of labour. He believed that the city made for cooperative social relations across races and cultures, bringing together diverse peoples precisely 'because they are different and thus useful to one another, rather than *because* they are homogeneous and like-minded' (Wirth 1938: 10). He commented that the abrupt transition between the divergent areas of the city, and their juxtaposition, made for 'a relativistic perspective and a sense of toleration of differences' (ibid.: 15). Cosmopolitanism was also thought by Chicagoans to arise from the dissemination and circulation of new images and ideas. Park (1926/1950a) believed that increasing literacy fed curiosity about distant lands, encouraging the desire to travel and seek new adventures in strange worlds far from home. He stated that this taste for adventure was not only seen among the upper classes and the literati, but was actually a mass phenomenon. Furthermore, the export of films meant that their audiences could see foreign people in action. Park thought that audiences thereby benefited from the intimacy of face-to-face interaction with alien others.

However, the detraditionalization facilitated and shaped by the new mobilities did not only occasion optimism among Chicagoans. During the late nineteenth century, the notion of 'mobility' had acquired negative meanings of excitability, and inconstancy of the imagination. For Chicagoans, as well as the possibility of a cosmopolitan outlook, the new mobilities brought troubling insecurities. Park thought that while contact with a new culture encouraged cosmopolitanism, it also left the individual stranded, directionless and without control (Park 1928: 888). He (1925/1952b: 68) described the restless search for excitement encouraged by new devices of locomotion, and added that 'this mobility is but the reflection of a corresponding mental instability'. Harvey Zorbaugh (1926/1971) emphasized the profundity of these insecurities in his study of rooming-house dwellers. These individuals were typically clerical workers and students, living in houses which had no communal area in which residents might meet. Their anonymity was exacerbated by the rapid turnover of both keepers and roomers, to the effect that nobody knew each other, and 'people come and go without speaking or questioning' (Zorbaugh 1926/1971: 101). Zorbaugh thought that this mobile anonymity produced restlessness and loneliness, and wrote that the roomer found 'neither security, response, nor recognition' (ibid.: 101).

Chicagoans believed that modern mobilities could be disorientating, as well as destructive of locally based social control:

> The mobility of city life, with its increase in the number and intensity of stimulations, tends inevitably to confuse and demoralize the person. For an essential element in the mores and in personality is consistency, consistency of the type that is natural in the social control of the primary group. Where mobility is the greatest, and where in consequence primary controls break down completely, as in the zone of deterioration in the modern city, there develop areas of demoralization, of promiscuity and of vice.
>
> (Burgess 1925/1967a)

They thought that liberation from neighbourhood and home-based control brought shifting values and new forms of social interaction. Within this line of thinking, mobilities facilitated anonymity, which in turn assisted the individual's indulgence of their deviant and criminal interests. Park linked gangsterdom to the automobile's undermining of the primary controls of neighbourhood vigilance and the individual's desire to maintain a good reputation, permitting, 'ubiquitous gangsters and bandits to be classed as public enemies abroad and continue to play the role of friend and benefactor among their neighbors, friends, and relatives at home' (Park 1934: 354).

Burgess (1925/1967b) argued that mobility encouraged, and made possible, promiscuity, because it enabled young people to frequent leisure venues located outside their local community in 'bright light areas'. In venues like these, there was no control by group opinion, as the revellers were largely anonymous to one another. Indeed, Burgess stated that the flapper was the product of the dance hall. The flapper was a 'wild', 'modern' 'new woman', indulging in hedonistic activities like smoking, drinking alcohol and jazz dancing. These forms of display and leisure entailed a rejection of normative feminine passivity within a new ethos of pleasure, glimpsed in the novels of F. Scott Fitzgerald. The modern woman as cosmopolitan urbanite was not valorized in Chicagoan discourses on mobilities and crime. Walter Reckless (1926/1971) also emphasized the anonymity brought by mobilities, and linked this to the distribution of 'commercialized vice' (prostitution) in Chicago. He explained that rapid transport and automobility made remoter areas readily accessible, with the effect that 'commercialized vice has gone with the tide of an outgoing pleasure traffic'

(Reckless 1926/1971: 194). Increasing mobility shifted the balance from primary to secondary contacts. Indeed, Burgess described promiscuity as, 'intimate behavior upon the basis of secondary contacts' (Burgess 1925/1967b: 151). This notion was also taken up by Paul Cressey in *The Taxi-Dance Hall*, a study of the disreputable establishments in which male customers paid for the pleasure of dancing with female employees. He found that the focus of activities was commercial and impersonal, with the attitudes of the marketplace over-riding those of romance. For Cressey, the taxi-dance girls, removed from home influences, were moved by the 'transient thrills of the day' (Cressey 1932/1971: 201). He depicted them as individualistic and opportunistic, bent on 'getting as much as possible for nothing' (ibid.: 207). A highly disapproving tone is evident in Cressey's analysis of the women who made a living from the taxi-dance, demonstrating perhaps too readily the traffic in women central to the reproduction of social relations. These works reveal the gendered construc-tion of the Chicagoan cosmopolitan urbanite, 'the city man, the man who ranges widely', is marked as male. Women tend to be present, if at all, as negative figures like the prostitute or immoral flapper. The invisibility of cosmopolitan women urbanites within this discourse is striking.

Diaspora, dislocation and marginality

Mobilities were seen by Chicagoans as both stretching and shrinking distances between 'home' and 'away'. They brought strangers close at hand, and by allowing the individual to roam further afield, often made oneself an anonymous stranger, with all the opportunities and discontents that strangerhood brings. Wirth thought that increasing mobilities encouraged individuals to identify with multiple social groups. He stated that they also brought rapid changes in status, as individuals associated in the different groups of the metropolis. According to Wirth (1938: 16), these everyday experiences encouraged the 'acceptance of instability and insecurity in the world at large as a norm', accounting in part for the urbanite's cosmopolitanism. However, Chicagoans also recognized that the obscuring and unravelling of distinctions between home and away multiplied experiences of social and cultural marginality, and produced ambivalent feelings towards both others and the self.

The notion of diaspora, which designates the condition of a group of people living scattered among others, derives from the Greek διασπορά, meaning dispersion. The retention of a sense of belonging to the homeland constitutes the basis of the contemporary usage of the notion (Cohen 1997). The term has hence been used both to refer to communities settled outside their homeland, and to draw attention to the ties maintained with that homeland. Chicagoans recognized something of both meanings, for instance Park (1939/1950: 102) defined the term as designating 'a nation or part of a nation separated from its own state or territory and dispersed among other nations but preserving its national culture'. They recognized that modern movements, because of the interpenetration of diverse peoples that they entailed, produced frequent experiences of cultural dislocation. For instance, Park (1926/1950b: 249) described the Oriental immigrant as undergoing 'a conflict of loyalty; a struggle to knit together the strands of a divided self'.

Postulating that a distinctive character-type was produced by these conditions, Park (1928) elaborated a notion of the 'marginal man', an unstable individual caught between two divergent cultural groups. He did not depict gypsies and hobos as marginal, reasoning that they maintained their ancient customs intact despite their wanderings, with the result that 'nomadic life is stabilized on the basis of movement' (Park 1928: 887). Instead, Park reserved the notion of marginality for the immigrant and the 'mixed-blood'. According to him, the marginal man was 'never quite willing to break, even if he were permitted to do so, with his past and his traditions, and not quite accepted, because of racial prejudice, in the new society in which he now seeks to find a place' (Park 1928: 892). Park (1930/1950) argued that cultural conflict was not just part of the process by which the individual is incorporated into society, but also integral to the processes by which their identity develops. He thought that the culture conflict experienced by every immigrant during their transitional period took the form of a conflict between old and new selves, which brought 'inner turmoil and intense self-consciousness' (Park 1928: 893).

Park's student Everett Stonequist (1937) further developed the concept of the marginal man. In doing so, he emphasized the predicament of the person of 'mixed-blood' over that of the immigrant. Like Park, Stonequist saw the marginal man as an individual who was freed from the sources of social control through his mobility, but also found himself vulnerable to uncertainties and stigmatization. He drew on the work of W.E.B. Du Bois, the first black sociologist, who in *The Souls of Black Folk* (1903) described the experience of 'double consciousness', in which the individual seems to regard himself through the reflections of two mirrors which present clashing images of him. Stonequist mused that the 'mixed-blood' is subject to both racial prejudice and culture conflict, the unsettling pull and pressure from both sides producing an ambivalent attitude of pride/shame and love/hate towards the self. He stated that the passing in and out of groups in which the marginal man is of uncertain status several times daily, gives rise to a double consciousness, a 'sense of always looking at one's self through the eyes of others, of measuring one's soul by the tape of a world that looks on in amused contempt and pity' (Du Bois 1903/1989: 5). Du Bois had described a continual sense of 'two-ness', of wanting to merge one's American and black selves, but without losing the older self-identity. Stonequist thought that adjustment to this predicament might take a number of different forms, and mentioned creative expression, 'passing', and becoming a minority group leader. In others, withdrawal and isolation were seen. Stonequist thought that in some people the conflict was only ever temporarily resolved, initiating in them a process of personal disorganization expressed in delinquency, crime, suicide and mental instability. It is clear that culture conflict was primarily construed by Chicagoans as a personal predicament, which met with individualized 'adjustments'.

The second generation is a category which expresses an ambivalent status between the nomad and the resident (Silverman 1992). It was a category given considerable attention by Chicagoans. Wirth argued that culture conflict was more prevalent in the second generation immigrant, who had a weaker attachment to the Old-World culture and a greater mobility than their parents. Park (1925/1950: 27) wrote that the second generation immigrant 'having lost or abandoned the older cultural heritages, is not quite in possession of the new', and linked this predicament to the origins of criminality. Clifford Shaw's *The Jack-Roller* (1930/1968) told the story of Stanley, the offspring of Polish immigrants, who lived in the deteriorated 'Back of the yards' area of Chicago. Both the rift between parents and child, and the disorganization of the local community, meant that Stanley was subject to ineffective control and drifted into theft and burglary. On occasion, Chicagoans depicted the immigrant child as indicative of a broader existential condition. Wirth argued that culture conflict was an endemic feature of urban existence, where 'contacts are extended, heterogeneous groups mingle, neighbourhoods disappear, and people, deprived of local and family ties, are forced to live under the loose, transient, and impersonal relations that are characteristic of cities' (Wirth 1931). Similarly, Park saw the immigrant and the 'mixed-blood' as exemplifying the existential condition of marginality, but generalized the experience to make it a characteristic feature of modernity. On this view, experiences of dislocation and the formation of diasporic attachments are common features of modern times. However, the overall effect of Chicagoan scholarship on culture conflict and crime was to essentialize certain readily identifiable people as marginal, reifying the notion of displacement.

Passing through: transitional spaces

Chicagoan work established a tradition of research into the connections between crime and place. This has particularly involved exploring links between residency and criminality. However, the Chicagoan corpus can also be read as supplying a notion of places as sites of travel experiences and encounters with others. It is true that Chicagoans saw certain areas of the city as especially prone to 'social disorganization', but this was a concept through which they linked *transience* of dwelling to criminality. The most crime-ridden areas of the city, in their view, were the sites of continuous arrivals and departures, which were only punctuated by brief periods of sojourn. The notion of transition employed by Chicagoans carried spatial and temporal connotations of intermediacy (betweenness), impermanence (temporariness) and a lack of grounding (rootlessness).

Chicagoans dubbed the slum area of the city, which seemed to be the place of the most troubling mobility, the 'zone of transition'. The slum was the point of first settlement for new immigrants. Furthermore, as Burgess (1925/1967a) pointed out, relocation out of this neighbourhood was more rapid than from other areas of the city. It was so undesirable that newcomers moved out as soon as they could afford to live elsewhere. This continuous process of influx and exodus made the zone of transition a place of turbulence and disorder. Burgess (1926/1971: 170) thought that slums were the most mobile, and least fluid, of all the areas of the city. This was because their inhabitants might come and go in continuous succession, but while living there they had a particularly limited range of movement.

The physical locale of the slum was linked by Chicago school scholars with cultural differences that they sought to theorize as passing away. The slum was the primary locus of what Chicagoans saw as the transitional institution of the immigrant community. In their classic study *The Polish Peasant in Europe and America*, William Thomas and Florian Znaniecki linked the 'wild' behaviour of Poles to the imperfect cohesion of the Polish-American community, which according to them could not provide adequate support and control. Thomas and Znaniecki depicted the delinquent child of Polish parents as a wild and amoral being, describing amorality as 'a condition of passive or active wildness in which behavior is not controlled by social customs and beliefs but directly conditioned by temperamental tendencies and swayed by momentary moods' (Thomas and Znaniecki 1958: 1777). The broader point being made through their discussion of crime concerned the weak control exercised by Polonia Americana over its increasingly independent and individualized peoples: 'The prevalent general social unrest and demoralization is due to the decay of the primary-group organization, which gave the individual a sense of responsibility and security because he belonged to something' (ibid.: 1,827). Spaces of belonging were hence envisaged by Chicagoans as more or less effective regulatory devices. This idea can be seen in Park's (1925/1967b) argument that delinquency was caused by the failure of community organizations to function, and his claim that the forces which broke up neighbourhood cohesion included the proportion of floating population, the racial and class composition, and the proportion of nomads and hobos. To take another example of this approach, Robert Faris (1938/1971) linked the isolation of disorganized communities like the rooming-house district and the slum to the incidence of mental abnormalities and illnesses.

These descriptions of the imperfection and failure of immigrant communities, and the wildness of their members, are telling. Chicagoan fascination with the criminogenic transience of the slum was judgemental. Park added to his (1926/1971: 6) definition of a slum as 'an area of casual and transient population', 'an area of dirt and disorder, of missions and of lost souls', the comment that its inhabitants were no longer persons. He (ibid.: 6) mentioned briefly that the slum was bohemian, a place where artists and radicals sought refuge from fundamentalism and the limitations of a philistine world. However, Chicagoans did not valorize the alternative values and lifestyles seen among the inhabitants of the zone of transition. For Harvey Zorbaugh (1929), mean streets and decaying buildings were characteristic of the slum, but so were distinctive types of 'human derelicts'. He depicted Chicago's bohemia, a world dominated by women and where gay and lesbian sexualities could find relatively open expression, as a place of sterile rebellion (Wilson 1991). The focus on the transitional milieu of the slum gave rise to the study of the gang, a casual grouping usually composed of immigrant boys, for whom play and adventurous roaming merged into delinquent acts. Frederic Thrasher (1927) depicted the slum as a site of social centrality for the reproduction of the marginal elective identity of gang member, as well as describing the defensive localism of gang members and its expression in racist attacks (Hetherington 1998, Adamson 2000). Yet as a way of understanding collective identities, the process of 'learning' theorized by the concept of differential association did not exclude earlier notions of contamination. In this respect, Chicagoan work crossed over with discourses of the 'dangerous classes' prominent in nineteenth-century France and England, 'The nineteenth-century fear of working-class ghetto-zones, it was believed, of criminality, disease and rebellion, was redirected towards immigrant ghettos in the twentieth century' (Silverman 1992: 78).

The Chicago school of sociology is remembered for having emphasized the importance of authenticity to ethnographic practice. Yet it seems that despite their approving discussions of cosmopolitanism, Chicagoans could not banish ethnocentrism and xenophobia from their own outlook. The myopic and distorting lens of the Chicagoan ethnographic eye arises in part from their largely unexamined status as visitors to the slums. Chicago scholars noted that the zone of transition was a commuter route, a pathway out of the business centre, which 'empties itself every night and fills itself every morning' (Park 1925/1952a: 171). Depicting the zone of transition as a place in which people were *en route*, Chicagoans rarely reflected upon the significance of their own transitional status. Chicagoans worked with an understanding of *verstehen* as a process of thinking oneself into an alien milieu. This disregarded the conditions of their own passage from home to away, as a visitor passing through, or a guest temporarily entering, the zone of transition.

Rolf Lindner has emphasized the significance of the 'art of looking' to Chicagoan ethnography, and stated that the principal aim of Park's sociology was 'to develop the ability to put oneself in the position of other people, in order to know and understand other people better and thus bring about mutual understanding (*verstehen*), a common universe of discourse' (Lindner 1996: 135). Chicagoan epistemology conceived of the scholar as able to be at home in the milieu of the other. Lindner explained that the process of *verstehen* was thought of as a form of empathetic insight into the inner world of others. But can one take the place of the other, see through her eyes, in this way? An important criticism made by Rob Shields is instructive here. He writes that the process of *verstehen* is 'directed towards a relation of identity between the researcher's and research subject's values. That is, the identification of Self with Other. "Speaking-with" is transplanted into "speaking as" that Other. The empathetic aspect of verstehen is a flaw which silences the Other by masking the difference between Self and Other' (Shields, cited in Diken 1998: 260). This insight by which one aims to see things from the viewpoint of others was not construed as a reflexive process in which one might also recognize the foreign within oneself.

Given the lessons of history, the grounding of Chicagoan optimism in notions of mobility and transitions, with the idea that migrants 'moved upwards and outwards on the escalator towards suburbia', now looks somewhat suspect (Graham and Clarke 1995: 157). Yet Chicagoan thought also appears problematic set against the standards of its own day, and particularly when attention is turned to its ethnoracial cast and underlying insistence on assimilation to the 'American way of life'. These presuppositions about mobilities, ethnic, religious and national forms of belonging, and identities, are further evinced in Chicagoan work on ethnic encounters and processes of assimilation.

Assimilation and ethnic encounters

Debates about assimilation were prominent in Progressive Era America. Assimilation, the action of making or becoming like, carries notions of conformity with the mores and daily practices of the established body. Park (1926/1971: 7) employed the notion of assimilation broadly to denote the individual's accommodation to the moral order of the community, writing that 'the life of the community therefore involves a kind of metabolism. It is constantly assimilating new individuals.' Assimilation was understood by Chicagoans to be a deep and gradual personality transformation. It occurred when, through a process of intimate association, individuals acquired common experiences and traditions:

> Assimilation is a process of interpenetration and fusion in which persons and groups acquire the memories, sentiments, and attitudes of other persons or groups, and, by sharing their experience and history, are incorporated with them in a common cultural life.
>
> (Park and Burgess 1921: 62)

Becoming part of a group is identified here with becoming like its members.

Chicagoans thought that the assimilation of both immigrants and black migrants was a particularly serious problem. For seven years, Park had worked as a press agent and ghostwriter for Booker T. Washington, a black spokesman who developed a theory and regime of racial self-improvement at the Tuskegee Institute in Alabama. Washington advanced a programme of assimilating blacks to an American ethic of self-discipline through vocational education and training. His politics took a conciliatory approach and aimed at gradual improvement. Washington believed that blacks should not campaign for the vote. He claimed that they needed to prove their loyalty to the USA by working hard without complaint before being granted rights. In his work as publicist and writer, Park drew attention to the successes of 'achieving Negroes'. This strategy was both an attempt to eliminate the harmful stereotype of the lazy Negro and a reflection of Washington's politics. Washington was heavily criticized by black intellectuals and political leaders of his day for his silence and submission with regard to rights. For instance, Du Bois devoted a chapter of *The Souls of Black Folk* to a critique of Washington's gradualism, stating forcefully that 'Mr. Washington's programme practically accepts the alleged inferiority of the Negro race' (Du Bois 1903/1989: 43). It has been said that Park's assimilationism meant that he neglected the significance of institutionalized discrimination, which was being discussed by other scholars at the time. Du Bois, as well as the Chicago-based Jane Addams and Edith Abbott, discussed workplace and housing discrimination, linking economic exploitation and racism centrally to the racial segregation seen in the city. Park paid scant attention to these exclusionary processes, depicting blacks as 'progressing up the economic ladder rather than being trapped by discrimination in the housing and job markets' (Sibley 1995: 150). During the period 1917–19, there were twenty-six bomb attacks on black residences in formerly all-white neighbourhoods or the offices of realtors who sold property to blacks (Tuttle 1974, Philpott 1978). This aggressive and sometimes deadly reassertion of the 'colour line' makes Park's myopia all the more striking.

Chicagoans distanced themselves from the 'melting-pot' notion of a new Americanism. This envisaged assimilation as a natural and unassisted process, a kind of 'magic crucible' from which a new singular national type emerged. The melting pot image of fusion threatened the submergence of separate ethnic identities. As Stonequist (1937) was later to point out, it was the members of minority groups that were generally expected to do most of the melting. The dominant group did not expect to have to adjust themselves to others. Indeed, assimilation entailed conformity to a specifically Anglo-Saxon tradition. However, I agree with Peter Kivisto that Park 'failed to articulate a discourse on reciprocal cultural influence' (Kivisto 1990: 457). For instance, *Old World Traits Transplanted* (Park and Miller 1921/1969) argued that their foreign heritage was useful in helping immigrants to adjust to American ways, but did not discuss what American culture itself might gain from these 'aliens'.

The Chicagoan view of American nationality envisaged the body of the nation as a mosaic rather than a singular type. The absorption of the melting pot meant repudiation of one's past. Instead of absorption, Chicagoans preferred a notion of incorporation. Park (1914) noted that there were two distinct historical meanings of the term 'assimilation'. The earlier of these denoted 'to make like', whereas more recent usage had the meaning of 'to take up and incorporate'. He challenged the assumption that the purpose of assimilation was the production of a national type based on homogeneity and like-mindedness. For him, the solidarity of modern states depended less on the homogeneity of their populace than on the intermingling of heterogeneous elements. Cosmopolitan solidarity consisted in a practical working arrangement into which individuals entered as coordinate parts, the mutual interdependence of each producing the corporate character of social groups.

Chicagoan assimilationism differed from the cultural pluralism professed by contemporaries like Randolph Bourne and Horace Kallen, who both emphasized the importance of encouraging the preservation of separate group identities. Kallen (1915/1996: 72), a Jewish philosopher, rigorously dismissed the assumption that a melting-pot process was underway. Instead of a singular new American race, Kallen wrote that the USA was stratified ethnically, with consciousness of dissimilarity widespread. He theorized a process by which immigrants at first find external differences a handicap so struggle to assimilate, but later undergo a process of dissimilation in which the life, ideas and arts of their native country become paramount. Kallen related this 'self-realization' to the American democratic tradition, and wrote that 'on the whole, American-ization has not repressed nationality. Americanization has liberated nationality' (ibid.: 88). Randolph Bourne (1916/1996), a literary critic and essayist, advanced a vision of 'transnational America', a new type of nation in which cultural differences would be maintained and the peaceful coexistence of hetero-geneous groups would arise. Against the melting-pot notion, Bourne pointed out the tendency for clusters of immigrants to emerge as they became more established and prosperous, and of their cultivation of the cultures and traditions of the homeland, writing that 'assimilation . . . instead of washing out the memories of Europe, made them more and more intensely real' (Bourne 1916/ 1996: 93).

In two studies undertaken for a Carnegie Corporation study of American-ization methods, Park made evident his view that ethnically specific institutions were valuable only as transitional measures. In *Old World Traits Transplanted* (1921/1969), he opposed demands that immigrants make an instant repudia-tion of their past. He argued that immigrants could build on their memories, using them as points of contact with Americanism. Old knowledge and experi-ences could assist in the interpretation of the new, in a process through which immigrants would come to identify with their hosts. However, this was only to entail a temporary toleration of the foreignness of immigrants, limited to the duration of their difficult period of adjustment. Park stated firmly that assimi-lation was inevitable, and only supported immigrant organizations to the extent that they facilitated the transition. In *The Immigrant Press and its Control* (1922: 468), he wrote that, 'the immigrant's language, like his memories, is part of his personality. These are not baggage that he can lose *en route* to his destination.' Yet he depicted the immigrant press as an important Americanizing influence, preserving old memories but also affording a gateway to new experiences.

These assimilationist notions are inherent in Park's theorizing of ethnic encounters. In 'Behind Our Masks' (1926/1950b: 247), he advanced the precept that 'race prejudice is a function of visibility'. He argued that when strangers meet, the type and not the individual is seen, and when racial differences are great the individual often remains quite unseen. This argument involved the presupposition that racial traits conceal the individual, and suggested that assimilation required the erasure of the external signs distinguishing one race from another. This concealment and camouflaging involved the immigrant learning enough of the vernacular, social ritual and outward forms of the adopted country to be able to get by. Park noted the superficial uniformity in manners and fashion of cosmopolitan groups, seeing this as accompanied by relatively profound differences in individual opinions, sentiments and beliefs. He therefore posited that the homogeneity of cosmopolitan groups mobilized and emancipated the individual to the extent that each person looked like the other, thus removing the social taboo on interaction and permitting the individual to move among strangers. Like Durkheim, he valorized an obscuring of racial differences, and a proliferation of individual differences. Cosmopolitan nationality would be the product of this process:

> In obliterating the external signs, which in secondary groups seem to be the sole basis of caste and class distinctions, it realizes, for the individual, the principle of *laissez-faire, laissez-aller*. Its ultimate economic effect is to subordinate personal for social competition, and to give free play to forces that tend to relegate every individual, irrespective of race or status, to the position he or she is best fitted to fill.
>
> (Park 1914: 608)

What was at stake in Chicagoan discourses was a shift from ascription to individualized achievement. It is evident that Park's assimilationism was closely associated with his liberal free market individualism. In contradistinction to Kallen's political philosophy, the logic of temporary toleration of strangeness was seen by Park as an instance of the democratizing process in action. Yet his purified vision of an individualized society with a competitive meritocracy was stained by those whom he theorized as unable or unwilling to assimilate.

Antipathy and indigestion: the unassimilable remainder

The gesture of ingestion entailed by the Chicagoan vision of assimilation into the American nation merits critical scrutiny. Park (1914: 611) was clearly aware of the nutritional associations carried by the term 'assimilation'. Nutrition is an everyday metabolic function rather than a disease process, hence Park wrote that, 'Ordinarily assimilation goes on silently and unconsciously, and only forces itself into popular conscience when there is some interruption or disturbance of the process' (Park 1914: 611). While the assimilation of foreigners was uncomfortable for them, and indeed Park (ibid.: 111) described it as 'slow, often painful, not always complete', it generally proceeded unnoticed by the (white) majority. Yet Park's theories construed everyday ethnic encounters with blacks and Asians as the cause of major indigestion.

On several occasions, he wrote that an unassimilable remainder, the sign of black and yellow skin, was an effective barrier to integration:

> the ease and rapidity with which aliens, under existing conditions in the United States, have been able to assimilate themselves to the customs and manners of American life have enabled this country to swallow and digest every sort of normal human difference, except the purely external ones, like the color of the skin.
>
> (Park 1914: 608)

Park thought that where race was indicated by external signs, these marks of difference supplied 'a permanent physical substratum upon which and around which the irritations and animosities, incidental to all human intercourse, tend to accumulate and so gain strength and volume' (ibid.: 611). According to him, the foreigner must lose the stigmata of difference that make him conspicuous and hence likely to attract the fear or hostility of the dominant group:

> the Japanese bears in his features a distinctive racial hallmark, that he wears, so to speak, a racial uniform which classifies him. He cannot become a mere individual, indistinguishable in the cosmopolitan mass of the population, as is true, for example, of the Irish, and, to a lesser extent, of some of the other immigrant races. The Japanese, like the Negro, is condemned to remain among us an abstraction, a symbol – and a symbol not merely of his own race but of the Orient and of that vague, ill-defined menace we sometimes refer to as the 'yellow peril'.
>
> (Park 1928: 611)

Becoming 'a mere individual', rather than a discriminated against minority figure, meant passing for white. On this view, blacks and immigrants must put on the mask of whiteness, which over the years has effected 'a succession of negations of man, and an avalanche of murders' (Fanon 1961/1990: 252).

Anxieties and hostilities towards Asian immigrants were given a powerful representation in the highly popular Fu-Manchu novels. Fu-Manchu, a Chinese man living in London, was 'the yellow peril incarnate in one man', combining tropes of mysterious exoticism with those of criminality (Rohmer 1913). He figured in the novels as a grave threat to both specific individuals and western culture itself. Park's normative assimilationism could only envisage that, because he could not put off his 'Oriental mask', the Japanese would always stand in for fear of Oriental otherness. For Park, those visibly different would inevitably fuel antipathy and attract prejudice. They could not, or would not, shake off the stigma of otherness. It appears from his writings that those visibly different were what the cosmopolitanizing order just couldn't stomach.

The problem of visible difference and the need for concealment and passing, as understood by Park, was not restricted to blacks and Asians. It included all newcomers, for instance Italians, the Irish, Scandinavians, Greeks, filipinos, Japanese and Chinese people, Poles, and Jews of various nationalities. He thought that dark skins attracted the most prejudice, but added that speaking in a foreign language closely followed as a sign of unlikeness and object of animosity (Park and Miller 1921/1969: 282). Indeed Park (1938/1950: 49) wrote of immigrants, 'everything that marks them as strangers – manners, accent, habits of speech and thought – makes this struggle difficult.' He (1926/1950b: 246–7) also stated that physical differences were both emphasized and reinforced by distinctive features of costume, manner, deportment and facial expression. Perceived strangeness marked out those who did not belong, leading Park to reflect that 'the un-American shoes and un-American beard of the immigrant arouse these emotions in us' (Park and Miller 1921/1969: 19). It appears that the logic of Chicagoan theory demanded the invisibility of difference, whilst simultaneously constructing the visibility of certain symbolic aliens as particularly threatening strangers.[1] Furthermore, as Sander Gilman (1991) explains, there is no possibility of those marked by signifiers of difference concealing themselves, 'Altering the Jew's external form may have provided a wider margin in which the Jew could "pass", but the Jew could never be truly at peace with the sense of his or her invisibility' (Gilman 1991: 192). Relationships between embodiment, identities and forms of belonging are considerably more complex than Park appears to have envisaged.

Writing on ethnic encounters, Park distinguished between two types of negative attitude toward foreigners, namely antipathy and prejudice. His concept of racial antipathy, 'an unfocused universal response to new experience which was seen as strange and potentially threatening', is somewhat akin to the later notion of xenophobia (Matthews 1977: 175). Park (1917/1950: 226) theorized racial prejudice as a defence-reaction, writing that 'we hate people because we fear them'. He thought that there was a curiosity, fascination and attraction towards the stranger, but also that the presence of the stranger inspired insecurity and aversion. Park thought that this feeling of fear and distrust tended to crystallize into a relatively stable attitude. This prejudice meant that negative judgements were pre-emptively made in advance of personal encounters. For Park, prejudice was associated with conservatism. It essentially consisted in a resistance to social change, and was especially manifested when others made efforts to improve their status.

Despite the brief recognition that prejudiced attitudes passed into the group culture, prejudice primarily appears in Park's writings as an individualized reaction. He also dismissed the role of prejudice and discrimination in perpetuating separate collective identities and institutions (Park and Miller 1921/1969: 306). Chicagoans undertook minimal analysis of institutionalized discrimination when theorizing new socialities. Filipinos were prominent in Cressey's discussion of secondary contacts in the taxi-dance hall. Yet he neglected the significance of panics about Filipino sexual aggressiveness and the extension of anti-miscegenation laws to them, facets of the Filipino diaspora which are described by San Juan (1994). Discrimination and victimization are also telling absences in Chicagoan work on relationships between foreigners and crime. As well as neglecting the importance of racism in housing and employment, they overlooked the role of racist practices in the criminal justice system. This omission was particularly remiss because events in the 1920s could readily have occasioned just this kind of analysis. A number of infamous criminal trials aroused debates about racial prejudice within criminal justice processes, and none more so than the trial of Sacco and Vanzetti. After a murder of 1920, several eyewitnesses claimed that the offenders responsible looked Italian, and the police set about questioning large numbers of Italian immigrants. Eventually Nicola Sacco and Bartolomeo Vanzetti, two anarchists, were arrested. They had good alibis, but the prosecution emphasized that all those called to provide evidence to substantiate these alibis were themselves Italian immigrants. The defendants' radical political views, as well as their having dodged the draft, were emphasized in order to frame them as unpatriotic and dangerous. After the sentence of death was passed on Sacco, he told the court in his faltering English that he was on trial because he was an Italian and an anarchist, and commented, 'You try to put a path between us and some other nationality that hates us' (Ehrmann 1970: 451). The case occasioned an international scandal, with people like Jane Addams, Dorothy Parker, Bertrand Russell, H.G. Wells and George Bernard Shaw campaigning on behalf of the convicted men. Nevertheless, Sacco and Vanzetti were executed, and were only effectively absolved by a proclamation of the Governor of Massachusetts in 1977.

The failure of the criminal justice system to protect blacks, or at least to punish the perpetrators of racist attacks, was also a cause of antagonism. Of the twenty-five race riots throughout the USA in the 'Red Summer' of 1919, Chicago saw the greatest number of casualties (Tuttle 1974). The violence in Chicago was precipitated by the drowning of a black youth, who had been stoned after drifting into an area of Lake Michigan tacitly reserved for whites. The police refused to arrest the white man thought to be responsible, and thirteen days of lawlessness ensued. The state militia were called in, thirty-eight people died and 537 were injured. Park was involved with the Chicago Commission on Race Relations, which was set up after the riots. He reflected that these violent events were a response to disturbing social changes, writing that 'as the public feels itself drifting, legislative enactments are multiplied, but actual control is decreased. Then, as the public realizes the futility of legislative enactments, there is a demand for more drastic action, which expresses itself in ill-defined mass movements and, often, in mere mob violence' (Park 1926/1971: 8). This comment about 'mere mob violence' indexes a blindness towards the colour of justice. This is all the more regrettable given that *The Negro in Chicago* (1922/1968) had described the police and the courts' hostility towards blacks.

Penal marking and national narratives

At the end of the twentieth century, an unprecedented volume of flows of people, images, capital and products cross borders of all kinds. They bring the reimagining and reconfiguration of geo-spatial, political and cultural entities and boundaries. Today's scholars work with a notion of differential mobilities, instead of the escalator notion of geographical and social mobility favoured by the Chicagoans. Additionally, enforced immobilities are evident in the use of imprisonment as a powerful form of containment shoring up an increasingly contested caste division (Wacquant 2001). This insight diverges markedly from Park's blindness to the colour of justice. Furthermore, the concept of diaspora as used by contemporary theorists departs from its Chicagoan meaning. Park strictly delimited a notion of the diasporic as a transitional and temporary experience, a finite period before the immigrant was received into the body of the American nation. Today, the notion of diaspora is defined against that of the nation-state:

> In assimilationist national ideologies such as those of the United States, immigrants may experience loss and nostalgia, but only en route to a whole new home in a new place. Such ideologies are designed to integrate immigrants, not people in diasporas. Whether the national narrative is one of common origins or of gathered populations, it cannot assimilate groups that maintain important allegiances and practical connections to a homeland or a dispersed community located elsewhere. . . . Positive articulations of diaspora identity reach outside the normative territory and temporality (myth/history) of the nation-state.
>
> (Clifford 1997: 250–1)

The contemporary notion of diaspora is hence incompatible with the Chicagoan vision of American nationhood as the site of cosmopolitan solidarity. Park's assimilationist conception of the diasporic moment is replaced by the notion of diasporic identities. The Chicagoan notion of cosmopolitan solidarity envisaged a purified nation of individuals.

The next chapter of this book moves the field of enquiry from criminological discourse to the communicational practices of mass public culture. The analysis also moves on from modern to contemporary punitive cultures. The argument presented addresses the displays through which the punitive subjects of the USA are presently convoked through emotive images of national trauma. As with the assimilationist discourses of the early twentieth century, national trauma is related to the disruption of a mythical homogenous national identity. The chapter looks into the ways in which vengeful victimhood is premised upon an emotive, privatized and familial citizenship.

4 Irony and the state of unitedness

Spaces of irony open out from within, and turn away from, the dominant public culture. They are to be found in media such as cartoons and literary works, as well as in everyday speech acts. Standard treatises on rhetoric inform their readers that the figure of irony consists in saying the opposite of what one really means. However, this commonplace definition is imprecise because irony comes about in a space between the said and the unsaid. It is hence a trope in which the border between said and unsaid is called into question. The ironic address becomes a site at which dominant truth claims are called to account. It is a rhetorical device which calls upon the audience to distance themselves from some commonplace notion. For the usual modes of interpellation an alternative idiom is substituted. This chapter engages with the strident discourses surrounding the execution of its first federal prisoner in four decades by the United States of America. The punitive subjects of this killing state are at present convoked through powerfully emotive images of national trauma, and promised closure through imposition of the death penalty. I demonstrate through analysis of some editorial cartoons how spaces of irony can effectively critique the state of unitedness of this vengeful 'America'.

Because it acknowledges what it also questions, irony is a dissenting mode of address. It looks to the customary meaning only to turn away from it. For me, this double movement gives the ironic mode considerable political purchase. For Søren Kierkegaard, who wrote a dissertation on the subject, irony was a mode of engagement in public life (Cross 1998). He used it to counter the social production of stereotypes, and taken as a whole his corpus mounts a prescient critique of the emergent mass society. The usefulness of this dissident rhetorical device in cultural and political analysis has not been lost upon others. In her book *The Queen of America Goes to Washington City*, Lauren Berlant (1997) suggests that the fantasy nation form both produces normative political subjectivity and creates public spaces of exaggeration, irony or ambivalence. Relatedly, she writes of a pervasive rhetoric of citizen trauma in the public culture of America, which, she argues, produces a 'cartoon version of the shaken nation'. The new figure of the victim-citizen addressed by a range of criminal-legal practices is, I believe, the product of what Berlant (1997: 2) calls politics by caricature, 'a farce-style moral and civil war between icons and hyphenated stereotypes'. This politics by caricature constructs what Berlant sees as 'extreme images of personhood' which nevertheless, she tells us, constitute modal points in the identity politics of western societies. Her analysis charts the ways in which a number of alternately demonic and idealized images and narratives came to dominate the official national public sphere of the US. It seems to me that this politics by caricature instantiates within the realm of legal practices what we might as well call a cartoon justice. This may well secure a popular mandate for punitive measures, but it also permits spaces of irony to be opened up. These have the potential to be transformative, for while irony opens out new discursive spaces, these are not safely located outside of, and at a distance from, the established, the mainstream and the canonical. This chapter looks into the iconoclastic force of irony, its capacity to question the evidences of the self-evidently iconic. What you will find below is an ironic reading of iconic images, a reading to which you are a party. I believe that this kind of subaltern reading can play a part in the constitution of critical counter-publics. Through the opening up of spaces of irony, we can engage with the dominant culture, we can camp on its terrain, but at the same time perform acts of disaffiliation.

The killing of Timothy McVeigh, the Oklahoma City bomber, occasioned a flurry of activity from editorial cartoonists.[1] His case was emblematic of a number of important developments in criminal justice philosophies and practices, occurring in similar forms across a number of western jurisdictions. The McVeigh case was central to several important changes in American criminal justice procedures. Congress passed the landmark Effective Death Penalty and Anti-Terrorism Act 1996, which made the death penalty more 'robust' through substantial habeas corpus reform. Basically, an 'effective' death penalty was linked by this statute to a diminished ability of the federal courts to enforce the constitutional rights of state prisoners (Steiker 2001). Secondly, new victim participation legislation was passed, overriding decisions of the trial judge and the US Court of Appeals, in the Victim Rights Clarification Act 1997. In these two legislatory changes, retributivism is linked to victim's rights discourses, a development seen in a number of western jurisdictions. The McVeigh case is also, and relatedly I would argue, associated with battles of various kinds over images. Days before the execution, an internet entertainment company sued the authorities for the right to show a live public webcast of the event.[2] Their demand, levied 'as citizens and as victims', was rejected by the court. However, Congress passed a special motion to permit survivors and relatives of the dead to witness the killing of prisoner 12076–064 by live satellite feed in Oklahoma City, 650 miles from the death chamber.[3] The execution was delayed by ten minutes while engineers fixed a technical glitch in the transmission. After McVeigh had been declared dead, the American President announced, 'today, every living person who was hurt by the evil done in Oklahoma City can rest in the knowledge that there has been a reckoning'.[4]

Today we are regularly presented with emotive 'iconic' images. These are appropriated into punitive discourses when an authoritative interpretation of them is promulgated, grounding a strident narrative in which trauma is necessarily followed by 'closure' attained through capital punishment. This discourse is indeed strident. It openly excludes dissenting voices even, for instance, the voices of those crime victims who do not support the death penalty. How can we counter this potent aesthetic? What alternative ways can we find of engaging audiences? In this chapter I take a look at some editorial cartoons, which were published in mainstream daily newspapers, as well as on the internet. They initiate what to my mind is a highly effective critique of the mass subject invoked as the subject of the killing state, as well as more broadly questioning the very iconicity of iconic images.

I am going to argue that the hegemony of politics by caricature is undercut by the cartooning of the political. Berlant, as I mentioned above, described the obsessive production within American public culture of alternately idealized and demonized figures. Many cartoons on the McVeigh execution dramatized the very prosaic rendering of the condemned man as evil, depicting him being welcomed into hotel hell by the devil. Others focused on the audience, and sent up the idealized iconic figures of the television viewer in a sports bar, or, as in the editorial cartoon by Doug Marlette, at home with the family (see Figure 4.1). This cartoon is loaded with ironic counter-meaning. As you can see, the device of caricature, which exaggerates and distorts a person's distinctive features to comic effect, is used to great effect by Marlette. In this instance, the image of the audience depicts a generic family unit. The family tableau shown here is every bit as revealing as the scene of *Las Meniñas*. The cartoon shows up in bold relief the primary constituency addressed by the politicians who claim that we should centre criminal justice upon victims. The framing

Figure 4.1 'Closure' is reproduced by the kind permission of Doug Marlette, Tribune Media Serivces©

of the OKC bombing as a specifically *national* tragedy foregrounded images of dead children and their grieving parents. The bombing, which took place on Patriot's Day, decimated the America's Kids Daycare Centre, killing nineteen babies and children. In the hours following the bombing, televised images of bleeding and dead infants being pulled from the ruins were broadcast far and wide. President Clinton took the opportunity to state, 'we were for a moment once again family, outraged and heartbroken' (cited in Linenthal 2001: 111). As we will see, the terms 'outraged' and 'heartbroken' are quite significant, evoking as they do the expressions of anger and grief following upon trauma to the 'heartland' of American public culture.

In the Marlette cartoon, the national citizens, the audience addressed as this 'America', hailed and greeted by the television anchor, occupy the fantasy space of domestic entertainment and harmony. This indexes nostalgic evocation of the suburban space of pleasurable consumption *and* normative nuclear familial relations associated with the advent of mass television ownership (see Spiegel 1992). This domestic snapshot also satirizes the heteronormative politics of the family, which one might evoke by mere mention of the Defence of Marriage Act. The cartoon sends up all those institutions, instruments, images and ways of understanding that make the hetero-familial both coherent and privileged. The national family, the 'America' hailed, welcomed, and which recognizes itself here as the audience, is privatized, coupled, gendered (in a spoof on the division of labour, she handles, literally, childcare, he drinks, ready for the office, his coffee) and hetero-reproductive. This is all written here in black and white. The cartoon makes explicit what Berlant and Warner (1998) identify as typically unmarked, as invisible and tacit, as the basic idiom of the social and the personal.

The cartoon also makes ironic commentary upon the mass subject invoked by discourses of trauma and closure. The goggle-eyed buffoons staring at the television screen prompt reflection upon debates about western public spheres. In his fascinating text *The Present Age*, Kierkegaard characterized the democratized culture of his day as productive of a phantom public sphere, writing: 'In order that everything should be reduced to the same level, it is first of all necessary to produce a phantom, its spirit a monstrous abstraction . . . and that phantom is the Public' (Kierkegaard 1846/1962: 59). According to Kierkegaard, this phantasmatic character of the public came about as the press engendered a realm of idle talk, curious yet ultimately disinterested amusement, and opinionated irresponsibility. This 'monstrous abstraction', he argued, is produced in the form of anonymous spectators, who are constituted as citizens through their consumption of mass media. People become riveted voyeurs, who, Kierkegaard complained, feel themselves bound by no commitments. The ironic idiom was, in a way, his means of undercutting the superficiality of the public of his day. Over the last decade, notions of the phantom public sphere have undergone a critical revival since the publication of an edited collection upon the subject (Robbins 1993). This stimulating text looked back to Walter Lippman's use of the phrase, when he argued in 1925 that the formation of citizens into the responsible, well-informed public of participatory democracy was deeply problematic. The Robbins book addressed the ways in which the subject of mass culture is invoked, an analysis also taken up by Hal Foster (1996) in his essay 'Death in America'. Foster writes that the mass subject of modern democracies is convoked both through a body, for instance that of a celebrity or a politician, and as a body, for instance as a collective traumatized by the same event. He reflects upon the making of what he terms the 'psychic nation' through mass-mediated disaster and death:

> the death of the old body politic did not only issue in the return of the total leader or the rise of the spectacular star; it also led to the birth of the psychic nation, that is, to a mass-mediated polis that is not only convoked around calamitous events (like the Rodney King beating or the Oklahoma City bombing) but also addressed, polled, and reported as a traumatic subject.
>
> (Foster 1996: 55)

The construction of the contemporary body politic within western societies combines both what Foster calls 'the spectacular star' and 'the psychic nation'. Convoked, addressed, polled and reported in wounded nationality, the images in and through which this kind of mass-mediated polis is constituted seem to have a sacrosanct quality about them. Editorial cartoons, however, are typically irreverent. As you can see, Marlette's image directly sends up the *esprit de corpse* which the traumatic subject supposedly lives out.

To convey the emotive character of wounded familial nationhood, and indicate the traumatic reconstruction of criminal justice practices of late, we can outline the discourses of trauma and closure, as they arose in the McVeigh case. Days after the Oklahoma City bombing, in a press statement, President Clinton both announced a national day of mourning and stated that the government would seek the death penalty for the bombers. Here the traumatic subject is also addressed as the subject of the killing state. Throughout the case these two interpellatory forms continued to be juxtaposed, as though the one necessarily implied the other. The trial itself featured searing testimony from survivors and the relatives of the deceased, far in excess of the detail needed to prove the corpus delicti or to establish the guilt of the accused. In addition, forty victim impact statements were admitted during the penalty phase, and these unusually included those from rescue workers as well as survivors and relatives of the dead. Four police officers gave testimony about their rescue efforts in the imme-diate aftermath of the blast. This entailed what the defence were to call 'graphic and gruesome' testimony about finding and removing the grievously injured and dead from the rubble. The police officers also spoke of psychological suffering that they had endured due to witnessing the scenes of carnage, terror and death. The jury, several of whom cried during the victim impact testimony, unanimously recommended that McVeigh be executed. During the minutes that it took to kill this man, ABC's *Good Morning* programme showed footage of survivors and relatives reading the victim impact statements that they had presented to the court. For the prohibited images of execution was substituted the figure of the traumatic subject, authorizing maximal retribution as just deserts for loss and suffering. It was through these extreme images of national familial trauma that US citizens were interpellated into a retributive community of grief.

In the Marlette cartoon, 'Closure' corresponds to restoration of the 'safe' familial space of secure meanings. Entertainment Network Inc, the company suing for the execution webcast, claimed that their proposed transmission could 'help to bring a sense of closure to this event for all of the Americans who were outraged and traumatized by this heinous crime'.[5] The national trauma of the attack was officially described as having 'literally brought home the impact of terrorism for Americans' (Department of Justice 2000). This official report described the huge shock for Americans to discover that they are not immune from massive-scale attack within their own borders. The report states that the shock was magnified by the location of the attack, inflicted right there in the 'heartland' of the country. The national trauma was hence depicted as one of anxiety, loss and fear because the bombing, 'changed the Nation's general sense of safety and insecurity'. In comments like 'OKC looks like Beirut', the bombed city was imagined as an alien landscape. The attack was described as the kind of thing that happens in 'hybrid' cities like LA and New York, but not in middle America, 'far from the country's urban edges, deep in the farm belt, a quint-essentially secure and American landscape' (*Life* 1996). The Marlette cartoon can be seen as a space of irony that exposes the familial politics of the wounded 'heartland way' in the memorialization of the bombing and the demand for the death penalty. Commemorative television programmes related recovery after the bombing to the reconstruction of a mundane family life. Victoria Johnson (1999) relates the imagined pastoral of Oklahoma to an idealized turn towards the home, in a privatized and familial model of citizenship. She shows how coverage of the anniversary of the bombing was infused with a fantasy politics of 'the normal'. Johnson argues that the typical narratives and images of victim-hood and recovery constructed a mythical heartland landscape. This was the scene of privatized citizenship, based in the observance and display of traditional gender roles within the heterosexual nuclear family. She hence argues that the notion of the heartland is less concerned with a specific bounded geographical locality, than with evoking the symbolic geography of a specific American pastoral ideal. This, she explains, is centred on a privatized ethic of church and family. The imagined rural safe space, inhabited by good citizens with an 'innocent' communal sensibility, injured by the bombing, is also evoked by the 'sacred' space of the Oklahoma Memorial. Within an hour of McVeigh's death, a plaque marking his execution was installed in the timeline. In her fascinating chapter on *The Simpsons*, Berlant (1997) reads narratives of the pilgrimage to Washington through analysis of an episode of the cartoon series. This tells a tale of the pilgrimage as a coming into being as a political subject. The initiation into the mythical rites of participatory democracy is, in Berlant's reading of the cartoon, an initiation into, and out of, naivete. The trip to the OKC memorial, made as a 'real' excursion or as an imagined journey through the images on its website, also figures as a political pilgrimage. While the spaces of irony in cartoons suggest a way out of naivete, the placement of the execution plaque sutures a closed narrative of victimhood, citizenship and revenge. The very sacredness of the memorial is produced in and through this emotive, privatized and familial citizenship.

As well as addressing the ways in which the subjects of mass culture are convoked, the contributors to the collection, *The Phantom Public Sphere* emphasized the multiple character of publics, with the formation of both dominant publics and subaltern counter-publics. These latter were envisaged as oppositional spaces opened up by subordinate social groups. I believe that irony can contribute to the alternative idiom that generates and sustains counter-public spaces. The notion comes with that of doubled audiences. Simply put, there is one audience that gets the gag, and another that does not, that is also the one being sent up. The ironist takes with him a discerning listener, or, to prefer a Kierkegaardian locution, one who is 'in the know'. The family figured in the Marlette cartoon, the unreflexive grinning blockheads, are those who refuse to read ironically. Kierkegaard argues that the subject of modernity is an ironic subject. One might remark that however much ironic reading is an ever-present possibility, encouraged by the existential conditions of western modernity, it is one that some people cannot countenance. As well as the Kierkegaardian ironic subject, an equally noticeable figure is the subject of ressentiment. This is the subject that moves from the wound to revenge, a subject that nostalgically seeks closure. Irony however, is a refusal of nostalgia, 'that fantastic longing for direct and absolute truths, for primal innocence, for transparent immediacy' (Shakespeare 1998: 97). The characters drawn by Marlette are the subjects of mass culture, interpellated as members of the dominant public. They happily, gleefully almost, misrecognize themselves as 'America itself' through the expansive address of the television anchor. At the same time, the cartoon works as a space of irony, a space of passage within which a critical audience can recognize itself in turning away from the brute literality of the term 'Closure'.

Iconic images, the psychic nation and the global village

While a psychic nation is produced as a mass-mediated polis convoked around calamitous scenes, with the global circulation of images the nation is no longer a boundary for this kind of imagined traumatic community. The McVeigh webcast case raised important questions about the political effects of viewing the mediated spectacle of the death penalty. Intriguingly, the case featured the theories of cult 1960s figure Marshall McLuhan, who wrote that through the flows of iconic images circulated by the new electronic media, people would reach out towards others with empathy and tolerance.[6] This McLuhanesque debate in the courtroom made a series of assumptions about the national and global collectivities effected by viewing images of punishment. McLuhan studied the effects of the electronic media, theorizing their transformative impact upon the dimensions of space and time. He argued that new media profoundly alter our relations to one another and to ourselves.

McLuhan's argument drew attention to the interplay between user and technology. Writing that the media are 'the extensions of man', he envisaged media as merged or fused with the person. Specifically, McLuhan depicted electronic media as the externalization of the human sensorium, or nervous system. He argued that these technologies brought the 'outering' of the central nervous system, which extends in a global embrace that abolishes space and time. This technological outering of the nervous system, he believed, involves us in the fate of the rest of the world. Electronic media therefore bring a depth participation that makes every action hugely consequential. McLuhan emphasized the potent effects of new media on subjectivities, values, indeed, he said, on everything, 'All media work us over completely. They are so persuasive in their personal, political, economic, aesthetic, psychological, moral, ethical, and social consequences that they leave no part of us untouched, unaffected, unaltered' (McLuhan and Fiore 1968: 26). For McLuhan, the new media change the scale and form of social relations and individual perceptions, fundamentally altering the experiential content of people's everyday lives. Electronic technologies dissolve divisions, create new interdependencies, and promote heightened forms of awareness.

McLuhan's book *The Gutenberg Galaxy* (1962) discussed the revolution in forms of social organization and identities brought by the dispersal of the mechanical printing press. He theorized three successive eras, namely the oral age, the print age and the age of electronic media. According to him, print culture brought a progressive 'innering' of the senses, promoting the rise of specialization and individualism. The Gutenberg revolution instantiated a principle of lineality, which produced private, separate man. He linked the dissemination of the printing press to individualist patterns of enterprise and monopoly, with a movement away from medieval guild structures. Print culture was also related by McLuhan to the bureaucratic and national centralization of power and the emergence of nationalism. He portrayed the dissemination of electronic media as a second revolution, bringing about simultaneity and continuous interaction and, he claimed, replacing the brief and privatized communications of the Gutenberg galaxy. In the world of instant and total awareness, a sense of separate and self-centred identity is impossible. The lineality of the print age is reversed with the 'outering' of the collective central nervous system. McLuhan's notion of the 'global village' theorized the increasing extent of worldwide and transborder interdependencies, and was most famously expressed in the phrase, 'the new electronic interdependence recreates the world in the image of a global village' (McLuhan and Fiore 1968: 67). He advanced a generally optimistic vision of the advent of electronic media, as bringing unprecedented opportunities for global interconnectedness. McLuhan associated the Gutenberg galaxy with detachment and non-involvement, and wrote that we live integrally in the electronic age, an era of the heightened awareness of consciousness:

Electric circuitry has overthrown the regime of 'time' and 'space' and pours upon us instantly and continuously the concerns of all other men. It has reconstituted dialogue on a global scale. Its message is Total Change, ending psychic, social, economic, and political parochialism. The old civic, state, and national groupings have become unworkable. Nothing can be further from the spirit of the new technology than 'a place for everything and everything in its place.' You can't *go* home again.

(McLuhan and Fiore 1968: 16)

McLuhan heralded an end to the atomistic strictures of parochialism through the global dialogue facilitated by the electronic technologies of his day. 'You can't *go* home again': he proclaimed the dissolution of the old forms of belonging, and looked to a new cosmopolitanism, in which one's home would no longer be limited to the exclusive and privatized space of the Gutenberg galaxy. Disrupting the established spatio-temporal order, electronic technologies would usher in unique forms of proximity. What was it about electronic media that promised this dramatic transformation? McLuhan argued for a historical shift from nonparticipational ('hot') to participational ('cool') media. Hot media, he told readers, are of high definition, replete with information and thereby low in audience participation. Cool media are quite the opposite, low on information and therefore engaging fuller active participation. Simply put, 'the hot form excludes, and the cool one includes' (McLuhan 1964/2002: 25). He saw this new participational environment as 'sensuous', 'tactile', 'tribal' and 'choric'.

McLuhan (ibid.: 218) wrote that in the Gutenberg galaxy, there is 'a place for everything and everything in its place', portraying this as an order passing away. According to him, by the 1960s, western societies were moving on beyond the terms of what Foucault, as I showed in Chapter 1, described as a carceral society, within which 'each individual has his own place; and each place its individual' (Foucault 1975/1991: 143). McLuhan contrasted the electronic age with the earlier era of ordering through individualization, seriality and separation. Electric speed, he argued, makes the world compressional, bringing together and merging cultural hierarchies and public/private spheres. In this process of implosion, there is an abolition of prior spatial distinctions and linear conceptions of time. With vertical, temporal and spatial implosion, formerly exclusive hierarchies and categories collapse in on themselves. Baudrillard, in a review of *Understanding Media*, described the impact of instantaneous communications as changing everything, 'Even causality: one passes from linear connection to configuration. Everything at once becomes contemporary and decentralized, a process of planetary synthesis installs itself ("implosion")' (Baudrillard 1967/2001: 40). A shift from lineality to acentred organizational forms, and increasingly rapid communications, brought about a profound set of cultural transformations that tended towards different and as yet unseen kinds of solidarity.

The link between McLuhan's concept of implosion and the cosmopolitanism of his vision was his notion of the tribal. McLuhan envisaged the world's collective future through a paradigm of retribalization. He thought that the instantaneity and proximity of 'our electronic involvement in one another's lives' would destroy the discrete empires of self and nation (McLuhan 1964/ 1994: 35). For McLuhan, in the global village, 'a simultaneous happening', there was a return to tribal emotions. Electronic media transform the patterns of interdependence, forming new communalities, 'electric speeds create centers everywhere. Margins cease to exist on this planet' (McLuhan 1964/2002: 99). McLuhan argued on occasion that technological innovations disturbed both individuals and entire social orders. The new sensory environment that they brought was difficult to adjust to, causing pain, misery and anxiety. He argued in *War and Peace in the Global Village* that new technologies 'bring on the cultural blues', threatening the identity image of individuals and nations (McLuhan and Fiore 1968/1997: 16). The fear and aggression that results from the dissolution of the old certainties escalates into war as a violent quest for identity. He also remarked in passing that in the global village we can become conservative reactionaries. On occasion he spoke of the 1960s as a time of unstable transition from the old to the new media age, an anxious time of a precarious interface between a declining fragmentary print culture and an emergent inclusive culture. More often though, he presented the global village as a democratizing, participational reality already in evidence. His work depicted the effects of the electrical retribalization of the West as generally salutary, emphasizing their holistic and liberatory potential. He claimed that electronic conditions fostered uniqueness and diversity as never before. The extreme and pervasive tactility of the new electronic environment, and especially the computer, would he thought promote 'a dialogue among cultures which is as intimate as private speech' (ibid.: 90).

McLuhan's notion of a global village predicted that electric implosion would compel commitment to and participation in the fate of others. Simultaneity makes us present and accessible to the rest of humanity, the field of inclusive awareness produces empathy and heightened responsibility:

> As electrically contracted, the globe is no more than a village. Electric speed in bringing all social and political functions together in a sudden implosion has heightened human awareness of responsibility to an intense degree. It is this implosive factor that alters the position of the Negro, the teen-ager, and some other groups. They can no longer be *contained*, in the political sense of limited association. They are now *involved* in our lives, as we in theirs, thanks to the electric media.
>
> (McLuhan 1964/1994: 5)

On this view, electric media brought a promise of improved race relations and a decline in inter-generational conflict; in short, a shift from hostile segregation to a new and striking awareness and appreciation of mutuality. Electronic media would bring into communication members of disempowered groups, as well as publicizing their plight to others. In *The Medium is the Massage*, McLuhan presented a graphic which depicted a man looking out at the reader from behind prison bars. The accompanying text claimed that detention as a form of punitive correction did not work well in an electronic world. According to McLuhan, enclosure as a means of constraint and classification was inimicable in the global village, a world of 'total involvement', in which the guilt for misdeeds was felt to be shared by all (McLuhan and Fiore 1968: 61).

McLuhan's book hailed the obsolescence of punitive detention. The McVeigh webcast case indicates the extent to which his utopian vision has not been realized. The Bureau of Prisons' case against the webcast was centred on 'the maintenance of security and good order'. The Terre Haute prison warden explained the significance of the secure order issue by stating that inmates might see the execution as dehumanising 'sport'. He stated that feeling devalued as persons, there was a danger that the inmates would become disorderly, leading to riots and disturbances. The court's ruling was based on emphasizing this danger of insecurity and disorder. The webcast was prohibited as a danger to the smooth management of a potentially unruly population. The issue before the court was not whether a webcast execution, or indeed the act of execution itself, would be dehumanizing. What mattered was the efficacy of secure containment. In this respect, the case seems to exemplify Zygmunt Bauman's (1998: 13) persuasive depiction of the American penitentiary as 'a laboratory of the "globalized" society'. Bauman wrote that incarceration in institutions like the Californian prison at Pelican Bay exemplifies the interconnection of localizing, space-fixing processes with globalizing ones. He argued that incarceration in today's post-correctional prisons represents the extreme expression of polarization endemic in a globalizing world. According to Bauman, estrangement is at the core of spatial segregation, limiting dramatically the view of the other. Estrangement casts the other into 'a condition of enforced unfamiliarity guarded and cultivated by the closely supervised space boundaries, held at a distance and barred regular or sporadic communicative access' (Bauman 1998: 108). These penal practices of estrangement seem far from the return of the choric predicted by McLuhan. Both death row, and the more general arrangement of western prisons as 'prisons of immobility', deny McLuhan's (1964/2002: 270) vision of 'our co-presence everywhere at once in the electric age'.

Capital punishment is perhaps the ultimate act of the 'factories of immobility', both in terms of the many years spent in estranged isolation on death row, and the eventual killing of the prisoner, an extreme rite of dehumanization. Death penalty procedures in the supermax high security units of today are the ultimate iteration of the 'waste management' model of contemporary penality. This notion of the prison as a penal dustbin figures inmates as contaminating trash, as rubbish to be isolated from contact and clinically disposed of. McLuhan emphasized the sensuousness and tactility of the electronic age, musing, 'perhaps touch is not just skin contact with things, but the very life of things in the mind' (ibid.: 117). The sensuous global *embrace* is a metaphor for the intimate connection of minds. It associates information and images with compassion, linking seeing with feeling. McLuhan associated tactility with empathy.

He related images of suffering to being 'touched' by the other, in the sense of being moved by the plight of the other to bring him or her into communication. On death row however, contact is only permitted with authorized correctional personnel. The condemned individual is 'literally made untouchable – a form of "toxic waste" . . . which must be contained until it can be disposed of in the prescribed manner' (Lynch 2000: 15). Arizona's prohibition on touch continues to the very moment of death. Even the last visit by relatives is conducted through a plexiglass screen, which forms a barrier against any final embrace. This policy seems a particularly vivid inversion of McLuhan's hoped-for return to a tactile culture. The legally delimited experience of solitary confinement has become the generalized philosophy behind entire prison facilities, which exist solely to incarcerate 'incorrigibles' for indefinite periods of time. The administration of the death penalty in America casts a spotlight on a carceral philosophy echoed in many countries. McLuhan's graphic depicted a black inmate looking out at the reader, expressing his claim that 'electric involvement' would improve race relations. However, the American prisons of today are highly racialized institutions. For McLuhan (1964/2002: 180), 'TV simply involved everybody in everybody more deeply than before.' However, viewing images of the policing and punishment of blacks does not automatically produce an ecumenical concern and a transformative politics. The Rodney King beating images, and those of the pursuit of O.J. Simpson, brought a highly divided range of responses (Jacobs 1996, Fiske 1998).

McLuhan wrote that 'margins cease to exist on this planet', but the person on death row epitomizes the extremes of contemporary marginalization. The fatal rejection of mutuality which the death penalty represents suggests that McLuhan's vision of the new media in a global village is not simply an incomplete project, or dream yet to be fulfilled. Jonathan Miller, an early critic of McLuhan, challenged the notion of a televisually constituted 'global village'. Rejecting McLuhan's claims about the new 'cool' media, he argued that the sensory features of electronic media do not bring moral and emotional involvement with the condition of distant others. Indeed, he wrote of televisual images, 'The viewer sits watching them all in the drab comfort of his own home, cut off from the pain, heat and smell of what is actually going on. . . . All these effects serve to distance the viewer from the scenes which he is watching' (Miller 1971: 126). The onus here is on TV viewing as distancing rather than being a mediated experience which tends towards 'total involvement' with the plight of others. The picture of American imprisonment that emerges from *ENI* v. *Lappin* diverges markedly from McLuhan's prophecy of involvement, responsibility and the increasing obsolescence of punitive detention.

Instead of McLuhan's inclusive vision of the viewing subject, the Marlette cartoon evokes what we might call iconic unmarked citizens. It shows up the tendency of official and mainstream discourses of criminal victimhood to construct a generic traumatic subject. These discourses frame privileged forms of victimhood in certain ways. They create images of the idealized victim, unmarked by any index of subaltern status, always constructed as innocent, and demanding strong measures of protection and tough penalties. This tendency is not limited to the sphere of criminal justice policy and practice. For example, Berlant more broadly relates the coupling of suffering and citizenship to the production of generic people, those iconic citizens, the white middle-class family. This frequent appeal to the generic traumatic subject gives me pause to reflect a little upon the iconicity of iconic images. Indeed, one could posit something like an iconomy, an economy of icons. Addressing this iconomy, we might think about who profits from these iconic images, for whose consumption they are particularly destined, in what circuits they are distributed and in what ways they are coded to interest their target audiences. This line of thinking moves away from that generalist register in which one remarks that iconic images are simply 'for everyone', that they are in themselves 'of and for the people'. The notion of an iconomy departs then from McLuhan's description of the icon as 'an inclusive compressed image' (McLuhan 1964/2002: 118). He emphasized the power of television images to involve *all* members of the nation. However, more recent scholarship emphasizes the fact that the spectacles which produce 'iconic intimates' rely upon illusions of reciprocity, participation and dialogue, creating what actually only amounts to a hallucination of nearness (Bhabha 1998). Furthermore, rather than involving everybody in everybody, iconic images both appeal to a mass subject, and are the focus of a number of competing readings. It is to these ironic counter-meanings that we once again turn.

Heroism, absurdity and irony

The supposedly sacred character of the icons of the OKC bombing, and their intimate connection with address to the vengeful traumatic subject, has been hotly contested. The mediated nature of iconic images renders them vulnerable to irony's edge, that is, to a profound questioning of their very iconicity. This exposes and challenges the particular viewing relations by which they function as icons. Basically, the ironic reading undercuts the relations of spectatorship that permit icons to operate within a familiar vocabulary and set of symbols. Ever since Northrop Frye's classic text *The Anatomy of Criticism*, the ironic mode has been linked to the portrayal of the hero within a scene of absurdity. The iconic image of the OKC attack, awarded a Pulitzer prize, was an amateur's photograph of a firefighter cradling the lifeless and bloodied body of a dead baby covered in dust, dirt and debris in his arms. This image was immediately identified as 'an American icon', as 'an American emblem for the sorrow of April 19' (Linenthal 2001: 145, Hamm 1997: 50). Not only did the image of Baylee Almon and the firefighter become the most popular memorial idea for remembrance of the tragedy of OKC, it was also the subject of an extensive memorabilia, including T-shirts, belt buckles, key chains, necklaces, statues and phone cards (Linenthal 2001). A controversial cartoon by Steve Benson, composed in protest against the sentencing of McVeigh to death in June 1997, redrew this 'American icon'. The cartoon showed the firefighter, whose nametag reads 'death penalty fanatics', holding the child. The child says, 'Please, no more killing', and the firefighter responds, 'Oh, stop your whining.' The resulting image was quickly denounced by a number of parties including the Oklahoma Governor as 'offensive', 'repulsive' and 'disgusting'. Alfred Whitehouse, President of the International Association of Fire Fighters, complained that the cartoonist had taken an image of heroism and tragedy and twisted it into something obscene. Benson however defended the 'brutal honesty' of his cartoon. This cartoon created quite a furore, with its very direct demand that its viewers take up a position *vis à vis* the appropriation of the iconic OKC image into a pro-death penalty agenda. The cartoon also uncomfortably exposes the relations of spectatorship central to iconicity, dramatizing its very constructedness.

Accompanying the contested politics of victimhood there was, as part of the killing of McVeigh, a battle over hero status. Something of this battle is played out in the Benson cartoon. A common device in irony is the naive hero, a credulous figure. In the cartoon, for the name-tag is substituted the label 'death penalty fanatics', just as for the identity of the individual firefighter, Chris Fields, was substituted the symbolic figure of heroism in tragedy. A fanatic is one marked by an intense, uncritical devotion. The Benson cartoon calls up the contested status of Timothy McVeigh as war hero and self-styled American patriot. Berlant (1997: 2), you may remember, described politics by caricature as, 'a farce-style moral and civil war between icons and hyphenated stereotypes'. Farce, a comic genre, engages its audiences through the performance of ludicrous confusions, improbable situations, and the display of exaggerated and stereotyped characters. These are all features of the McVeigh case. Foucault wrote that armed power particularly solicits public participation as onlookers when the person punished is an enemy within, a citizen or subject of one's own nation. McVeigh was, as some of the popular books put it, *One of Ours*, an *American Terrorist*, an *All-American Monster* (Serrano 1998, Michel and Herbeck 2001). Not only was the OKC bomber an American citizen, he was also a decorated Gulf War veteran, trained by his government to defend the nation against its enemies. He was sent to the Gulf War as a top gun, a highly skilled gunner in a high-tech infantry force. He was the gunner of a Bradley fighting vehicle, a formidable battle machine that carries three guns. The largest of these fires TOW (tube-launched, optical-tracked, wire-command-link-guided) missiles at targets over a mile away. McVeigh saw active duty in Operation Desert Storm, during which heavily armed forces pushed through Kuwait, decimating in a mere four days their poorly trained and ill-equipped opponents. The Allied force was equipped with highly sophisticated night-vision technology and vastly superior fire power, 'the ground fighting in which McVeigh would be engaged was more of a high-tech turkey shoot than a war' (Michel and Herbeck 2001: 72). McVeigh had not fired at a human being before Desert Storm. For him, 'sitting in the turret of the camouflage-colored Bradley, peering into the padded viewfinder was like being turned loose in the world's greatest video parlor' (ibid.: 63). On the second day of the ground assault his crew spotted a dug-in enemy machine-gun nest. When an Iraqi soldier momentarily came into view McVeigh fired from over a mile away, exploding the soldier's entire upper body and killing another man standing nearby. He was awarded the Army Commendation Medal for this sharp-shooting at an enemy too far away to inflict any damage, and from death row told reporters of his guilt and disillusionment after the attack. A man from the war zone, McVeigh was the hero who killed the distant enemy. Yet he brought back from that deadly exchange, from that dangerous and foreign wild zone, a fury at America's extravagant violence. His attack on the federal government building was also designed as revenge for the excessive use of force against 'enemies within' at Waco and Ruby Ridge. Refusing a stay of execution, the government was keen to depict McVeigh as 'an enemy of the Constitution'.[7] Immediately after the death penalty was passed, Congress rushed through legislation to prevent him from being buried with military honours in the sacred space of a national cemetery, to forestall this desecration of the space designed to remember and honour the nation's war heroes.[8] McVeigh's last statement was read outside the prison after his death, its words the text of a nineteenth-century poem:

Invictus

Out of the night that covers me,
Black as the Pit from pole to pole,
I thank whatever gods may be
For my unconquerable soul.
In the fell clutch of circumstance
I have not winced nor cried aloud.
Under the bludgeonings of chance
My head is bloody, but unbowed.
Beyond this place of wrath and tears
Looms but the Horror of the shade,
And yet the menace of the years
Finds, and shall find, me unafraid.
It matters not how strait the gate,
How charged with punishments the scroll,
I am the master of my fate:
I am the captain of my soul
(W.E. Henley 1875)

Into the cacophony following the execution came this striking poem, which conveys ideas of stoicism and forbearance through adversity and suffering. In the context of its use as McVeigh's last statement, it also reads as unapologetic, as a determination to stand by his convictions. The secular idiom of the work levels a challenge to the dogmatic rhetoric of righteous vengeance, evil and damnation. Idealized generic victims are demarcated against stereotyped villains. Yet the figure of McVeigh contains elements of both hero and fanatic. The 'sorrow of April 19' is rewritten here as the opening scene of a revenge movie, similar in a way to *Collateral Damage* (Warner Brothers 2001). In this film, Arnold Schwarzenegger plays a family man and firefighter who seeks revenge after the authorities fail to bring to justice the Colombian rebel who bombed a building, killing his wife and child. The hero turns avenger, but in doing so can he remain hero? Critics fiercely objected to the proximity imagined between firefighter-hero and vigilante. The battle over heroism in the Benson cartoon, like Marlette's caricatured audience, evokes the familial politics of vengeful victimhood. The firefighter cradles the dying child in a fatherly and protective pose, but responds harshly to its plea. The paternal state does not look well as a killing state.

The firefighter cartoon demonstrates clearly the caustic effect, the bite and the cut, of irony. Responding to enraged denouncers, Benson stated, 'art is intended to grab you in the gut and to twist', and explained that his cartoon was intended to bring about introspection and self-examination (cited in Moore 1997). Quite unimpressed with this explanation, Whitehouse for the firefighters retorted, 'at a time when the healing process has begun and all of those who were touched by the Oklahoma City bombing are trying to bring closure to this tragedy, Mr Benson and United Features Syndicate by their callousness, have opened some deep wound.' Well, in a way, this objector has hit the nail on the head, for irony disrupts the (violently) therapeutic register of 'closure'. As I mentioned above, there is a certain traumatic force of irony, which particularly proceeds, I believe, from its staging and provocation of moral ambiguities. Relatedly, Kierkegaard speaks of 'the wound of negativity', the wounding character of irony, of this nothingness that calls borders and limits into question, which 'disrupts one's myths of innocence and immediacy, of community and self-inclosure' (Shakespeare 1998: 111). The Benson cartoon makes plain the cutting edge of irony. Paul de Man (1969/1983; 1977/1996) emphasized this disturbing aspect, arguing that irony produces the permanent interruption of narrative. He added that ironic consciousness is not reassuring, pointing to its tendency to gain momentum and unravel all customary distinctions. Irony is neither curative nor reconciliatory. Ultimately, it defers closure.

Irony and the subject of mass culture

The Marlette cartoon shows the home restored as a safe and cosy site for the domestic consumption of distant violence. The figures, these couch potatoes, are Berlant's infantile citizens. Naive, passive and infantilized, they are also the consumers of this televised entertainment, the index market for the AT&T, Toyota, and Outback Steakhouse advertisements that punctuated the coverage of McVeigh's execution. The Marlette and Benson cartoons put on display, but also question, the Baudrillardian subject, the subject who is saturated with information and images, riveted by the latest kind of reality TV. Baudrillard argues that the media implode into the mass consciousness, obliterating distinctions between public and private, and replacing them with an increasingly pervasive media space. The subject, he claims, is reduced to a terminal within an all-consuming circulation of the hyper-real. Hence for Baudrillard, new media bring the neutralization of meaning and the emasculation of politics, with the collapse of all critical distance. Though Baudrillard's work is usefully provocative, I do not believe that the media are always already antimediatory. As you will have gathered from this chapter, I prefer to work with a notion of doubled audiences. There is, as I have hoped to demonstrate to you, much critical mileage to be gained from addressing the figure of an ironic reader, from calling upon one who can, and will, read between the lines.

Ironic spaces are one way in which the critical distance that Baudrillard claims is an impossibility can be engendered. Because irony is sited in the in-between, on that edge which is also a point of passage, the spaces of irony are media. Occupying a middle position, they effect a conveyance and a communication. The ironic is therefore a space which mediates, and it constructs an alternative media space. It is a mode of address suited to the formation of counter-public spaces, those sites in which an alternative idiom develops. These new discursive spaces engage with the mainstream and dominant public sphere, seeking to reinscribe its terms. Irony contributes to this task, as a device by which dominant discourses can be challenged in their habitual and hegemonic vocabularies, for, as Rorty (1989: 74) points out, 'the opposite of irony is common sense'. Because irony unfolds within a logic of repetition and negation it counters the iterative construction of dominant terms. As an effective counterfoil to the populist appeal of common sense, irony suspends the assumed commonality of that which is called the common*place*. It points towards other spaces, turning away towards an elsewhere. The figure of irony undercuts the claim to singularity and sameness within this prefix 'uni' to the state of unitedness. It questions the constructions of belonging, of togetherness and of ecumenical concern through which imagined traumatic collectivities are addressed as victim-citizens. The McVeigh webcast case questions the association of the internet with a democratic electronic agora. This area of inquiry is also addressed in the following chapter, which considers the impact of new media upon penality through analysis of the extensive online communications around several notorious murder cases. Once again, these are linked to the construction of new collectivities.

5　The internet, new collectivities and crime

Internet communications about crimes and punishments performatively construct new collectivities, in a process which begins to reconfigure the modern outlines of penality. This chapter explores internet communications around several notorious murder cases, with an eye to their invocations of group membership and exclusion. A century ago, Emile Durkheim argued that through outraged talk about scandals and crimes, members of a community are bonded together. In his theory, the expression of angered feelings and hostile opinions formed a constitutive link between shared sentiments and group solidarity:

> We have only to notice what happens, particularly in a small town, when some moral scandal has just occurred. Men stop each other on the street, they visit each other, they seek to come together to talk of the event and to wax indignant in common. From all the similar impressions which are exchanged, and the anger that is expressed, there emerges a unique emotion, more or less determinate according to the circumstances, which emanates from no specific person, but from everyone. This is the public wrath.
>
> (Durkheim 1893 cited in Giddens 1972: 127)

For Durkheim, when the enraged passions aroused by a crime are communicated between members of a social group, they reinforce its values. Condemnatory statements were envisaged by him as a form of civic duty because through them the collective morality is reinstated. Anger, a passion excited by injury to the group's moral tenets, confirms membership of the group. At the same time, this fury solicits severe and exclusionary punishment, marking the repudiation from belonging of the offender. A powerful and univocal public wrath arises through meetings and visits among the local group, built up from talk between its members.

In Durkheim's theory, outraged expressions, severe punishment and a rigid collective morality, were emblematic of 'primitive' premodern societies. The communicational conditions of late modernity depart radically from the mechanical solidarity linked by Durkheim to angry talk and severe punishment. As I also mentioned in Chapter 4, the time-space compression and disembedding wrought by contemporary technologies brings new proximities, and forms of affiliation and exclusion. Cyberspatial technologies permit rapid communication over vast distances and across regional, national and continental boundaries. Durkheim emphasized the relationship between angered crime talk and the genesis of a public wrath in local communities. As outlined in Chapter 2, he did not discuss the transformation in relations between punishment and communication brought by print culture. A theory of punishment and communication for today must go further still, addressing the shift from print to electronic culture. What happens when people meet each other in cyberspace to discuss and debate a murder? What happens when people outside the limits of a traditional face-to-face community, and beyond earlier borders of locality and nation, talk of a notorious crime? Can we assume that through communicating in this distant yet proximate way, people 'wax indignant *in common*'?

A premise of reflections on the internet and penality must be that cyberspace provides an important medium for new forms of sociality and belonging. The kinds of proximity and intimacy made possible through cyberspatial communications disrupt earlier notions of *communitas*. It seems that a different 'order of closeness' arises through the complex connectivity brought by online communications (Tomlinson 1999). Penality has conventionally been thought in terms of the bounded entities of local community and nation-state. The penal practices of today however are shaped by the myriad ways in which global networks and flows, exemplified by the internet, reconfigure the significance of the nation-state. Online communications move in a space of flows, hence the spatiality of the web is defined by connection rather than distance. In what ways do the connections and forms of belonging performed through online communications shape the punitive practices of today? It seems that the new media have not brought the 'sensuous global embrace' anticipated by McLuhan. With cyberspatial communications, 'territories dissolve, collectivities lose their borders', but tolerance and concern for the fate of the other does not necessarily thereby ensue (Bogard 2000: 28). This chapter explores the characteristics of the extensive online communications around several controversial murder cases, and reflects upon their likely impact. The killings in question took place in North America and England, but were the subject of global scrutiny and debate. Online communications about murders include email, campaigning, informational and memorial websites, newsgroups, chat rooms, petitions, polls, poems, cartoons and satirical commentary, photographs and games. To a certain extent these are ephemeral cultural forms, rapidly changing and widely dispersed across the net. Nevertheless, internet communications about crimes and punishments performatively construct new collectivities of various kinds, in a process which begins to reconfigure the modern outlines of penality.

A study of the internet, punishment and the emergence of new collectivities must be informed by the literature on electronic media. A commitment to libertarianism is prominent within several of the most well-known books on cyberspatial communications. These typically associate the internet and email with ideals of free speech, and furthermore with processes of democratic revival. This chapter begins with the notions of sociality and identity advanced by two persuasive theories of internet and society. These are Howard Rheingold's vision of altruistic virtual community, and Manuel Castells' claim that the internet is a medium of networked individualism. Contra Castells' theory, online communications are, according to my research, an important site for the contestation of group values. Indeed, it is through this very contestation that new forms of collectivity are imagined and performed. Cyber-communications are seen as practices through which various forms of national and transnational identities are both displayed and moulded, through images and ideas about belonging and being alien. Online talk about murders does not display the compassionate practices of Rheingold's 'virtual community'. Some speculative links are postulated between the complex connectivity of internet and the penal escalation seen in many western countries.

The electronic agora

Many of the writers on internet and society profess their faith in the potential for online communications to foster democracy. Two prominent contributions of this kind by Rheingold and Castells portrayed the internet as an agora, as an electronic form of the Athenian market-place in which citizens met to gossip and debate political ideas. As concerns the kind of social interaction and bonds arising within this agora, the two books gave contrasting descriptions of virtual community and networked individualism. It is worth looking in some detail at these two prominent contributions to the debate on the net, before considering in what respects cyber-communications around murders fit with or depart from their ideas.

In *The Virtual Community*, Howard Rheingold presented a utopian vision of online communications as a source of renewed mutuality and potent vehicle of progressive social change. Rheingold (1994: 5) summarized virtual communities as 'social aggregations that emerge from the [internet] when enough people carry on those public discussions long enough, with sufficient human feeling, to form webs of personal relationships in cyberspace.' According to this definition, virtual communities are milieux where in addition to social interaction taking place, new kinds of group membership are imagined and displayed. Through 'feeling' discussions on internet bulletin boards and chat rooms, new forms of belonging develop, and Rheingold emphasized the possibility of altruistic values developing. This optimistic approach to the effects of the internet was inspired by an explicitly communitarian and liberation politics. Online communications figured in *The Virtual Community* within the context of a quest for countercultural forms of belonging based in egalitarian social relations. As a 'network of networks', the internet was for Rheingold analogous to grassroots organizing for social change. He depicted virtual communities as a source of solace, advice and material assistance to those who solicited these forms of empathy and support. The virtual community not only supplied a strong sense of communion, but also harboured great potential for collective decision-making and action. The conversation and publication that takes place through cyberspatial communications was shown by Rheingold to take the form of a process of group problem-solving that created salutary values in the process. Virtual communities hence provided a promising vehicle for transformative social action.

Rheingold promoted a notion of virtual communities as alternative social spaces. He thought that the web of citizen-to-citizen communications central to the notion of representative democracy was being denuded by the domination of commercial mass media. Indeed Rheingold went so far as to say that commercialism had 'polluted with barrages of flashy, phony, often violent imagery a public sphere that once included a large component of reading, writing, and rational discourse' (Rheingold 1994: 13). Online communications, he believed, brought a political challenge to the corporate dominance over mass communications through the promise of electronic democracy. Cyber-libertarianism was an important constituent of Rheingold's vision of virtual community. His call for constitutional protections to be extended to the US portion of cyberspace exemplifies his association of free speech with the electronic agora of which he dreamed. Rheingold did not posit electronic democracy as an automatic effect of the dissemination of the internet. For instance, he saw the dominance of large corporations like Microsoft, and the possibilities of enhanced state surveillance, as threats. Like McLuhan, Rheingold thought that new communications media would shape people's beliefs and perceptions, moulding individual personalities, but he also described the internet as 'a conduit for and reflector of our cultural codes . . . our images of who "we" might be' (ibid.: 11). He warned that computer-mediated social groups would only be liberatory if the technology was employed 'intelligently and deliberately by an informed population' (ibid.: 4). In sum, Rheingold offered a utopian notion of cyberspatial communications as a medium through which new ethical collectivities would emerge, based in active adherence to values of free speech and collective responsibility for others.

In *The Internet Galaxy* (2001), Manuel Castells rejected Rheingold's notion of virtual community, and stated that instead the internet promotes networked individualism. Castells argued that the net supplies a key lever for a transition in which vertically organized corporations and centralized bureaucracies are increasingly displaced by networks, that is, by sets of interconnected nodes. Taking up McLuhan's aphoristic style, Castells announced that 'the network is the message'. He also substituted McLuhan's turn of phrase 'the Gutenberg Galaxy' by the 'Internet Galaxy', as a way of naming the new world of communication that emerges when the internet enables the communication of many to many on a global scale. This notion of an 'Internet Galaxy' did not only express the massive proliferation of internet users during the 1990s, but also denoted the restructuring of core economic, social, political and cultural activities by computer networks. In analysing the new forms of online sociality, Castells' starting premise was with the internet's purposeful design as a technology of free communication. He described the internet's early origins in North America, and depicted internet culture as suffused with a pervasive ideology of individual freedom and openness. Castells stated that whereas the early proponents of virtual community heralded the advent of unbounded sociability, as the internet diffused into mainstream society its impact on sociality became less dramatic. He made the strong claim that 'societal interaction on the internet does not seem to have a direct effect on the patterning of everyday life' (Castells 2001: 119). Castells argued that place-based sociability was fading away before the emergence of the internet, in a shift towards relationships based around affinities with others, in which networks substitute for places. For Castells, if we are to understand the forms of social interaction in the 'Internet Galaxy' we must redefine the notion of community, rejecting its traditional and accepted meaning of an organizational form based in the sharing of common values. The displacement from community to network postulated by Castells saw online communities as ephemeral forms of sociality through which only weak ties are formed. The emergent form of the 'Internet Galaxy' is, according to Castells, one of networked individualism, a social pattern of 'me-centered networks'.

Castells' vision of the 'Internet Galaxy' linked this new communicational world to the development of democracy, and like Rheingold he believed that cyberspace could bring people together in a public agora. He argued that while the internet contributes to democratization, it does not provide a simple technological fix to the crisis of democracy. For him, the internet is a contested domain in which a battle for freedom is fought against the domination of media corporations and the persistence of state control. In sum, Castells related his picture of a distinctively libertarian 'internet culture' to the rise of a new form of sociality which he called 'networked individualism'. There is cause for suspicion of this evocation of a singular internet culture. Rheingold wrote of a particular kind of place, a virtual community with a caring libertarian ethic. Castells moved from this idea of a distinctively communitarian locus to the notion of a space of flows, emphasizing connection rather than location. Communications on the murder cases studied demonstrate complex connectivity rather than virtual community. However, Castells' emphasis on individualism and his extrapolation to democratic revival, are also questioned.

Rheingold and Castells did not discuss online communications about crimes, trials and punishment. How far does this area of internet traffic accord with their notions of electronic agora, virtual community and networked individualism? Online communications about murders demonstrate a complex series of proximities between free speech discourses, infotainment media and penal escalation. They display forms of technological populism rather than representative democracy or individualism. For instance, online polls epitomize the difficulties with the notion of the internet as the locus of democratic fora: 'Do you approve or disapprove of the release of Jon Venables and Robert Thompson?' 'Should the identities of James Bulger's killers be revealed?'[1]

The internet has been hailed as a new political force able to transform electoral politics. Dick Morris (1999) announced that cyber-communications made possible a return to Jeffersonian direct democracy, technologizing the notion of people making their own decisions at town meetings. The diminished role of intermediaries and the increase of direct popular participation would bring, according to Morris, the empowerment of a 'Fifth Estate' made up of all citizens online. Voting on sites like Vote.com would bring direct democracy by popular referendum. Yet even this highly optimistic author sounded a warning about the effects of cyberspatial communications upon the judicial process. He thought that internet activity around trials was likely to produce 'interactive kangaroo courts or a popular lynch-mob psychology'. Online polls are a form of entertainment more than of democratic decision-making. The punitive pleasures invoked by commercial polling are evident in several complaints upheld by the UK regulatory body Independent Committee for the Supervision of Standards of Telephone Information Services (ICSTIS) against Planet Telecom in 1998. ICSTIS received a number of complaints arising from 99,522 'Myra Hindley Vote' and 411, 100 'Paedophile Vote' promotions sent out as unsolicited faxes to private homes and businesses. These voting com- munications tend to solicit a gut response by the use of emotive images and rhetoric. For instance, the 'Paedophile Vote' fax read, 'Paedophiles in your neighbourhood? Is it any of your business??? Should we castrate them all?' They seldom offer much information on the issue at hand. They are instances of a soundbite society in which political argument is simplified to quick snatches of words and images:

> A sound bite society is one that is flooded with images and slogans, bits of information and abbreviated or symbolic messages – a culture of instant but shallow gratification. It is not just a culture of gratification and consumption, but one of immediacy and superficiality, in which the very notion of 'news' erodes in a tide of formulaic mass entertainment. It is a reality anaesthetized to violence, one that is cynical but uncritical.
>
> (Scheuer 2001: 8)

Soundbite society, according to Scheuer, not only erodes democratic forms of communication, it also favours right-wing politics. This begs the question of the relationship between new media and the punitive drift of the last two decades, within which penal populist modes of engaging audiences have been explicitly recruited into electoral politics.

Online communications about crimes and punishments display the charac- teristics of 'tabloid justice', a media form in which legal proceedings are presented as entertainment by an obsessive media establishment for a riveted public (Fox and Van Sickel 2001). In tabloid justice, the news and civic educa- tion roles of media are undermined by a focus on the titillating and shocking aspects of a story. In this media frenzy, major legal and political issues are obscured by 'a cacophony of commentary, prognostication and confrontation' (ibid.: 5). A fascinated public witnesses trials, which often bring the aggravation of social cleavages through the media's polarizing coverage styles, crudely pitting blacks against whites, men against women. Subject selection and presentation format are dominated by a market-driven imperative to supply shocking images, and to structure narrative in brief and dramatic narrative segments. This typically results in 'fast-paced, dramatic, superficial presentations and simplistic explanations' (Surette 1998: 73). Despite western beliefs in the free exchange of ideas, 'democratic imperatives are strikingly absent in the present news environment' (Fox and Van Sickel 2001: 9). The internet plays an important part in the spread of tabloid justice. It permits anyone to act as reporter or publisher of images and information, to transmit material on any topic to a potentially global audience, as well as allowing people to participate in real-time conversations with distant others. These communicative features of the internet are central to contemporary tabloid justice, fostering 'an essential technological populism' (ibid.: 111). Fox and Van Sickel were concerned with the extent to which the media disseminate distorted images that undermine public confidence in criminal justice. This perspective envisages an authentic, unmediated representation of criminal justice, in which the public could be rightly confident. I prefer a notion of mutual implication between media and justice system. On the one hand, criminal justice is highly mediated, suffused with ideas and images that come from the media, and on the other, the output of the mass media has depended for two centuries on the proceedings of the criminal justice system. In the communication culture of late modernity, it is problematic to draw a boundary between the two. It is a moot question as to the part played by this reciprocity within the recent penal escalation seen in many western countries.

The internet, free speech and penal escalation

The extensive online communications around murders invite speculation about the relationship between the technological populism of internet and penal escalation. The murder cases of Woodward, Homolka and Thompson and Venables all involved debate about new media and their impact upon criminal justice. A relationship between punitive populism, vigilante desires and acts and media flows was discerned by some, albeit an unclear one. Others however sought to wholly dismiss any connections, vigorously defending a vision of the democratizing force of the internet. The three cases played an important part in the framing of 1990s internet culture. This was due to the heavy net traffic reporting and debating the crimes, trials and sentences, as well as the use of the net to announce a verdict in one case, and the imposition of media bans in the other two. In connection with the three cases, the relationship between the internet and justice processes was debated in courts, newspapers and on the net itself. The precise terms of the debate changed a little on each occasion.

Woodward was a teenage English nanny tried in Boston, Massachusetts for the murder of Matthew Eappen, a young child in her care. Her trial was tele-vised live, and the ratings-oriented coverage made the testimony of Woodward and the advocacy of her celebrity lawyer Barry Scheck into major media events. The images of these moments of the trial were given a greater volume of coverage than the complex medical testimony. Woodward was convicted of second-degree murder and the child's parents made an emotive and vengeful victim impact statement. However, the trial judge overturned the verdict, and substituted a conviction of involuntary manslaughter, ruling that Woodward had acted in confusion, fright and bad judgement rather than malice or rage. A court official emailed the judge's decision to around twenty media organizations, who immediately published it on their websites. Announcing the verdict in this way figured the net as a powerful informational tool. However, the judge's statement also acknowledged the populist character of media. He noted the huge press and public interest in the case, and insisted that justice must ignore this pressure, stating, 'in this country, we do not administer justice by plebiscite'. He also emphasized that the court could not consider the feelings of the relatives of the victim when considering the question of liability, although he wished to acknowledge their 'indescribable pain'. The case was accompanied by extensive activity on the net. Informative sites sprang up, sometimes accompanied by sound and videoclips of courtroom proceedings including a quicktime movie of Woodward breaking down when her original sentence was announced. There were heated debates in newsgroups, as participants denounced the 'babykiller' or the hostility of the child's parents. Some sites invited you to 'rageback', to 'vent it now' and 'blow off some steam'. Others constituted a campaigning web-ring seeking 'Justice for Louise' by popular vote, and invited donations by credit card.

The judge later sentenced Woodward to 279 days' imprisonment, the time already served by her in custody. Television and internet images of the sentencing employed a split screen format to juxtapose the scene of a pub in Woodward's home village with the Massachusetts courtroom. This brought the virtual co-presence of jubilant villagers and distraught Eappen parents. The performance of national identity was one of the most noted ways in which web-users discussed developments in the case:

> Louise, as a British subject being tried in the US, became a symbol for national differences between the US and the UK. . . . What was seen in some of the newsgroups discussing the Louise Woodward case appeared to be not so much a case of cultural homogenisation as a polarization or playing out of difference, and national identities appeared to be solidified rather than dissolved by the contact.
>
> (Hine 2000: 114)

Hine associated online communications on the Woodward case with situated performances of national identity. Online communications on the Homolka and Bulger cases also performed various forms of national and transnational collective identities.

The Homolka case of 1993 saw a controversial ban in Canada on publication of the details of a murder trial. Karla Homolka and Paul Bernardo, commonly known as 'Killer Barbie and Ken', are a Canadian couple who engaged in a series of videotaped sex murders. Procedural failings in the police investigation and the concealment of vital evidence by the defence meant that Homolka was offered and accepted a plea bargain, in which she testified against her ex-husband. This 'deal with the devil', as it became popularly known, won her immunity from prosecution on a murder charge. She was tried for manslaughter, with prosecutors at her trial portraying Homolka as a beaten wife, and reluctant accomplice of a sadist. Following Homolka's subsequent conviction and the imposition of a twelve-year sentence, videotapes showing the crimes which had been concealed by Bernardo's lawyer were turned over to the authorities. The Ontario Court of Justice imposed a strict ban on publication of the Homolka case details until the trial of her ex-husband had taken place.[2] The media parties to the case cited the freedom of the media under s.2(b) of the Canadian Charter of Rights and Freedoms. They called for open justice, and stated that transparency was especially important in this case because of the plea bargain struck by Homolka. The judge allowed the ban solely on the basis that a fair trial for Paul Bernardo necessitated the measure, to allow an impartial jury to be found. However, the ban was subverted by transborder flows of information and gossip, through which the details of the crime were 'ferociously available' (Shade 1996: 20). A newsgroup on Usenet, a worldwide bulletin-board system, was set up to enable discussion of the case and the ban. This produced a collage of rumours and speculations, which slowly formed a picture of the crimes, a narrative circulated by email as a lurid FAQ (Frequently Asked Questions) list. An anonymous remailer in Finland (a service which receives email and resends it after removing all traces of the original source) was used extensively, being out of Canadian jurisdiction. Despite universities preventing access to the newsgroup, and police seizing newspapers and intercepting television signals, there were many ways for people to gain access to the prohibited information. Toronto residents with television antennas could pick up the broadcasts about the trial from Buffalo, and Canadians streamed across the border to purchase and read the coverage in US newspapers.

An issue of *Wired* magazine supplying information on how Canadians could find the illicit information was banned in Canada. In protest, the magazine's president called up the phrase 'information wants to be free', quoting Stewart Brand, a key counterculture figure, and co-founder of the virtual community described in Rheingold's book. Freedom of expression campaigners celebrated the cyberspatial subversion of the ban as a triumph for libertarian activism. Analyses like the following were typical:

> 'In cyberspace, nobody knows you are a dog,' says one canine to another in a popular cartoon exemplifying the indirect nature of electronic contact. . . . Nobody has any reason to believe what you say you are, and nobody has any way of holding you responsible for your actions without your cooperation. . . . Boundaries erected by nations or companies may work to hinder the free flow of material, but to the free flow of information these boundaries are artificial. . . . A typical case that got a lot of media coverage

is to do with the Teale–Homolka trial. . . . The government was helpless at this demonstration of information wanting to be free. . . [3]

This kind of response to the ban typically avoids discussing the actual specificities of the communications made, and instead cyber-libertarian phrases are repeated as magic mantras with a self-evident, unassailable logic. A singular democratic internet culture is evoked, 'the internet spirit', instead of any analysis of the kinds of communications around the Homolka case and their various likely effects.

Illicit online communications about Homolka's crime merged together gory details, punitive expressions, and salacious titillation about the 'homicide blonde', or 'killer babe'. A 300,000 signature petition was presented to the Senate of Canada in 1995 demanding a public inquiry into the Homolka investigation and plea bargain, as well as insisting that all Homolka's privileges in prison be revoked and that she serve the full twelve-year sentence.[4] The Attorney-General ordered an inquiry, the report of which addressed in great detail the juridical transformation of Homolka from depraved sex killer to battered woman beaten into murder (Gilligan 1996). A range of violent and vengeful websites were set up, as well as campaigning sites protesting the plea bargain. These debated Homolka's motivations and demanded more severe punishment. For instance, one webpage announced, 'Folks, we have a histrionic, psychopath hybristophile. Karla is #NOT# the pseudo-psycho-compliant-battered-post-traumatically-stressed-and-otherwise-nice-girl-victim that the Bernardo prosecution portrayed.'[5] The most reported upon threat site was the 'Karla Homolka Death Pool', its ominous subititle 'When the Game is Over, We all Win.' Another, 'Karla Homolka Sucks', featured a photograph of Homolka, which bled if you 'bashed' it by mouse-clicking.[6] Homolka's lawyer told the press of his growing fears for her safety because of the internet death pools, stating that she would be an easy target for someone wanting to shoot her through the wire fence surrounding her prison. By law, all Canadian federal prisoners must be released after serving two-thirds of their sentence unless officials can prove that they are likely to kill or cause serious harm. Homolka's parole hearing took place amid hostility and scandal, after photographs of her attired in evening dress at a birthday party in prison were published in the press. Calls were made for the 'liberal' federal government to repeal the law on automatic early release. After the authorities ordered a psychiatric assessment, Homolka was refused parole on the grounds that she posed too great a risk of violent reoffending, and that she refused to recognize her own sadistic role in the killings. Her lawyer's protest that the authorities were capitulating to media-fuelled public vengefulness emphasized a complex interplay of vengeful communications and cyber-libertarian activism.

The complexity of relations between the technological populism of internet and aspects of penal escalation becomes all the more visible when analysis turns to the Bulger case. A ban on publishing or broadcasting details of the new identities of the two young men who had been convicted of the murder of James

Bulger was made in 2001. This was made after a UK court heard evidence that sections of the media were inciting people to commit revenge attacks against them. The injunction restrained any publication or broadcast of any description, image in any form, photograph, film or video recording of them since their arrest in 1993.[7] Giving or soliciting any description of their appearance, voice or accent, the divulging of their new names, and any information on their past, present or future whereabouts, was also prohibited. However, the ease of circumventing the ban via the internet, and the existence of many websites and bulletin boards making death threats, were widely reported by the international media. The mother of the murdered child told the press,

> Anyone with a computer will be able to read details. They will be recognised and found out under any new name. Every minute they will have to look over their shoulders. That is some comfort to me – to know they will always be haunted and hunted.[8]

After the ease of these potentially unlawful online communications was described in the media, the injunction was amended to clarify its applicability to the internet. The onus of the amendments provided that service providers must take reasonable steps to prevent the publication of contemptuous material.[9] These measures included checking what was being posted on servers, as well as taking steps to remove offending material or to block access to it. The injunction has to date resulted in one prosecution. In *Attorney General* v. *GMNL* [2001], the publisher of the *Manchester Evening News* was fined for contempt of court after an article appeared in the newspaper and on its website, giving information relating to the whereabouts of Thompson and Venables (*Guardian*, 4 December 2001). The site had been jammed for hours with users logging on to see the illicit information.

Free speech campaigners immediately issued media releases condemning the ban, and denying the potency of relations between cyberspatial flows, vengeance and vigilantism, 'the internet, ISPs and Net-users are not to blame for any retribution against Venables and Thompson. . . . The likelihood is that hate on the internet – or in any other medium – is not going to inspire hate where it didn't already exist.'[10] This perspective obscures the role played by the populist technology of the internet in the vengeful fury surrounding notorious crimes, and particularly in this case to the intersection of cyber-libertarianism with the extra-legal actions of vigilantes. It seeks to reassert the approach that McLuhan's aphorism, 'the medium is the message' had replaced, viz., that it is merely how media are used that matters. The cyber-libertarian view typically erects simple oppositions between good uses/users and bad uses/users of the net, assuming that these can be readily identified.

A British documentary shown a week before Thompson and Venables' parole hearing, *Unforgiven*, showed a close-up of email icons on a screen, the mouse positioned over 'reply', with modem noises and a voiceover saying 'the internet is almost impossible to police'. An interview with the press agent for the Justice for James Campaign was shown, who denied the organization's responsibility for a recent photograph of Thompson unlawfully in circulation. He insisted that such an action was not an official act of the campaign group, but also refused to condemn distribution of the image, 'I should have to say to them that they should not circulate it in Britain. Whether they decided that the internet was so big that it couldn't be stopped is a matter for them. . . . If somebody abroad wanted to do it, then we couldn't stop them.' There is a proximity between the claims of cyber-libertarians and vengeful/vigilante activists, who both argue that the internet cannot be controlled, often invoking notions of the medium's spacelessness and timelessness. However, a considerable body of literature now strongly challenges these assumptions, depicting the complex spatialities and temporalities of the internet, and describing various forms of both internal surveillance and interdictory control.

As an acentred network, the internet offers zones in which illegitimate communications can flow relatively unrestricted, beyond, 'the limiting quality of context, community sanctions and the ability of moral arbiters to limit debates and censor topics through the threat of local sanctions' (Shields 1996: 1 and 4). However, while online communications do indeed undermine the bounded entities of old, new spaces and borders emerge there. A simple equation of cyberspatial communications with democratic revival would hence be erroneous, 'cyberspace is not spatially preordained to nurture democractic fora and to threaten the power of the state' (Herbert 2000: 102). Notions of freedom, spacelessness and the impossibility of control should not therefore furnish the premises for analysis of online communications. Internet enthusiasts may continue to place great emphasis upon the medium's promotion of democratic ideals. Yet the analysis of online communications around notorious murder cases demonstrates the dangers of assuming that the internet will bring post-national democracy and harmony (Barwell and Bowles 2000). Cyber-libertarian claims that the net plays no part in the punitive threats and vigilante activism directed at murderers rest upon highly questionable premises about free speech and democracy. Like the pro-death penalty websites described by Mona Lynch (2002), online communications around notorious murders tend to show up the affective, symbolic character of punitive cultures. Their rhetoric tends towards a denial of interdependencies, essentializing and repudiating criminals through highly simplified and formulaic narratives.

Cyber-communications and new collectivities

Online communications about the release of the newly anonymous Bulger killers depart from the notions of both virtual community and networked individualism. The ethic of care and responsibility evident in Rheingold's discussion of the virtual community is not the norm of practice in online communications in this case. While debating and maligning the Bulger killers on the internet does not attest to the communion found by Rheingold, neither does it support Castells' thesis of networked individualism. Contrary to Castells' argument, these online discussions do involve the contestation of group values. Analysis of online talk about a murder found it to be reactionary, conventional and normative, despite the received notion of the democratic character of the internet (Aycock and Buchignani 1995: 187). This was the case with much of the online traffic on the Bulger case. Some participants evoked what might be called a transnational vengeful network, which vociferously condemned the murder and demanded severe punishment of its perpetrators. A small number of others indicted punitive excess as barbarism, often invoking notions of primitivism versus civility and appealing to notions of universal human rights. Soundbite culture's image-based flows reconstitute selves and communities into image-oriented performances, products and presentations (Slayden and Whillock 1999). Net communications around the Bulger case demonstrate the performative construction of various kinds of collective identities. They indicate the emergence of new forms of sociality, less permanent and more intense, informally networked, 'small, mobile and flexible groupings – sometimes enduring, often easily dissoluble – formed with an intensive affective bonding' (Lash 2002: 27). These explosive extraterritorial communities are volatile, transient and single-purpose, and Bauman (2000: 199–200) writes, 'their life-span is short while full of sound and fury'. He adds that their potency is derived not from their durability but from the strong emotional investment demanded by their precarious existence.

The appeal to a transnational vengeful network was typically focused on florid yet formulaic messages about the crime's 'inherent evil', employing vivid depictions of the horror of the murder. One online petition from a British site stated, 'There can be no doubt that the murderers of James Bulger and little Sarah Payne are simply evil people.'[11] Bulger and Homolka sites featured online petitions, bulletin boards and polls, through which contributors from all over the world made a range of violent threats. The site most prominently reported by the news media carried a petition addressed to the 'General Public'.[12] The petition, which demanded that the release and anonymity rulings be undone, displayed thousands of signatures, and took the form of a message-board. Messages posted by signatories from all over the world included the following:

> Attack these 2 monsters as soon as their photo is released to the public (USA)

> You can't hide forever . . . you will be found. They should be hounded to the ends of the earth and persecuted till the day they take their own miserable rotten lives (UK)

> Someone must know where they are. Let's find them and get it over with already (Australia)

> I believe in the Bible, they should be executed so god can Judge them (USA)

> if you are old enough to kill in such a manner u should be treated as an adult would be and spend life in prison (USA)

> To let these boys go is to put all children in the world in danger (USA)

> An eye for an eye, a tooth for a tooth (England)

Each of these postings made a gesture of national location or affiliation, producing an image of a geographically dispersed network of vengeful and vigilante voices. The punitive network was partly constituted through the petition's circulation via a link in a chain email, passed on from one angered person to the next. The populist force of the petition was emphasized in its claim to be the organ of 'People for Jamie Bulger'. The petition author wrote, 'I would like people all over the world to band together and demand that this be undone.' Although many of the postings readily employed expletives and sexually explicit language to make violent threats, the petition signatories repeatedly claimed the authority of 'justice'. A few signatories condemned the 'ill-informed and vengeful' messages posted on the site:

> You people are all twisted. You would honestly take the lives of two more people to avenge the death of another, where is the logic in that, how does it help anyone by making more people suffer? (UK)

> It seems to me that every single one of you people have nothing between your ears . . . you people are just as sick as what they did back in 1993. What SATISFACTION does it give you to have them killed? (UK)

> Do we care that thousands of people needlessly die EVERY DAY in the third world, NO, but because there is someone to BLAME, we love it and all join in the fun. (UK)

There were no replies to the few critical postings. The site did not permit dialogical communication, a prominent instance of the soundbite culture.

The 'have your say' invitation of online petitions and polls does not solicit discussion. These communicational forms indicate that the existence of disagreement and contestation does not mean that the internet should be characterized as an essentially democractic medium. Indeed, analysis often shows online communication to produce a resounding silence indicating lack of interest, or to take the form of a shouting match, 'Cyberspace . . . on a day to day basis is about as interactive as a shouting match. Offering freedom from sanction and the power of anonymity and untraceability, cyberspace becomes not an environment for rational discussion, but a soapbox for extreme opinions' (Streck 1998: 45). The cacophony of dismissive assertion and insult seems to be found more often than interested exchange and listening dialogue: 'Hyper-connectivity brings more and more people in touch with each other faster yet it does not bring them closer together. . . . Those visitors who do not merely lurk exchange lengthy diatribes or random utterances, without any incentive to engage others' (Noveck 2000: 19). The internet is hence not essentially a medium of deliberative, thoughtful dialogue.

Other populist net communications included model protest letters, and an online ribbon campaign.[13] One email petition stated, 'The Love-Bug virus took less than 72 hours to reach the world. I hope this one does too.'[14] The Justice for James campaign official website supplied a model text letter to encourage visitors to write to politicians, the Lord Chief Justice, the Chairman of the Parole Board and the Queen, to ask for the pair to be 'properly punished'.[15] This site claimed the authorizing voice of the mother of James Bulger on its index page. There were several webrings, which linked together kitsch Bulger memorial pages. For instance, the site lovingyou.com presented a poem 'Jamie Bulger', 'I know that I am looking for the day When they die and go to hell For killers never get their way.'[16] Another memorial, on the 'God hears you' site, employed an angelic iconography, with a photograph of 'Jamie' flanked by two flying doves, on a background of cherubs.[17] These memorial and tribute sites readily idealized James as a 'little doll' and 'angel'. While listening to piped music, visitors could read '*the* story' of James's murder, which told them,

> He may be from Britain but this nightmare has happened here in the states also. . . . Tell us what you think, we are trying to petition the government to stop this anonymity. Australia refused to take these boys and we want the rest of the world to do the same, so they will remain in Britain and will be fearful all their lives.

Despite these invocations of a transnational vengeful network, cyber-communications around the Bulger case did not evince the univocal public wrath and punitive zeal theorized by Durkheim. There were comedy simulations ridiculing the sensationalized mass media role in the case. One of these posted pretend photographs of how the pair look now.[18] There were sites which lambasted the political exploitation of the Bulger killers phenomenon, for instance 'Mr Blair Congratulates Bulger Case Bullies', and 'Venables and Thompson to be rehoused in gothic, torch-lit castle on remote mountainside.'[19] Messages solicited by BBC News Talking Point included those calling for the identification of Thompson and Venables and those denouncing calls for vengeance and further punishment, for instance 'the bloodlust and mob mentality that some people are showing sickens me' and 'the psychotic baying for the blood of these two boys disgusts me'.[20]

Online talk about the Bulger and Homolka cases involved plenty of 'flaming', as postings and discussions in chat rooms and newsgroups took the form of vitriolic exchanges. Wallace (1999) argued that the characteristics of the internet medium, and especially the disinhibitory effect of perceived anonymity, escalate aggression. She added that communication patterns on the net mediate against consensus. Yet rather than seeing the internet as a medium particularly suited to stimulate rage and aggression, these online communications indicate the vigorous performance of various kinds of belonging and exclusion.

Cyber-communications, compassion and exclusion

The non-dialogical postings and frequently vitriolic flaming that characterized online communications around the Bulger case are a far cry from the egalitarian and compassionate communications described by McLuhan and Rheingold. Rheingold (1994: 17) wrote of a 'tacit understanding [that] sanctifies the virtual space' of parenting in his virtual community. He described the parenting conference as the 'heart' of this virtual community, a place at which information was shared, emotional support and solace was sought and gained, and collective action was organized. He detailed the comfort and fellowship arising from membership of this online group, identifying this as a sense of communion, arising from a commitment to others. A network of Bulger online clubs can be found on the web. These depart markedly from the 'compassional and compressional' spaces associated by McLuhan (1964/2002: 91) with electronic retribalization. Several of the postings on the People for Jamie Bulger online petition made comments like, 'I am the mother of a two-year old. Need I say more.' This kind of message employed an identification as parent as a basis from which to demand severe punishment. A series of exchanges in two of the Bulger case online clubs reveals parenting as a position from which ethical and moral debate arose:[21]

DEBATE-CHAIRMAN: if Thompson and Venables were your own children would you still feel the same way?

AMAZED28: if Jamie was your child would you be so loving to the killers?

AMAZED28: this is only the opinion of a mother. Cause a mother is one that should be a mother to all children even if they are not her own!

DEBATE-CHAIRMAN: it seems that you are also saying, 'a mother is a mother to all children – except children who do evil things' – like Thompson and Venables. In that case where do you draw the line?

AMAZED28: my answer to how would I feel if Thompson and Venables were my sons I would want them punished. A punishment that fit the crime not that fit their age.

DEBATE-CHAIRMAN: On what basis do you judge the value of a person. . . . Imagine you are a mother and have two girls. One of them is a well behaved child, but the other is a little horror. . . . Which of those two children is more 'valuable' to you? Is one of them less 'valuable' than the other because she is less well behaved?

MEGS_1_1999: I think if I was Jamie's mother I would not be able to forgive them for needlessly taking away my son.

TXMAMAOF2: I can't imagine what Jamie's mother is go'n thru or if she will EVER forgive these boys for tak'n her son. . . . I just hurt for her, my heart aches for her.

In the debate in this Bulger online club, parenting as an ethic of responsibility, commitment and compassion is being contested. To whom can comfort be extended? Should care and assistance be withdrawn in certain circumstances? The postings from Megs and Tx reinstate an inconsolable maternal voice. The figure of the mother of the murdered child is used to evoke the just and natural character of vengeance, a justice in which the offender can receive no consideration or affection. This debate in the Bulger online club is also concerned with what kind of network the clubs can form. This is not a sanctified space like Rheingold's parenting group. Can the networks and web-rings provide a medium for debate? Can they allow compassion?

The pitting of exclusionary penality against an ethic of compassionate refuge was prominent after extensive speculation that British authorities were planning to send the newly anonymous Bulger killers to Australia, New Zealand or Canada. This news, first reported in December 2000, brought angry headlines demanding: 'No haven for Bulger killers', 'No sanctuary for Bulger killers', 'Keep Out'. Should the arrival of the Bulger killers be welcomed as a compassionate act, or refused as a reinscription of colonial history? Many of the terms of the debate figured in the following Editorial from *The Age*:

> The era of the penal colony is over. The rehabilitation of child murderers is an agonising problem. It should not be exported. . . . This murder of a child by a child shocked the world, and the memory of it has continued to do so ever since. . . . It might be argued that if Australia were to accept one of the youths it would be a compassionate act, in principle no different from participation in international witness-protection programs. But Venables and Thompson are offenders, not witnesses, and there would surely be something odd about granting them what amounts to asylum while extremely stringent entry tests are imposed on others who come here in search of asylum but have no criminal history. Four of Australia's six states were once British penal colonies, and many Australians are descended from people who, like Venables and Thompson, wanted a home where their past did not matter. But neither of these things means that Britain ought to be able to export a social problem it does not want, as it once transported convicts it did not want. Transportation has passed into history, which is where it should remain.[22]

This episode indicates the interconnections of penality with the spectre of the colonial history of Australia, as well as an anxiety about border controls and the exclusion of 'undesirable' immigrants. Notably, refuge for the Bulger killers was typically refused as a reinscription of colonial history by deploying the contemporary waste management model of penality. As one online poll put it, 'should countries like Australia have to take our rubbish?'[23]

Crime victims' associations expressed vehement opposition to the proposal, with one spokesman stating, 'allowing Thompson and Venables in would set a nasty precedent for resuming transportation of criminals to Australia. I don't think there'd be any other country in the western world that would have them after such an intolerable crime.'[24] The Australian press reported that Canada had indicated that it would not welcome Thompson and Venables.[25] By late December, the *Guardian* was reporting, 'Countries spurn Bulger killers' and quoting Helen Clarke the Prime Minister of New Zealand as saying, 'I would have thought the days of the penal colony were over.'[26] The immigration minister invoked section 501 of the Migration Act 1958. This states that an individual will fail the good character test if they have a substantial criminal record. Yet on Christmas Eve the *Herald Sun*'s headline stated 'EVIL PAIR COULD COME (and we would never know).'[27] The new twist in the story was that their new anonymous identities backed up by 'fake' documents and records could enable Thompson and Venables to sneak past Australia's good character requirement. Thompson and Venables could evade recognition as the stigmatized bearers of a criminal record through the subterfuge of an inauthentic, yet officially approved and fully documented, new identity.

By January, the Australian press was reporting that an email was circulating in the nation's workplaces and homes protesting at the release of the Bulger killers from custody.[28] 2001 was the centenary of Australian federation, and Brisbane's *Courier Mail* editorial noted the ironic timing of Britain's use of Australia as a 'dumping ground' during the centennial celebrations of Australian independence. The editor referred to the country's strict policy on expelling foreign criminals, and insisted that the government 'make it clear Australia is no longer a convict settlement and we do not want Britain's undesirables'.[29] A petition was presented to the Australian House of Representatives in March 2001, which demanded that Thompson and Venables be denied entry to Australia.[30] 'Not in our backyard', a Kiwi student organization prosaically demanded.[31] Online polls on Australian and Kiwi sites questioned whether Thompson and Venables should be identified.[32] The Labour Party immigration spokesman told television journalists that a written guarantee should be demanded from the British government that Thompson and Venables would not be given new identities and spirited into Australia, stating, 'Australia is no longer a dumping ground for criminals – we stopped that 150, 180 years ago.'[33] We see here the repetition and reiteration of the waste disposal model of penality over the notion of migration to a place of compassionate refuge.

The editorial from the *Age* spoke of the oddness of the idea of granting asylum to the Bulger killers. A refugee is a person fleeing life-threatening circumstances. Dame Butler Sloss's ruling stated that the threat was clearly in evidence. The international press reported Thompson's and Venables' terror of vigilante attacks. The first responsibility for protection of the individual lies with that person's country of nationality. The Bulger case questions the UK's ability to protect vilified criminals, given that the court stated that attack could come from any quarter, and made its ruling *contra mundum*, openly against all under its jurisdiction. Furthermore, it was widely reported that the cross border flows of the new media could readily disseminate information contravening the injunction, effectively undermining the court's powers. The question of the state's obligation to protect its nationals concerns both behaviour that it tolerates and behaviour that it commits. It hence calls up questions of the state's complicity in the persecution of the Bulger killers. Ultimately, refugee status largely comes about through a contrast between the laws of the country of origin and those of the asylum country. Australia, like the UK, shifted towards retributivism in juvenile justice over the 1990s. This would problematize Australia as a refuge that could provide asylum for Thompson and Venables.

These ideas were not discussed in the furious outbursts around the migration of the Bulger killers, which typically restated the precedence of border controls over humanitarian assistance. Australian immigration policy has been closely focused on control practices, which assert an exclusionary national sovereignty approach to refugees, for over a decade. The policy of mandatory detention has been legitimized by the spectre of criminals sneaking into the country:

> many of these people who are coming over, or at least some of them, who destroy their identification, who destroy their documents, who in fact are not who they say they are, which could mean that you could well be allowing terrorists or criminals into the country.
>
> (Con Sciacca cited in Wares 2001: 157)

The prospect of the Bulger killers landing in Australia, two men whom its government would seek to exclude, evoked the figure of Australia's immigration control practices, and their controversial application to asylum seekers. Despite established international obligations, these practices of refugee recognition apply exclusionary and punitive border controls of various kinds to those perceived to threaten Australian nationhood (McMaster 2001). This national sovereignty approach is premised on Australia controlling whom to admit, rather than on the needs of individual refugees within a discourse of compassion and hospitality. Politicians and victims' rights groups appealed to an exclusionary nativist notion of Australian citizenship, as well as a transnational anxiety about the presence of 'faceless killers' in the midst of the community. These demands for threatening difference to be marked and repudiated suggest a postcolonial reading of the communications about crime and punishment. The transportation of convicts for profit was an integral part of the cultural economy of colonialism. Today, the global trade in images and ideas about criminals is an important part of the postcolonial negotiation of borders and forms of belonging, as well as the emergence of complex forms of territoriality.

Punishment, communications and the internet

This chapter has elaborated some dimensions of punishment in the contemporary communications culture. It has been argued that cyber-communications bring new forms of imagined co-presence and connectedness, which question the Durkheimian association of the passion of punishment with locally or nationally based *communitas*. Instead of the compassional practices associated by Rheingold with virtual community, online talk and images about murders tends to be hostile and combative. However, this does not constitute a univocal public wrath. Situated performances of affiliation and exclusion are seen, both national and transnational. A complex set of relations between cyber-communications about serious crimes and processes of punitive escalation has been described. The formulaic messages of a soundbite culture that have been discussed often depicted gruesome and frightening images of injury and death. The next two chapters of this book move on to address the pervasive gothicity of contemporary discourses of retributive penality. The analyses presented address the ways in which the complex relations between punishment, culture and communication develop within, and remake, legal logics.

6   Punishment and the powers
of horror

In her recent novel *Border Crossing*, Pat Barker painted two scenes becoming
all too familiar within the iconic order of contemporary culture:

> He switched on the news. The Kelsey murder was the second item. Close-
> ups of flowers left at the scene of the crime, blowzy chrysanthemums,
> 'Love' in blue ink dribbling down a wet card. Then pictures of a white van
> accelerating rapidly, pursued by angry crowds.
>
> (Barker 2001: 176)

These two news images evoke the dramatic iconography within which penal
practices have been displayed on our screens over the last few decades. This
chapter takes further the analysis of the changing aesthetics of punishment in
contemporary culture. It explores another aspect of the aesthetics accompanying
the recruitment of the punitive subject in vengeful victimhood. The analysis
turns to the gut responses solicited by the gothic textual and pictorial practices
with which true crime fiction, news reporting, notorious murder cases and penal
policies are suffused. The powers of horror are a prominent feature of retributive
penality, and engage audiences in disgusted and fearful fascination. These
feelings touch us as *visceral* passions, begging the question of how these 'raw'
emotions are implicated in calls for retribution and the fearful agenda of public
protection. Gothicism writes crime and punishment through tropes of terror,
menacing shadowy figures, gruesome injury and trauma, and melancholic
haunting. Barker's images, of mournful tributes left at the crime scene, and of
an angry mob chasing a prison van, invoke vengeful victimhood. These emotive
scenes display the remaking of earlier distinctions between legal and extra-legal,
public and private.

Gothic narratives of crime and punishment are a product of the age of mediated spectacle. Emerging in the nineteenth century, they replaced the theodic
discourse of penitent sinner with one of monstrous otherness. The conventions
through which they were presented encouraged a fascination with the infliction
of pain and suffering upon the offender. Using a rhetoric of hyperbole and
increasing detail of bloody violence, they worked to 'shock the reader into an
emotional state that mingled fear with hatred and disgust' (Halttunen 1998: 3).

Over the last two hundred years, gothic has taken slightly different forms. In late modernity, it is particularly inflected by the increasing centrality of victims within the criminal justice system. Today, gothicity interpellates postsocietal and transnational collectivities through a rhetoric and imagery typically unmarked by locally based affiliations. The aesthetics of punishment in the iconic age promulgates essentialized images of faceless 'evil' predators who are anywhere and everywhere. There are also discourses of regional and national trauma, for instance the theme of 'sorrow on Merseyside' after the killing of James Bulger. An 'RIP JAMES' banner was held aloft as the crowd at Liverpool FC observed a minute's silence in remembrance of the child. However, these situated public performances of local affiliations begin to be shaped by transnational and postsocietal images, which lament generic innocent victims and evil killers everywhere. As I indicated in Chapter 5, through the complex connectivity of the internet, these discourses are circulated across vast distances. They link users who display mourning for Matthew Eappen with those who wish to display grief at the death of James Bulger, those who want to cyberbash or letch over the 'evil bitches/killer babes' Karla Homolka and Myra Hindley, and connect the fans of Charles Manson, Ronnie Biggs and the Krays. The gothic is eminently suited to these communicational forms, with its oppositions between idealized victim and monstrous stranger.

Late modern gothicism, true crime and penality

I am not the only one to have noticed the pervasive gothicity of crimino-legal practices. For instance, Mike Nellis (1988) described how the retelling of the Moors murders as mass entertainment repeatedly emphasized the macabre and sinister aspects of the tale. Colin Sumner (1991) has argued that crime- and detection-reporting and television shows are an important feature of late modern Crime Wars, a highly publicized semi-participatory game through which conservative ideologies of crime and justice are reiterated and reinforced. He notes the daily bombardment with stories of horrible murders and heroic policing, accompanied by salacious interpellations and snippets of rapid, unexplained action. Ian Taylor (1999) opens his book *Crime in Context* by noting the prominence of gothicism in popular cultural representations of crime and punishment. He sees the large collections of popular crime literature in high street bookstores, movies and prime-time television series as indicative of a powerful 'commonsense' interpretation of crime. This insistently focuses representation on the individual criminal and depicts him or her as acting under the influence of evil or personal pathology. He adds that these genres exercise an influential social presence. I want to emphasize that gothicism is not confined to the cultural narratives that circulate as stories and images in popular representations. Rather, gothic tropes are embedded in the practices of crime control and legal institutions. The florid textuality through which crimes are represented in popular culture both shapes, and is derivative of, the gothicity of legal judgments and penal policies. The processes in which crime and punishment are dramatized through a gothic register of horror hence demand scrutiny of the nexus between law and the literary/visual. A process of mutual implication pertains between the 'real' and the 'fictive', through the merging of news and political debate with entertainment as infotainment. For instance, high profile cases are frequently retold by novels, films and television series, and conversely journalists and politicians draw upon the textual styles of horror fictions. It is therefore as necessary to explore the powers of horror in contemporary penality as they are invoked through the texts and images circulated in true crime genres, newspaper articles, television programmes, websites and movies as it is to examine the gothicism of statutory changes, individual legal judgments and policy statements. More than this, an understanding of the dynamic mutual relation, and hybridizing fusion, between the two, is merited.

The visceral passions aroused by both the murder of James Bulger and its punishment are discussed in this chapter through a reading of Pat Barker's fascinating novel *Border Crossing* (2001), a book that tells a story which, in effect, reopens the Bulger case. Gothic tropes are at the core of the Bulger killers case, which concerned a crime that first came dramatically to light in 1993 with the abduction and murder in Liverpool of a two-year-old child by two ten-year-olds, Robert Thompson and Jon Venables. The event developed into a hotly debated mediated spectacle, reported across the world. The ensuing series of trials brought legal contestation over the aesthetics of retributive punishment.[1] The courts were asked whether the politician setting the term of imprisonment had lawfully taken into account hostile 'public opinion' evidenced by 21,281 coupons from a tabloid and a petition signed by 278,300 people. Lawyers for the boys took the government to the European court, arguing that the trial, and the release of their names and photographs, had been inhumanly degrading and intimidating. Interestingly, the European hearing addressed at what point the spectacle of suffering becomes unlawful. Although the court found that neither the trial nor the sentence were inhuman and degrading, the dissenting opinion of several judges insisted that vengeance against children had no place in law. The judges were told of the attacks on the prison van by a jeering and violent crowd, the boys' terror of being looked at in the dock, and their great distress upon hearing that their identities had been released to the media. Thompson and Venables were released during 2001 with new identities and a protective anonymity order, as the media circulated dramatic stories and images of enraged vigilantes. As discussed in Chapter 5, the anonymity order and its modifications for the internet depicted the dangerously populist force of the mass communications media. Vigilante attacks on these 'faceless killers' were repeatedly represented as a frighteningly uncontrollable menace. Given the highly charged atmosphere in the aftermath of the murder of James Bulger, and the changes in juvenile justice that followed fast on it, it is unsurprising that the concept of moral panic seemed to assume a new topicality. However, to understand the potent seductions of the gothic, we need to move on from the concept of moral panic. I take up Julia Kristeva's notion of abjection, which sees the powers of horror as provoked by that which breaches borders.[2] The movement from moral panic to abjection enables us to bring into bold relief the changing relations between victimhood, criminal justice processes, the media and state control.

Beyond the catastrophic register of moral panic

The concept of moral panic has provided an incisive means of theorizing connections between popular cultural representations, the hostile reaction to certain crimes, severely punitive responses in individual cases, policy shifts and new legislation, and the restoration of threatened collective values. Placing itself in a sceptical trend as opposed to the canonical tradition of mainstream criminology, this approach refused to see the meaning of crime and punishment as self-evident. Through an intellectual strategy of unmasking and debunking, the connections between outraged sentiments and the functioning of the control system would be laid bare. The first text to outline a theory of moral panics was published by Stan Cohen in 1972. More recently, Cohen (2000: 40) has written that the term 'folk devil' is more benign than befits the processes through which the monsters of today are manufactured, writing that, 'the moral panic line is crossed when the problem is seen as too horrible and its risk too threatening for mere cultural boundary-setting'. To fathom the depth of emotion surrounding the Bulger case, and to understand the pervasive gothicity of contemporary discourses and practices, we need to move on from the concept of moral panic.

The term 'moral panic' has been used extensively to characterize the hostile reactions of the media, public and agencies of social control to various forms of social disturbance and deviant behaviour. Cohen's book paid considerable attention to the links between the way in which acts and events were represented and the emotional reaction that this representation fostered. He theorized moral panics as written and experienced through a register of the catastrophic rather than the gothic. Cohen argued convincingly that an orientation of disaster was prominent in the emotional and intellectual standpoint from which the actions of the Mods and Rockers were depicted and evaluated. Following the use of disaster models, he found that the typical response to a catastrophic event demonstrated phases of rescue and recovery. However, contemporary penality departs markedly from the narratives and metaphors of the catastrophic. It is a convention of the gothic that there can be neither rescue nor escape from a besieging horror. Furthermore, rather than recovery, the gothic attains its formidable effects through repetitive themes of obsession and haunting.

There are several more specific reasons why the gothic characterizes the heated emotionality of contemporary penality more appropriately than the catastrophic register of moral panic. Firstly, the notion of moral panic theorizes a temporary and aberrational over-reaction. In *Folk Devils and Moral Panics*, Cohen (1972/1980: 9) supplied a definition of moral panic that has by now become a classic, 'Societies appear to be subject, every now and then, to periods of moral panic . . . the condition then disappears, submerges or deteriorates and becomes less visible.' We can see that for Cohen a panic has an immediacy and a rapidity of escalation, but just as quickly it passes away. He posited that a moral panic can sometimes produce 'long-lasting repercussions', and this suggests that he did not theorize a purely ephemeral phenomenon. In sum, although its consequences may linger, the affect itself is short-lived and volatile. In contrast to the fleeting moral panics theorized by Cohen, heavily punitive crime measures of various kinds have proliferated across several western societies of late. Rather than being a marginal phenomenon, punitive policies, practices and representations are an established feature of numerous western cultures. Cohen's argument conveyed a sense of an unusual and brief flare-up of alarm. In his theory, anxiety is spatio-temporally circumscribed, and panic originates in locally defined interests. In contemporary society, potentially fearful events are far more ubiquitous and commonplace than the concept of moral panic admits (Ungar 2001). The new sources of social anxiety, for instance those associated with nuclear and chemical hazards, are both transnational and imperceptible. These two features also contribute to the transformed meaning of the old sources of anxiety. As concerns penality, today's representations of crime increasingly depict a universally threatening universe (Reiner *et al.* 2000). Put simply, typical images of crime and criminal justice imply that danger can come from anywhere, at any time. Contemporary mainstream culture codes crime as a lurking menace, a powerfully gothic construction.

The notion of the folk devil, the figure which Cohen depicted as the focus of a moral panic, provides a further reason for dissatisfaction with the theory. Cohen (1972/1980: 194) stated directly that his theory required the visibility of the folk devil. In his argument, the clarification of moral values and normative contours works through the construction and demonization of 'distinguishable social types':

> In the gallery of types that society erects to show its members which roles should be avoided and which should be emulated, these groups have occupied a constant position as folk devils: visible reminders of what we should not be. The identities of such social types are public property and these particular adolescent groups have symbolized – both in what they were and how they were reacted to – much of the social change which has taken place in Britain over the last twenty years.
>
> (Cohen 1972/1980: 10)

In *Folk Devils and Moral Panics*, the Mods and Rockers provoked anxiety, and were subjected to extreme control measures, because they became readily identifiable symbols of social change. They became seen as the bearers of a specific and threatening youth culture, the subversive presence of which was marked by their distinctive styles of clothing. Furthermore, Cohen's theory addressed collective episodes of juvenile crime/deviance in their connection with the phenomenon of particular youth cultures. The process of making Thompson and Venables notorious however was marked by the incongruity between child

BLACKBURN COLLEGE LIBRARY

and monster, between appearance and attributed essence, occasioning a 'trauma of the visible' (Young 1996).

A third problem with adopting moral panic theory concerns its supporting notion of the criminal trial as a boundary-setting ritual. Cohen's study emerged out of the labelling perspective, and hence emphasized the significance of the dramatization of evil to the folk devilling process. The public degradation ceremony particularly noted by him was the criminal trial, which he envisaged as a demonstrative boundary-setting performance. For Cohen, the criminal trial is a stage upon which the deviant is publicly labelled, and through this event makes the transition to folk devil status (Cohen 1972/1980: 106–7). To date, the Bulger case has given rise to five court cases, several artworks, plays and novels, and a profusion of mass media depictions. These rituals and representations typically depict the case through the rhetoric of a trauma that can never be healed. Public displays of grief, misery and pain produced a melancholic remembrance of the event, seen in the Home Secretary's comments upon the release of Thompson and Venables:

> I offer my deepest sympathy to the family of James Bulger. The circumstances of the killing were horrific and had a profound impact throughout the United Kingdom and beyond. . . . The murder of James Bulger was a terrible event for his family and for the whole nation.
>
> (Blunkett, *Commons Hansard*, Written Answers,
> 22 June 2001)

Moral panic theory is focused on the folk devilling of the demonized criminal. A viewing position of imaginary victim departs markedly from that of moral entrepeneur. Furthermore, this is not a matter simply of 'response', as envisaged by moral panic theory. There is an increasingly central place of the victim *within* the legal process. This occasions, as I demonstrate below, a confusion of the boundaries within the victim–protector–predator triad, a destabilization of the terms upon which its fragile triangulation is founded.

This brings us to my final reason for departing from moral panic theory, which concerns its assumptions about consensus and control. In this theory, folk devilling constructs or reasserts consensus in society, hence moral panics are a key resource of the control culture of their day. Although societal reaction is not homogenous, the moral panic involves the assertion of a consensual model of society (Cohen 1972/1980: 65 and 75). This operates as a powerful form of social regulation. In *Policing the Crisis* (Hall *et al.* 1978), moral panics were also linked to the manufacture of consensus. They were envisaged as political phenomena that supported the orchestration and mobilization of authoritarian rule. Yet the emotional dynamism of the Bulger case suggests that public reaction is not simply orchestrated by, or incorporated into, the systems of control and governance. One difference between the authoritarian populism described so eloquently in *Policing the Crisis* and today's gothic populism derives from the incorporation of real and imaginary victims into the criminal justice process.

A further difference is that demonized individuals and groups hotly dispute their framing as folk devils, and in doing so contest moral boundaries. The consequences for the relationship between social reaction and social control are weighty ones according to Ungar (2001: 277), who writes that, 'social regulation processes have become less predictable and more fractious'. The initiating and/or directing role of authorities in the escalation of a panic cannot be assured. Indeed, the authorities themselves may become the target of moral outrage, and often try to dampen the perceived threat. A further complicating factor concerns the roles of the mass media and of late modern commodification. Hall *et al.* (1978) envisaged the mass media as a vehicle for the transmission of dominant ideology, representing the definitions of the powerful. The communications environment of late modern media brings a high degree of interactivity, which facilitates the emergence of new collectivities. The principal responses described by moral panic theory were campaign groups, and changes in legislation and policy. Vigilante avengers engaging in actions over which the authorities seem to exercise limited control did not figure.

We turn now from folk devils to faceless killers. Instead of a notion of criminal trials as boundary-setting rituals performed before condemnatory audiences, we must address the incorporation of literal and imaginary victims. We also move from ideas of the control system's powerful management of consensus, and organization of a cycle ended by orderly recovery, to the contestation of moral categories and the fractious instability of social regulation processes. These reconfigurations are displayed in discourses which depict threat and danger as all around us. Pat Barker's *Border Crossing* draws upon this gothic aesthetic and permits reflection upon the abject state of criminal law in contemporary punitive cultures.

Faceless killers, dereliction and realist horror in *Border Crossing*

Gothicism narrates crime and punishment in a sensational manner, accomplishing its potent effects through titillated fascination and excited revulsion rather than the soberly didactic. I have referred to the passions of the Bulger case as visceral. Not only does the notion of horror embrace both experience and imagination, the corporeality of horror is indexed in the Latin root of this word (*horrēre*), which can be translated as 'to bristle' or 'to shiver'. Horrēre conveys the way in which the hair at the nape of the neck stands on end during moments of excitation. The sensation of horror is located precisely at the boundary between psyche and flesh, and reveals emotional expressions to be embodied practices. This corporeal liminality of horror makes it, and its effects, difficult to contain, as gothic's narratives 'spill over from worlds of fantasy and fiction into real and social spheres' (Botting 1996: 168). When a warder describes Danny the ten-year-old murderer as 'a horror', Tom Seymour the psychologist looks up a definition of this term, and writes it into his clinical notes:

Horror
1 (A painful feeling of) intense loathing or fear; a terrified and revolted shuddering; a strong aversion or an intense dislike (*of*); *colloq*. Dismay (*at*) **2** The quality of exciting intense loathing and fear; a person who or thing which excites such feelings; colloq. A mischevious person, esp. a child.

(Barker 2001: 36)

Although horror can be defined, can be designated, explained, and placed, through words like loathing, fear, terror, revolt and aversion in dictionaries, it cannot be tied down or readily made out in Barker's story. Tom initially rejects the notion of horror, inimicable as it is to professionalism and an objective viewpoint. Yet he does not figure in the novel as a detective who coolly unravels the truth of Danny's crime, and categorizes and contains danger. The chilling tale that follows is written through a series of gothic conventions which undermine any reading position of comfortable detachment.

A generically gothic landscape, 'desolate, alienating and full of menace' frames the opening of Barker's tale (Botting 1996: 2). Tom is walking through a quayside area beside a river, which smells rotten and is edged by thick, black, stinking mud. Derelict and burnt-out buildings, closed off by barbed-wire fences, bear warning pictures of guard dogs, and 'DANGER. KEEP OUT' notices. Danger cannot be fenced off and contained in this novel, as symbolized by Barker's vivid evocation of a misty sea-fret over the Tyne, suggesting not only an ominous landscape, but a miasma symptomatic of disintegrating boundaries (Ellman 1990: 181). The scene is reminiscent of Ian McEwan's (1975/1997: 76) canal in 'Butterflies', as a place where dereliction, danger and crime are inextricable, with 'brown stinking water' running along the backs of windowless and deserted factories. In 'Butterflies', the canal is a prohibited space away from the suburban rows of houses, a 'somewhere else' that the murdered girl had been banned from visiting. However, in *Border Crossing*, Tom lives in the dilapidated quayside area; dereliction places the decaying remnants of the past in the present, the immediate, the everyday, and the proximate. The novel troubles the border between decay and juvescence, between ontologized difference and the possibility of both personal and collective change, between revenge and rehabilitation.

The novel dramatizes both the threat posed by Danny, a young man who killed an elderly woman when he was ten years old, and the threat to him of exposure by the media and vigilante attack. Put plainly, the reader is faced with both fear of, and fear for, Danny. Tom rescues a young man from drowning himself and discovers that it's Danny Miller, at whose murder trial he had given some rather damning evidence. Danny is now known as Ian Wilkinson, and has been released on life licence. A sense of foreboding and ominous tension is built up from the outset, and Tom is uneasy and sceptical, suspecting that Danny may have plotted the meeting. The past casts a menacing shadow over the present. Chris Baldick writes that the gothic effect combines, 'a fearful sense of inheritance in time with a claustrophobic sense of enclosure in space . . . to produce an impression of sickening descent into disintegration' (Baldick 1992: xix). In *Border Crossing*, Danny is trapped as the past comes back to threaten him through his awful struggle to remember and understand his crime. He is also menaced by his past through the terrifying pursuit of the mass media and brutal vigilantes who continue to hunt him down.

As the tension mounts, the reader gleans more hints of the macabre nature of Danny's crime, his troubling behaviour while in custody, and his antagonism towards Tom. Away from home, Tom wakes suddenly in the night to hear a series of shrieks, which confuse and alarm him. He wonders whether they are the screams of a woman or a child. It seems that the shrieks are probably the pained and fearful cries of a snared rabbit, yet Tom remains unnerved, struck by the fragility of order, comfort, security and well-being. Riding home on the train, his wife calls to say that Danny has arrived unexpectedly at their house, and seems to be disturbed. This news provokes what Tom sees as an irrational element in his mistrust of Danny; 'the screams of the snared rabbit lingered in his mind' (Barker 2001: 163). Yet when he gets home, Tom finds that it is Danny who is trapped. A similar murder has revived media interest in his crime, and his old school photograph has been shown on television. Barker gives readers a keen sense of Danny's feverish terror:

> 'It's going to open up again,' Danny said, his voice strangled with misery and fear. Already he'd seen on television all the things that had happened to him: fists beating on the sides of a police van, shouted threats, the blaze of publicity, nowhere to run, nowhere to hide. . . . He looked deranged, slack mouthed and sweating, but there was no doubting the reality of the fear. Tom could smell it on him.
>
> (Barker 2001: 165 and 192)

In a classically gothic scene, which dramatizes the fantasmatic investments of the discourses of public protection and crime prevention, Barker extends the deep sense of menace to Tom:

> the wind moaned about the house. Somewhere a gate was banging. . . . He got up to look. Pulling the curtain back, he saw what at first he took to be his own face reflected in the glass, until a sudden movement dislocated the illusion. Pale features, lank wet hair, distorted by streaming rivulets of rain. . . . Probably he should phone the police, but there wasn't time. . . . Better check the back-garden door was bolted.
>
> (ibid.: 190)

This scene imaginatively echoes the ghostly face at the window in Chapter 3 of *Wuthering Heights*. In Lockwood's nightmare, the spectre of Catherine appears at a window, tapping, wailing and pleading to be admitted to the house. This apparition fills Lockwood with terror, and he is awakened by his own scream. He reacts violently, smashing the window and dragging the ghostly hand across a broken pane until blood drenches the bedclothes. This confusion of spectral and material terrifies Lockwood, and he 'tried to jump up; but, could not stir a limb; and so yelled aloud, in a frenzy of fright' (Brontë 1847/1995: 26). He tells Heathcliff that the spectre was a fiend who would probably have strangled him, but then hastily dismisses it as a trick of his sleeping imagination. Tom is quite awake when he receives his visitation, and he does not envisage his intruder as a ghost. He imagines that this 'somebody out to get you' is probably a peeping tom or a burglar, although it could also be a stalker, a vigilante or a journalist. The window is a border so fragile that you can see right through it, yet the identity of this intruder cannot be made out. No screams of horror issue forth from Tom, but in mute fear he secures the perimeters of his dwelling through bolts, locks and a burglar alarm. Tom is not sure at first whether the face at the window is his own reflection. This vignette hints towards the fearful investments of the discourse of crime prevention, warning us not to think of it as a rationalist discourse, contrasted to the cathected discourse of retribution.

According to Freeland (1995), realist horror is characterized by a displacement from plot to gruesome spectacle, showcasing the spectacular nature of monstrous violence. The fearful suspense in reading *Border Crossing* comes from the narrative withholding of the spectacle of violence. Horror also emanates from the multiplicity of the threats of violence, for instance the threat that Danny might attack Tom, and the lurking menace of vigilante assaults. Just as the menacing Tyne quayside in which *Border Crossing* opens is not a space in which threat and fear are contained, violence and danger are not simply condensed within the figure of Danny Miller. The narrative may be contrasted in this respect to Iain Banks' *The Wasp Factory* (1984), noted for the goriness of its depictions of violence. This novel tells the tale of Frank Cauldhame, who while a child vengefully murdered a younger brother and two cousins. This is a story of terrible violence, to body, to identity, to sanity, but this violence stays within the family and on the island owned by it, and reaches a kind of spectacular firey resolution at its close. The threat and danger in *Border Crossing* is more contagious, and more frightening for not being shown. Danny, afraid he is being followed, and too scared to go home, stays the night at Tom's house. Remembering the unnameable horrors of his crime, he goes into a borderline psychotic state and nearly sets Tom's house on fire. Hours later Tom opens his door to a yelling, pushing, clicking press pack, which Barker (2001: 201) eloquently describes as 'a swarm of killer bees'. Danny fears the arrival of vigilantes, aware of the hatred that some people still harbour for him. Eventually, the police arrive and take Danny away, but there is no sign that his new identity will be any safer.

So, just who is the villain of the piece? Freeland (1995) wrote that the monsters created by realist horror seem to have a certain possibility, as ordinary people turned killers rather than supernatural beings. The gothic imagination of the nineteenth century rendered the murderer grotesque, a being separated from the normal majority by an impassable gulf (Halttunen 1998). There has been a realignment of the locus of monstrosity. Unlike in former days, the monstrous bodies of today retain a certain familiarity, abhuman rather than inhuman. Judith Halberstam writes of the contemporary gothic imagination, 'Monstrosity no longer coagulates into a specific body, a single face, a unique feature; it is replaced with a banality that fractures resistance because the enemy becomes harder to locate and looks more like the hero' (Halberstam 1995: 163). In *Border Crossing* the enemy is indeed 'hard to locate', in a narrative that depicts both a 'faceless killer' and faceless vigilantes, as the boundary between victim and predator unravels.

Border Crossing troubles the border between decay and juvenescence, between ontologized difference and the possibility of resignification, between revenge and rehabilitation. In the terms of the narrative, will Danny recover and be able to re-enter society successfully? Will the press and the vigilantes ever leave him alone? Patrick McGrath writes that 'the gothic revels in ruin, whether it be architectural, moral, biological, ontological, or psychic' (McGrath 1997: 154). The end of Barker's novel brings demolition of the derelict quayside area and its redevelopment. Even the river loses its stagnant taint, symbolizing a tentative possibility of justice, a justice of new beginnings. This fragile opportunity, which Barker (2001: 216) depicts as 'precarious, shadowed and ambiguous, but worth having nevertheless', imagines a way out of the claustro-phobic horror of the gothic. In a sense, *Border Crossing* deconstructs the fictions of otherness drawn by contemporary culture, in which difference is inscribed as monstrosity. This revisioning imaginatively rewrites borders and boundaries, the places of encounters with others, as sites of negotiation and translation. Yet these are risky encounters. Barker surrounds her reader with an ominous sense of terrible fatality, drawing us into a threatening and hazardous future written and re-written over by the dark shadow of the past. Past and present are as unclear as the future, 'the river was a confusion of overlapping rings and bubbles, too turbulent to reflect the blackening sky' (ibid.: 132). At the close of the novel, the possibility of change, of reinscription, remains a mere possibility, and no narrative closure is offered.

The chilling scenery and terrifying violence of the gothic fictions through which crime and punishment are represented and remembered confront the reader with their status as *imaginary* victim, ridden by anxiety, haunted by nightmares. Given the potency of the gothic, scholars of contemporary penality require critical tools that focus them on the permeability and reconfiguration of borders, and especially that between legal and extra-legal. It is with this set of problems in mind that I turn to Kristeva's notion of abjection.

Abjection and the powers of horror

The concept of abjection theorizes the powers of horror, relating them to the horror of that which breaches boundaries. Unlike in moral panic theory, abjection theorizes the ambivalent response of disgusted fascination, describing an extremely strong feeling that is both somatic and symbolic. The abject, a complex *mélange* of affects, thoughts and sensations with no definable object, is 'a composite of judgment and affect, of condemnation and yearning' (Kristeva 1982: 10). It disgusts, sickens, and inspires loathing, repugnance, nausea. Combining both violent denial and pleasurable fascination, the abject cannot be admitted or assimilated by the subject, who is simultaneously drawn towards and repelled by it. The concept hence foregrounds the ambivalent viewing position of the spectator, seen for instance in the 'dreadful delight' identified by Judith Walkowitz (1992) with discourses of fear and danger in the city. The abject persists, and is not simply excluded once and for all; what is expelled can never be wholly obliterated. Instead of seeing criminal justice processes as denunciatory boundary-maintaining rituals, Kristevan theory addresses how, 'the abject emerges when exclusions fail, in the sickening collapse of limits' (Ellman 1990: 181). The abject reveals the radical permeability of borders, and horror arises from flows, the liminal and the in-between.

Kristeva's analysis is particularly intriguing because when describing the abject as that which breaches borders, she uses crime as her example, writing that crime reveals the abject fragility of the law. She portrays crime against children as particularly abject, citing the image of a pile of children's shoes at Auschwitz. By the same logic, crime committed by a child is also abject, accounting for the difficulty of reconciling the notion of childhood with violent criminality. Recall for a moment the warder's description of Danny as a 'little horror' in *Border Crossing*, and Tom's impotent recourse to the dictionary. There is, as Marina Warner (1994) told the audience during her Reith lectures, a considerable ambiguity to these denominations: 'little horror', 'little devil', 'little monster' and, one might add, 'little terror'. She observed that the figure of the bad child has surfaced repeatedly throughout modernity, with the troubled constitution of a distinctively modern category of childhood. Yet in the late twentieth century, Warner added, the child is depicted far more than ever as a menacing enemy, with the increasing (and increasingly problematic) insistence upon childhood innocence. Through events like the killing of James Bulger, she explained, the child is saturated with all the power of projected monstrousness to excite repulsion and terror.

Instead of producing the denunciatory folk devilling of distinguishable social types, it seems to me that a crime committed by one child against another is doubly abject. For this very reason, the murder of James by Jon and Bobby elicits a hyperbolic disbelief; it is 'worst than worst, a new superlative in horror' (Morrison 1997: 21). This notion is supported by Sarah Kember's (1995) analysis of the effect of the abduction footage. She writes that the surveillance technology had failed to police the boundaries between those to be protected and those to be protected from, the blurred images challenging the desire for mastery and control. The ensuing binary construction of James as child, and Jon and Bobby as somehow non-child, is problematized by recent documentaries which have discussed their anguish and terror in police interrogation and at trial. For instance, when extracts from the taped police interviews were played on television, viewers could hear the real record of their confessions, used as evidence at trial. Their babyish voices, their weeping, screaming and terrible wailing as they made admissions, hugging their parents and police officers, are preserved on these tapes.[3]

The horror of this confusion in the victim–protector–predator triplet is exacerbated by the repetitive recourse to gory images of corporeal violence. The gruesome evocation of James' injuries seeks to circumscribe and condense injury in him, and hence limit compassion to him. Yet there is more still to the potency of these forensic and mass media reconstructions of terrible injury. The demand for an increased penal tariff in the Bulger case repeatedly reiterated frightening images of the tortured and dismembered body of a dead child. What punishment could suffice when confronted with the hanging lip, torn eyelid, scalp reddened by brick dust, boot marks on the cheek, splashes of paint in the eyes, leaf stuck by blood to a naked foot, the question mark of sexual abuse and the transected torso? Linking the corpse to the terrifying collapse of boundaries, Kristeva depicts the corpse as intolerable, the ultimate in abjection. The insistent recourse to gory images within gothic penality works through gut response, through brute facticity. It cannot ground the emotional narrative closure of consensual denunciation.

Kristeva stated that both crime and revenge are abject, displaying the law's fragility. In gothicized cases like the Bulger, Hindley and Spanner rulings, the liberal myth of humane, reasoned and just law is exposed as a screen, and law's violence comes strikingly to view.[4] On this view, the law does not erect and maintain clear boundaries. Horror arises as the edges between things collapse and their contents flow out and mingle, threatening defilement of both the mythical rule of modern law and the rational public sphere of civilized conduct and dialogue. Gothicism is a powerful set of conventions within which the reconfiguration of the boundary between the legal and the extra-legal, and the texture and norms of public space are played out.

The abject aesthetics of punishment

This chapter has sought to ascertain something of the meaning and the power of gothicity in contemporary penality. I have argued that the aesthetics of punishment in contemporary culture is an aesthetics of abjection. Ultimately, the mediated spectacle of punishment seeks yet fails to inscribe a logic of limit, border and enclosure. The boundaries between victim, predator and protector, between legal and extra-legal, break down. So, the logic of separation, of border and enclosure, must be repeatedly enacted and performed, as that which seems to be excluded returns *from within*. This produces the impossibility of marking boundaries; all is overtaken by the continuity of flows, 'according to the logic of separation, it is flow that is impure' (Kristeva 1982: 102). The aesthetics of punishment has taken changing forms, and in contemporary culture is remade with the incorporation of the victim into criminal justice processes. Martha Nussbaum (1999) argues persuasively that disgust attains a prominent place in criminal law at present. On his part, Mark Seltzer (1997) describes the obsessive public gathering around scenes of violence, shock and trauma, and argues that this fascination indicates a breakdown of boundaries between the public and private registers of experience. The abject aesthetics of punishment in contemporary culture marks the remaking of the practices that constitute both legality and public space. Nowhere is this set of developments played out more dramatically than in 'emotional' high-profile criminal cases.

A number of scholars, writing of the gothicity of the serial killer genre increasingly popular since the 1970s, have linked it to the retributive escalation of punitive cultures. Ingebretson (1998: 27) links these cultural products to, 'a rubric of social fear which is politically very useful'. Similarly, Freeland (1995) writes that realist horror fuels a conservative agenda, by creating a climate of fear in which everyone is a potential victim. Gothicity can usefully explain the visceral tug of the powers of horror, but we should also note the instability of this aesthetics. The next chapter of this book also shows that spectacles of severe punishment mediate an abject display. Yet gothicity is not inevitably the motor of conservative penal agendas, or at least it cannot be contained within them. Ultimately, this aesthetic does not succeed in securing the poetic justice of severe punishment as just proportionality.

7   The shadow of the death penalty

Michel Foucault once remarked that, 'the practice of the public execution haunted our penal system for a long time and still haunts it today' (Foucault 1975/1991: 15). This spectre returns, of course, only at the margins of his text. Nevertheless, the powers of horror retained a distinctive place within penal modernity. This chapter rejects contemporary liberal narratives that frame western penal change in terms of civilized sensibilities, increasing humanity and penal leniency. The analysis presented explores how, for more than a century, British penality has been haunted by the shadow of the death penalty. The spectral presence of deadly punishment within Britain, and the emergence from the 1960s of a new aesthetics of 'life means life', are traced. Through a reading of Myra Hindley's case, one sees how death is written into the law in new ways. From modern times the spectacle of the state's power of life and death has been accompanied by legal logics that no longer respect the limitless fury of sovereign power. However, in Hindley's case, the gothic of 'life means life' is revealed as one in which the ultimate penalty knows no bounds. This breaching of the limits of law reconfigures the very meaning of legality itself. Under the shadow of the death penalty, it seems, the aesthetics of punishment is an aesthetics of abjection.

Two principal theses are outlined in this chapter. Firstly, I show that the aesthetics of punishment in contemporary culture leads us to discard the narrative of penal leniency inherent in the notion of abolition. However, I also emphasize that the poetic justice of the logic of proportionality is destabilized by the display of severe punishment. The punitive display of a maximal penalty cannot be fully incorporated into conservative agendas of punitive escalation, except as a logic which constitutively transgresses its own limits. This penal rationale becomes supplemented by discourses which engender viewing positions of imagined victimhood as a basis for the recruitment of punitive subjects. In addition, as I have endeavoured to show in this book, the mediated spectacle of retributive punishment is made palatable to the subjects of mass culture as a set of practices that mark gender, race, sexuality and religious difference. In this chapter, a connection between the spectacle of severe legal punishment and that of femininity is traced. This demonstrates how in some modern displays of exemplary retributive and deterrent punishment, a potent relationship between violence, spectacle and femininity pertains. Yet the severe punishment of a woman not only legitimates, but also uncomfortably reveals, the violence which underpins state authority and is written into the law. I hence argue that under the shadow of the death penalty, the aesthetics of punishment becomes an aesthetics of abjection. By an aesthetics of abjection, I mean that the mediated display of severe punishment mingles the legal and the extra-legal in a number of novel and striking ways. This process produces the remaking of the terrain and boundaries of legality itself. The severely punitive display is hence a movement of passage, both transgressing the boundary between legal and extra-legal, and enabling us to recuperate moments of instability within the texts and practices of law. These expose and render vulnerable the authorizing procedures of modern law and state rule, opening up a way for subaltern readings.

The Moors case and British penality

Myra Hindley, described by the courts as 'uniquely notorious', was subject to a 'whole life' tariff, which imposed punitive lifelong detention upon her, and she had been in prison for four decades upon her death in 2002.[1] She is one of the 'Moors Murderers', involved with her lover Ian Brady in the torture and killing of several children, who were buried in shallow graves on the moors north of Manchester during the 1960s. These child murders took place during the last days of the English death penalty for murder. To be precise, the Murder (Abolition of Death Penalty) Act received the royal assent just eleven days after Brady and Hindley were charged with the crimes. Several months later, the case brought the first trial for 'mass murder', as their crimes were then called, since the passing into law of the Abolition Act. Nearly all of the bestsellers on the Moors case remarked on the 'irony' of the murders being revealed simultaneously with Parliament's passing of the 'No Hanging Bill'. As one popular book put it, 'the law is, by its own new law, *forced* to spare them' (Williams 1967/8: 343; my emphases). The last two death penalties in England had been imposed only a year before, when two men were hanged inside Walton and Strangeways prisons. Not only was the death penalty still being carried out at the time of the 1965 legislation, it was only temporarily suspended at first. Clauses within the statute initiated 'abolition' as a provisional five-year experiment. The Act hence did not command permanent abolition. Within the suspension clause, the terrifying ritual of the rope would return after 31 July 1970, if another affirmative resolution had not been made law by that time.[2] Several motions for the restoration of capital punishment were debated during this interim period, and relatives of the Moors children were prominent in the campaign to bring back the noose, just as they have more recently been active in the victim's rights movement. The beginnings of abolition were closely linked to this high-profile case, and with it to the passing into the public arena of vengeful desires and vigilante acts.

The 1965 Act not only removed the ritual of hanging, it also provided for an alternative penalty for murder, the mandatory sentence of life imprisonment.

But could this experimental penalty furnish a substitute for the forceful effect of killing by the state? The author of a bestseller on the Moors case wrote, 'When the Moors trial ended, we did feel a lack of catharsis: something violent should have happened to put an end to violence. Throughout, we were missing the shadow of the rope' (Johnson 1967: 89). This 'something violent', something missing, this 'shadow of the rope' has haunted British penality ever since. 'Suddenly at 5.30 the fight to end hanging was over' (*Daily Mail*, 29 October 1965: 9). The passing of the Abolition Act was described in the press as something of a disappointment, as quite an anticlimax. The noun 'abolition', a term that designates the act of abolishing a system, practice or institution, is derived from the Latin *abolere*, meaning 'destroy'. However, acts of abolition and decriminalization have been linked by scholars to the remaking of violent penal practices rather than their outright elimination. Reading press coverage of the Abolition Act throws up a striking juxtaposition, which is quite suggestive, 'End of hanging. Lords pass homosexuality bill by 65 votes' (*Manchester Guardian*, 29 October 65: 2). This newspaper headline puts the shadow of the death penalty and the enforcement of homosexual invisibility (Moran 1996) into close proximity. Rather than enacting penal leniency, the Abolition Act and the Sexual Offences Act 1967 remade the heteronormative and juridical strategies by which the state rules.

In Hindley's case it seems that the death penalty for murder has been superseded by a *dead time*, a life-cancelling penalty. Rather than seeing abolition as a progressive process of reform, punctuated by 'landmarks' in 1868, 1957, 1965, 1969 and a final culmination in 2002, one can trace a successive re-inscription, in which death is written into the law in different ways. There is a reconfiguration of the spectacle of the ultimate penalty and the state's armed power of life and death. The Abolition Act, while prohibiting a violent but swift death by hanging, did not give back life to murderers, but rather allowed for the 'condign punishment' of life imprisonment. The retention of a notion of justly severe punishment has frequently meant invocation of the Moors murderers, for instance listen to the words of Lord Hailsham's dictum:

> Murder, as every practitioner of the law knows, is not necessarily so, but consists of a whole bundle of offences of vastly differing degrees of culpability, ranging from brutal, cynical and repeated offences like the so-called Moors murders to the almost venial, if objectively immoral 'mercy killing' of a beloved partner.
> (Lord Hailsham in *R*. v. *Howe* 1987 1 AC 417 at 433)

In the late 1990s, Hindley brought three judicial review proceedings. In successive rulings the courts linked the purported 'evil inherent in this crime' to a justice that necessitated the ultimate in penal severity. The political punishment established in *Hindley* through the blurring of executive and judicial powers, has been depicted as an aberrational departure from an otherwise dispassionate rule of law (Schone 2000). However, through *Hindley* a broader and gendered politics of exemplary, retributive and non-rehabilitative punishment is made visible and contested, a politics within which the affectivity of law is writ large.

Law's violence and the mediated spectacle of the murderess

The persistence of the death penalty has been poorly addressed within the established account of penal modernity. For instance, David Garland (2001) depicts modern penality as a trend of rationalizing and civilizing processes, recently thrown into reverse. He hence characterizes contemporary punitiveness as the reappearance of the 'oddly archaic' and 'downright antimodern' (Garland 2001: 3, 133). Garland associates modern penality with decency, humanity and compassion. He notes that these sentiments were more prevalent among policy-making elites than in the general public of the day, and admits that modern penality included strong punishment for heinous crimes, but his account is dominated by a model of compassionate correctionalism (ibid.: 35). Nevertheless, an argument can readily be made that modern punishment should be construed as a redistribution of law's violence rather than its diminution. Public hanging was ended in England by the Act to Provide for the Carrying out of Capital Punishment in Prisons, 1868. Vic Gatrell (1994) notes the rhetoric of civility and humanity in the appeal for removal of a barbarous spectacle that accompanied the passing of this legislation. Yet he also describes the presence of punitive voices emphasizing the terror bonus of hidden executions. He writes that whereas the 1868 Act ended the plebeian, carnivalesque festival of public execution, this did not constitute a humane moment in British history:

> A civilizing process may redeploy, sanitize, and camouflage disciplinary and other violence without necessarily diminishing it. . . . Inside prisons for a century yet, murderers continued to be strangled on ropes too short or ropes too long, dying more dreadfully in private than in public, in chilly proceedings with crowd support withdrawn. . . . Hiding horrors did not end them.
>
> (Gatrell 1994: 590)

Gatrell gives an account of the strong persistence of punitive voices calling for retributive capital punishment. He describes the limiting of the death penalty to murder as having made it more awesome and its execution within prison walls as based in maximization of its deterrent horror, its imagined terrors presumed to have greater effect. Gatrell hence writes of the 1868 Act as producing a displacement of law's violence, rather than its diminution.

Central to this displacement, I believe, was a profusion of popular represen-
~ital punishment, both factual and fictional. Thomas Mathiesen
the term 'synopticon' to designate those mediated practices
the many watch the few, and argued that synopticism permitted

the formation of a new class in the public sphere, one of VIPs, stars and reporters. However, he did not outline the relationship of synopticism to penality, nor did he discuss the gendered character of spectacle. During modernity, and to this day, the performance of law's violence has not disappeared from view, becoming principally witnessed in mediated form. When the public spectacle of the scaffold receded from view after a statute of 1868, the death penalty was retained in Britain for a century, the execution of its deadly act then hidden within prison walls. The condemned cell and the noose remained, their terrors to be imagined. These rituals of state killing gave rise to a fascinated literature. A popular press, at all levels of literacy and cost, circulated sensational news of crimes, trials and punishments, in increasingly graphic detail. The *Illustrated Police News* established in 1864 is emblematic, engaging the reader with melodramatic depictions imagining how criminals felt and behaved at their execution. When capital punishment for the crime of murder was abolished in England and Wales in 1965, the ghostly afterlife of the public spectacle of the scaffold lingered on in the substitute of life imprisonment, which has developed into a dead time communicated to others through mediated spectacle.

The gendered character of the spectacle of modern punishment has been noted by some feminist histories. Judith Knelman (1998: 250) writes that by the 1830s, a pattern of the public vilification of murderesses had been established, through which 'part of a transgressive woman's punishment was public scrutiny'. In popular representation, murder by men figured as frightening whereas that by women was coded to arouse indignation. Through sensationalized narratives that made spectacle of the murderess's aberrance, the violence through which law is founded and practised was concealed (Duggan 2000). Murderesses were depicted as more monstrous and inhuman than male killers, but also subjected to a disgusted fascination, as dramatized in Margaret Atwood's *Alias Grace* (1996). This text is a historical novel on the case of Grace Marks, a Canadian woman convicted as an accessory in the murder of her employer during the 1840s. A fellow servant named James McDermott was hanged for the crime, but Grace's death sentence was commuted to life imprisonment. Campaigners insisted that she had been an unwilling participant in the killing. The book is based on the account of Susanna Moodie, who visited the celebrated prisoner in Kingston Penitentiary in 1853 and wrote from memory her story. Atwood emphasizes the voyeuristic fascination inherent in popular, medical and penological discourses on the murderess, linking this to the ambiguity of the notion of a woman who kills, '*Murderess, murderess*, he whispers to himself. It has an allure, a scent almost. Hothouse gardenias. Lurid but also furtive' (Atwood 1996: 453). The pleasure taken from the display of this dangerous allure is evident in Hindley's case, and is important to the aesthetic of the penalty imposed upon her.

By the mid-eighteenth century, an English murderess had figured as uniquely cruel within the mediated spectacle surrounding her trial and her execution. Furthermore, the disqualification of the woman's own story of the killing, as a feminine and hence duplicitous and unreliable account, was central to the vilification directed at her. Mary Blandy was convicted in 1752 of the murder of her father by arsenical poisoning. He had died after eating food into which she had placed powder from a 'love philtre'. Blandy told the court that her lover had given her the potion, saying that it would make her father approve their marriage. Over thirty pamphlets survive through which narratives of the crime were circulated and consumed. An early-twentieth-century account of the case emphasizes the widespread fascination, 'the story of Miss Blandy was upon every lip . . . the eyes of the whole nation were turned to the tragedy. . . . Mary Blandy stands alone and incomparable – pilloried to all ages among the basest of her sex' (Bleakley 1905/2000: 44, 70). This account repeats the description of Blandy as 'a sombre-hearted woman', 'an iron-hearted, remorseless demon-woman' (ibid.: 61, 70). Heinzelmann (1994) writes that by the mid-eighteenth century, jurisprudential and theological narratives were invested with the authority to make judgements about truth and lies, whereas novels, biographies and autobiographies were deemed implausible, questioning as they did the basis upon which authoritative narratives established their power. She argues that anxiety and tension were particularly heightened when the author of a narrative was a woman, with women deemed suspect in their capacity to authorize faithful representations of reality.

Heinzelmann illustrates her argument through an analysis of Blandy's case, in which the state assumed prosecution (ordinarily an action pursued by relatives) and the possibility of a charge of petty treason was raised. Petty treason was conceptualized as a crime attacking the natural, civil and spiritual relation between superior and inferior, for instance through the murder of a master by his servant, 'A crime against the familial patriarch thus constituted a "petticoat" version of a crime against the King and his State' (Heinzelmann 1994: 318). At trial the prosecution advanced a narrative of filial betrayal, depicting this as a grave social and political threat, and gendering Blandy's crime through a rhetoric of undaughterly, unnatural behaviour. The story of treasonous betrayal was given additional authority by the prosecution's deployment of notions of divine providence, through which the murderess had been revealed. By contrast, Blandy's own narrative, in which she claimed that she had been duped by her lover, adopted the model of the sentimental novel, a fictional genre in which a woman was characterized as the helpless victim of man's sexual deceit and aggression. This sentimental narrative, Heinzelmann argues, situated Blandy even more oppositionally to the dominant jurisprudential and theological discourses through which she had been condemned to death. Her protestation of innocence, relying as it did on the conventions of the sentimental novel, was read as the absence of a true confession, received as a fiction only further aggravating the depths of her wickedness. As Heinzelmann remarks, the individual and semi-fictional narrative was feminized as set against an apparently trans-cendent jurisprudential narrative of the crime, a narrative both authoritative and ultimately fatal for Blandy. Bearing in mind these aspects of the gendered character of the spectacle of punishment, we can move on to address the movement from the death penalty to the aesthetics of life imprisonment.

Life as death: the Abolition Act and the whole life tariff

The dead time penalty imposed upon Hindley arises from a complex logic of permission and prohibition at work within the 1965 Abolition Act. The prohibition of capital punishment enacted by s1(1) of the statute, with its injunction that 'nobody shall suffer death' as a punishment for murder, only veiled the continuing force of the state's power of life and death within penality. In the case of the Moors murderers, the penal practice of *life as death* in the penalty of life imprisonment was present from the first. Sentencing Brady, the trial judge departed from the accepted phrasing to announce, 'I pass the only sentence which the law *now* allows, which is three concurrent sentences of life imprisonment.' This moment at which the law commanded the new severe exemplary punishment was hence marked by a look back at the penalty that once had been. The very first moments of the Moors murderers' punishment brought a look over the shoulder at the deadly force now put behind the law of the day. In this gesture of looking back, of putting behind, the sentence writes that which had been into the continuing lawful infliction of punishment. Reporting the murder convictions of Brady and Hindley, the media featured an integral story about the meaning of their sentences. The *Guardian*'s (7 May 1966) headline summed up the story with the phrase, '"Life" can mean what it says.' The article informed readers that the Home Office had affirmed that the new sentence of life imprisonment for murder could indeed mean custodial detention for the remainder of the inmate's natural life. This enactment of 'abolition', commonly taken as the culmination of a civilizing trend in modern penality, authorized the continuation, albeit in new guise, of penal severity. The Act's passing allowed the terror of death to pass into penality, but, through veiling, death passed in as a shadow. If the Abolition Act veiled the new forms of deadly violence within penality, in doing so it also made possible contestation. A veil is not simply a concealment, rather it stands metonymically for that which is covered. The effect is that while working as a metaphor for prohibition, it also destabilizes the terms upon which that prohibition depends. This textual instability at the heart of the Abolition statute has meant that the penalty of life imprisonment is permitted to mean *both life and death*.

During the late 1990s, Hindley brought three successive proceedings before the High Court, the Court of Appeal, and the House of Lords, seeking to overturn her whole life tariff.[3] Lifelong imprisonment from which a murderer can never be rehabilitated is a penalty that the government has vigorously defended over the last two decades. In *Hindley*, the category of whole life imprisonment as an irredeemable dead time is maintained, yet the extent to which this penalty shows the law 'passing beyond itself' is masked by the notion of periodical review of the tariff. The Court of Appeal's ruling stated that the Home Secretary had finally accepted that a category of irrevocable lifers was not lawful and hence would periodically reconsider each whole life tariff. In these hearings, the legal imperative of periodic review was juxtaposed with the argument that certain crimes are so bad that a whole life tariff is necessary. This required the reiterative depiction of Hindley's crimes as incontestably heinous, reaching its apotheosis in Lord Steyn's rhetoric of the diabolical:

> even in the sordid history of crimes against children the murders committed by Hindley, jointly with Ian Brady, were uniquely evil . . . the two murders of which she had been convicted in 1965 were the culmination of a series of five murders committed by her and Brady. They abducted, terrified, tortured and killed their victims before burying their bodies on Saddleworth Moor. . . . The pitiless and depraved ordeal of the victims, and the torment of their families, place these crimes in terms of comparative wickedness in an exceptional category. If it be right, as I have held it to be, that lifelong incarceration for the purposes of punishment is competent where the crime or crimes are sufficiently heinous, it is difficult to argue that this case is not in that category.
>
> (R. v. *Secretary of State for the Home Department, ex parte Hindley*
> [2000] 2 WLR 730; 2 All ER 385)

Against its own logic of legality, the Lords ruling suggested that as 'uniquely evil' Hindley's crimes are so grave that no kind or degree of 'progress in prison' could ever qualify her for release. This premise was stated directly by Viscount Bridgeman during debate in the Lords, advising the House that he spoke on this matter not only personally but also for his party:

> There can surely be no question that Hindley's deeds plumbed a depth of cruelty and depravity which to the vast majority of people in this country was quite unimaginable. . . . We have crossed the borderline beyond which any idea of tempering retribution does not fall to be considered.
>
> (*House of Lords Hansard*, 4 May 2000, col 1,185)

Ultimately, the focus of the rulings lies in the premise that the exceptional gravity of the punishment lawfully rests in the 'uniquely evil' character of Hindley's crimes. Unlike in the spectacle of the *ancien régime*, exemplary punishment of Hindley is constructed as proportionate. Instead of the display of penal excess and asymmetry, the logic of 'just deserts' is applied. The reiteration of the 'inherent evil' of her crimes seeks to screen law's violence rather than legitimating it. Nevertheless, Hindley's case reveals the violence within this strategy, and repeatedly shows the law passing beyond itself.

Dead time and the spectacle of suffering

In *Discipline and Punish*, Foucault wrote that as well as a judicial act, the public execution of the *ancien régime* was also a political ritual, in which sovereign power was reactivated through the display of exorbitant force. He discussed *la supplice*, the horrible corporal punishment that was part of the penalty for all serious crimes. This, he explained, was not random or chaotic, but rather a calculated art of pain, calibrated with regard to the gravity of the crime and the rank of both the criminal and his or her victims, 'death-torture is the art of maintaining life in pain, by subdividing it into a "thousand deaths"' (Foucault 1975/1991: 33–4). He wrote that torture was intended to mark the victim, to brand the criminal with the signs of infamy. Torture did not reconcile; on the contrary, it traced on the body signs that must not be effaced, and that others must remember. Its infliction must be both spectacular and excessive. Foucault claimed that a trace of torture remained in modern criminal justice, but that this was increasingly enveloped by the non-corporal nature of the penal system. He wrote of the gentleness of modern punishments, focusing his study upon the noiseless and discreet technologies of disciplinary power. By the time of *The Will To Knowledge*, he was writing of the relation of power to death in modern democratic societies as benevolent, a power focused on maintaining, maxi-mizing and extending life. However, as in the case of Dreyfus discussed in Chapter 2, modern penality involves a mediated spectacle of suffering. Modern penality touches both a material and a discursive body, indeed the body of the criminal is specularized, as a condensed symbol of the political order (Hyde 1997). Hyde discerns in the US death penalty of today the construction of an abstracted, distanced body, removed from the direct apprehension of the reader/viewer. In contradistinction to this absent, distanced body, a body that one might kill in cold blood, the punishment of Hindley worked through a visceral immediacy, in which readers/viewers are invited to relish the spectacle of her pain and suffering. In this way, the force of law is coercively and violently inscribed upon and into the body, communicating forms of state power that incorporate populist punitiveness.

Letters to the press sent by Prisoner 964055 in the 1970s include the following words:

> Something is slowly dying inside me, and it's the will to live. . . . What is life for? To die? Then why not kill myself at once? No, I'm afraid. Wait for death until it comes? I fear that even more. Then I must live. But what for? In order to die. I can't escape from that circle. . . . I have served society in good stead as a scapegoat and whipping boy for far too many years. I can only see the light in the tunnel diminishing until nothing remains but a bottomless black pit of despair. Is society going to be compensated for being thwarted of the rope by my perpetual imprisonment? Is my life going to be sacrificed?
>
> (Hindley cited in Wilson 1986: 168–9 and 174)

Over these words is cast the shadow of the death penalty. Hindley's plea makes visible the reconfiguration of exemplary punishment as a dead time of uncertainty and vilification.[4] In the days of capital punishment, the waiting time between a murder conviction and the hour of execution tended to last for around a month. The executioner Albert Pierrepoint told the Gower Committee that it normally took nine to twelve seconds from the time the hangman entered the condemned cell to the pulling of the lever activating the drop. The act of killing itself was either instantaneous, or took a few minutes. By contrast, the *dead time* of life imprisonment is a protracted death. If Hindley had reached the average life expectancy for an English woman, the term of her incarceration would have amounted to over fifty years in custody. Retributive life imprisonment also involves repeated symbolic acts of killing. Dead time brings over again the re-enactment of rituals of social death. This reiterative denunciation and passionate expulsion began from the start of their sentences. Williams wrote that the continued existence of the Moors murderers unhanged was hard to tolerate, but added that they were in truth no longer really alive. Brady and Hindley, he explained, died at the moment when they were arrested, when policemen first gave them, 'the look people give in the zoo, at some unfamiliar and repulsive beast. The look which will confront them henceforth and for ever' (Williams 1967/8: 344). The dead time of life imprisonment also brings the symbolic civic death of disenfranchisement. Furthermore, some lifers endure repeated violent attacks in prison; Hindley underwent plastic surgery to her face after one assault. These violent acts are echoed by the death wishes of vigilante fantasy circulated in the mass media. Carol Ann Duffy's 'The Devil's Wife', in one brief and intense section of the poem imagines Hindley's experience over the years of these death wishes, 'In the long fifty-year night these are the words that crawl out of the wall: Suffer. Monster. Burn in hell' (Duffy 1999: 45). Extreme vilification figured as an inherent part of the *dead time forever* penalty imposed upon Hindley. The *Sun* published a double-page exclusive in March 2001, celebrating the coup of the first photographs of Hindley for seven years. The headline, 'Myra's Turn to Feel Pain' was accompanied by a sub-heading announcing 'Evil Moors Murderer in Hospital'. The new pictures were large telephoto-lens images of Hindley on her way to hospital for a leg operation. In one image Hindley was shown hobbling along between prison warders and grimacing, with the caption 'She Suffers.' This was displayed next to the 'Her Torment' image, in which she is seated in a wheelchair with her hand on her leg. The images of the murderer who suffers in physical torment are not invitations to feel compassion for her; rather, they command readers to relish the spectacle of her pain. Both Brady and Hindley have undertaken legal battles against press vilification, which celebrates their ill health and indulges the pleasure of imagining their painful deaths, but have received no redress and hence implicitly no protection.[5]

Populism and iconicity

The relationship between the populist engagement of punitive subjects and Hindley's case was raised but ultimately obscured by the courts, which recognized that she felt:

> a hostage to public opinion, condemned to pass the rest of her life in prison, although no longer judged a danger to anyone, because of her notoriety and

the public obloquy which would fall on any Home Secretary who ordered her release.

(*R* v. *Secretary of State for the Home Department,*
ex parte Hindley [1998] Q.B. 751)

Her counsel argued that Hindley had been, 'singled out for special treatment due to her notoriety and unpopularity'. However, the court simply stated that the Home Secretary had not relied upon (that is, had not stated) the potentially improper motive of 'public opinion' in his reasons for the decision. Nevertheless, a detailed analysis is readily conducted of the practices of display through which Hindley was held 'hostage to public opinion'. This exercise entails teasing out connections between the populist engagement of a collectivity of vengeful victims and iconicity. Iconicity is the writing of particular individuals and places as culturally resonant, their iconic status performatively constructed and reinforced through identificatory and dis-identificatory effects. Marshall McLuhan wrote in the 1960s that with the advent of electronic media we had entered the age of the icon, which he described as 'an inclusive compressed image' (McLuhan 1964/2002: 118). The inclusivity of the icon was related by McLuhan to his belief that electronic media generated communal, deep participation. McLuhan, whose work was given more extensive treatment in Chapter 5, theorized the icon as the medium of a sensuous embrace, through which the viewer of the image reaches out compassionately. He emphasized the human interest dimension of news in the electronic age, asserting that new media like television fostered an immediacy of participation in the experience of others. He linked electronic media to a heightened awareness of the fate of the other. For instance, he associated the viewing of images of deprivation and suffering with empathetic engagement, writing, 'to see a photograph of the local slum makes the condition unbearable' (ibid.: 214). The iconic images that are mass-produced and rapidly circulated through contemporary communications technologies emotively engage viewers. However, the sensuous global embrace of compassionate concern and empathetic involvement anticipated by McLuhan has not resulted from these flows of images. McLuhan did not envisage iconicity as an engaging display within which ambiguous forms of difference are marked.

The Moors murders were popularly described from the outset in terms of their haunting indelibility, as 'a crime that must live for ever in the annals of infamy' (Sparrow 1966: 9). Yet to figure as eternally memorable, these crimes have been retold over again within a complex economy of cultural production. Hindley's iconicity came about through the reiteration of two principal tropes, namely the horror and evil of her crimes, and a traumatic remembrance of the burials on the Moors. These two gothic tropes are increasingly prominent features of retributive punishment, as discussed in Chapter 6. The dominant writing of Hindley as evil, monstrous and irredeemably bad, was particularly linked to the persistent reproduction over the years of her police identification photograph. Central to the sense of drama within the aesthetics of her case is the repeated display, even forty years on, of this image. Reporting the conviction of the

Figure 7.1 Police identification photograph of Myra Hindley, 1965. © PA Photos, London.

Moors murderers on Saturday 7 May 1966, the newspapers and television channels first displayed the mugshot (see Figure 7.1). This has become an iconic image in the sense that an icon is known as or through an image, or set of images, rather than through their 'actual reality'. Hindley sought to have the mugshot replaced over the years with images of her as she aged, for instance those of her studying in her cell. However, the photograph from 1965 is invariably used. Here is Hindley's memory of the mugshot being taken:

I was kept in a small office with three police people who refused to speak to me. I was tired and afraid. When we left the room they led me down what seemed like endless flights of stone stairs dimly lit with sixty watt bulbs. I thought I was being taken to a dungeon somewhere. Then we came to some doors and a policeman kicked one of them open. I immediately thought they were going to interrogate me so I clenched my teeth hard. Suddenly there was a flash of light in my face. I was in that cell for the purpose of having a police photograph taken.

(BBC *Modern Times: Myra Hindley* 2000)

From this account, the mugshot is an image that condenses law's violence and the fearful coercive power of the state. However, it has been deployed over the years as 'the face of evil'. This image trapped Hindley, as Gordon Burn (1991: 24) put it in his novel *Alma Cogan*, as 'a stranger in a snapshot of myself'.

Analysis of Hindley's iconicity requires recognition of the gendered conventions of the aesthetics of punishment. In her depiction as grotesque, Hindley's mugshot becomes suffused with the horror of perverted femininity. In marked departure from McLuhan's idea of a sensuous embrace of the iconic, this image 'tears across the boundary of sexual difference' (Birch 1994: 53). The mugshot of Hindley invokes the destruction of boundaries, threatening a crisis of sexual difference. In threatening existing conceptual boundaries, the femininity of Ruth Ellis, the last woman hanged, and Hindley, these two bottle-blonde murderesses, 'could only appear as an outrage, as something inappropriate and out of place. . . . If not essence, femininity can be only trapping or mere show' (Rose 1993: 51). Reflections on the Moors trial typically lingered over the staged appearance and deportment of Hindley. One bestseller mused, 'she was dark, once; now she is a Nordic blonde . . . in the dock, she has a great strangeness' (Johnson 1967: 23). Another told of Hindley regarding the court with, 'a faintly scornful stare which she has learnt from film posters and close-ups on television. An empty look. Plastic Messalina' (Williams 1967/1968: 341). The Lords did not consider the relation between the mediated spectacle of Hindley's aberrant femininity and her notoriety. This would be to raise the spectre of the gendered character of punishment under the criminal law, questioning the rational neutrality of the logic of proportionate 'just deserts'.

Over the years of her incarceration, different kinds of popular cultural representations contested the relationship between Hindley's crime, her punishment and her femininity. In the 1970s, the Moors murderers became cult figures for the alternative art and music scene, appropriated into a counter-cultural challenge to mainstream values. In 1977 a band calling themselves the Moors Murderers which featured Chrissie Hynde recorded 'Free Hindley', the lyrics stating, 'Myra Hindley was nothing more than a woman who fell for a man.' The Sex Pistols 1978 single 'No One is Innocent' made number 6 in the pop charts, the vocals including, 'God save Myra Hindley God save Ian Brady Even though he's horrible and she ain't what you call a lady.' A popart image of Hindley was then used in the Pistols film *The Great Rock 'N' Roll Swindle*.

Crass's 'Mother-Earth' of 1989 proclaimed, 'She's the antimother. . . . Its Myra Hindley on the cover. . . . On the pages of the Star . . . the single mugshot from the past ensures your fantasy can last and last.'

Over the years these kinds of representations have been the target of literal and figurative attacks. This assault upon their 'offensive' and 'disgusting' character has included the denunciation of plays, songs and visual representations.[6] Gordon Burn's novel *Alma Cogan* (1991) juxtaposed the media constructions of a glamorous music star and Hindley the demonized murderess. In the novel, Cogan comes across newspaper coverage about Hindley, a huge image of the infamous mugshot splashed across the page, 'as usual, Hindley looks like a composite, an identikit, a media emanation, a hypothetical who never existed in the flesh' (Burn 1991: 100). News of the Moors case continues to dominate the news, and Cogan reflects on the television coverage, 'That she has an existence independent of the image that has represented her for twenty-one years – the trowel nose, the defiant eyes, the peroxide hair – is a mystery that seems hard to get to grips with' (ibid.: 163). Burn describes the artefacts and images kept of both celebrities and notorious criminals, ambiguously melding them together as commodities supporting a fascination with the spectacle of femininity.[7] Alison Young (2000) reflects upon the viscerally 'disgusted' response to these works, analysing Marcus Harvey's artwork *Myra*, a large painting of the police mugshot constructed in imprints made from a cast of a child's hand. The exhibition of this work coincided with Hindley's 1997 appeal against the whole life tariff. Young describes the pleasure taken in the imagination of Hindley's annihilation, with the *Sun* writing, 'Myra Hindley is to be hung in the Royal Academy. Sadly it is only a painting of her.' She reads these violent and repulsed responses as the shudders and recoils of abjection, the desire and imperative to expel that which threatens, as the image dramatizes uncomfortably the relations of spectatorship central to Hindley's iconicity.

Hindley's severe penalty prefigured a series of slippages between victimhood and electoral politics and between retribution and vigilantism. The prominence of the Moors families in the campaign to restore capital punishment began a series of links between politicization and populism. Just a month before the Moors trial opened, Patrick Downey, uncle of Lesley, stood against Sydney Silverman in the 1966 General Election. Silverman was the Labour MP whose Bill had become the Murder (Abolition of Death Penalty) Act. Downey stood against him in his constituency of Nelson and Colne on a bring-back-hanging platform, 'There was a strong emotional background, for the papers had been full of the details of the horrible and macabre murders of two children whose bodies had been found buried on the Pennine Moors not so far away' (Hughes 1969: 183). Downey's campaign was extensively publicized, and he was interviewed by British and North American television networks including BBC, ITV, NBC and CBC, as well as many domestic and overseas print journalists. In Silverman's speech on the second reading of the Abolition Bill, he stated: 'We do not govern ourselves by referendum. We do not, in matters of life and death, decide what is just or unjust by an unconsidered reaction taken on the street corner, in the club or the pub. No part of our criminal law has been so decided' (*The Times*, 23 December 1964). Downey's electoral campaign emphasized populist politics, for instance he told the press, 'a national plebiscite should have been taken before hanging was abolished' and 'why didn't they ask our opinion about the death penalty? They know most people want it' (cited in Hughes 1969: 185, 186).

The trials of serial murderers in the 1960s also saw public expressions of revenge and vindictiveness. Press and popular books told of the lynching mood in town during the trials, for instance one book reproduced as typical the following exchange between strangers in the street, 'I'd bloody 'ang 'em meself . . . 'Anging's too good for them. Let me get my hands on them and I'll show you what I'd do' (Marchbanks 1966: 152). There began a blurring of the boundary between severe legal punishment and vigilantism, so that vigilantism no longer figured as a straightforwardly extra-legal set of behaviours. During the committal proceedings, photographs were circulated in the mass media of Patrick Downey having to be restrained by the police when he ran and tried to pull open the door of the car taking Ian Brady from the court to the remand centre (ibid.: 32). The fascinated and furious presence of women was repeated over and over again in the press, 'several hundred people, mostly women with shopping bags, had waited hopefully for the 60 public seats in the Chester Castle courtroom' (*Sun*, 20 April 1966: 5). After the trial, 'two dozen policemen tried to hold the crowd back but women hammered on the windows of the van carrying them as they drove past. There were boos and shouts of "Hang them"' (Potter 1966: 198).[8] Over the years documentaries, and true crime programmes on the case have shown over again the grainy black and white television footage of these scenes, with local women in headscarves saying, 'a life for a life'. This co-mingling of legal and illegal threatened exposure of the mimetic relation between crime and punishment, but has been obscured by the framing of vengefulness and vigilantism as based in a salutary politics of grief.

The related trope in the iconicity of Hindley links the desolate moorland graves to a melancholic narrative of perpetual suffering. Sightseers thronged to the moors during the search for bodies, the press reporting a continuous line of cars for hours on end and people arriving in coachloads (*Sun*, 18 October 1965 and 25 October 1965). The Moors case saw the first televised police press conference in British criminal history. This led to two press conferences each day, which were attended by eighty-five global correspondents (Williams 1967/1968: 326–7). An international press corps descended on the moors, with reporters from publications like *Time*, *Paris Match* and *Stern* recording the search for bodies and capturing images that have since been circulated repeatedly. A textual strategy of infotainment was used by many of the journalists reporting on the Moors case.[9] For instance, a headline in the American magazine *Time* read 'Ghosts on the Moors', its epigraph quoting the scene from *Wuthering Heights* in which the melancholy ghost of Cathy appears at the window, and telling readers, 'the ghost of a child walked the bleak Yorkshire moors last week, just as did that of Cathy Linton in Emily Brontë's novel of a century ago.

This time the child was real, and murdered' (*Time*, 5 November 1965: 43). *Time* is a news weekly, and this article illustrates the blurring of the factual and the fictional, of news and information with entertainment, as infotainment.

Emlyn Williams' bestseller quoted from these lines of Emily Brontë's poem 'Hope and Despondency' in its epilogue:

> I dream of moor, and misty hill
> Where evening gathers, dark and chill
> For, lone, among the mountains cold
> Lie those that I have loved of old
> And my heart aches, in hopeless pain
> Exhausted with repinings vain
> That I shall greet them ne'er again.
> (Brontë 1846/1992: 3)

These are the words of the figure of despondency, a grieving father. Williams only quoted lines 18–24 of the poem. The lines are part of a conversation about death, burial, bereavement and trauma. They are followed by lines in which the voice of the figure of hope are heard. This is the voice of the man's daughter, who comforts him and persuades him not to dwell despairingly on the grave and the bodies. The child advises her father that he himself has taught her that sorrow is useless. In the last stanza of the poem the father responds, telling his hopeful daughter that she has spoken wisely. Williams printed neither the words of the child nor the closing agreement of the father. In silencing these words he figured the meaning and power of the Moors murders through the force of inconsolable grief. Williams' epigraph is emblematic of the potent links between trauma, imaginary victimhood and penality that come about through the Moors case. The remembrance of the Moors murders figures the moors as a deeply cathected space, a site around which narratives of suffering, sorrow and anger are built up. The moors figure in the textual practices of case law as a cathected space in their reconstruction as crime scene through the practices of criminal detection. Both forensic reconstruction and popular remembrance write trauma in public space, evoking a violent past and memorializing suffering through emotive representational practices.

The moors were typically figured as a space of fear and terror in many popular representations of the murders, 'black and brown wilderness, lonely and frightening in its endless folds of peat and rock-clad hills . . . four hundred square miles of peat, rock, bog and furze; rolling planes of destruction' (Marchbanks 1966: 88 and 90). This evocation of a barren place of awesome stillness, black rocks like tombstones, and mournful sighing winds continued into the 1980s. Wilson's popular books *Devil's Disciples* (1986) and *Return to Hell* (1988) emphasized the fables about the moors as a legendary place of violence where the devil's children steal and murder babies, a haunted place of terrifying ghostly screams, 'a place to fear, a no-man's land of fable' (Wilson 1986: 5 and 1988: 110). During the years of child abductions from Manchester, both local and national media painted a chilling picture of how the children had 'disappeared without trace' from public spaces, sometimes in full daylight. The press reported the panic of families when their children had not returned, and the police's inability to apprehend the 'monster' responsible. Women police officers went around the schools in Manchester lecturing the children not to talk to strangers (Marchbanks 1966: 24 and 144). A friend of Lesley Downey appeared on a Granada television children's programme appealing for information. Wilson (1988) worked as a journalist in the area throughout the time of the disappearance of Manchester children. He describes local people's fears for their children as thousands of Lancashire Constabulary posters were displayed bearing the question, 'Have you seen this boy?' One neighbour of John Kilbride was quoted as having said, 'It's as if the ground had opened, and swallowed him up' (cited in Williams 1967/8: 25). Press reportage on the missing Moors children described appeals for search volunteers. Leaflets were put through doors asking householders to search their premises and handbills were given out. These disappearances, and the eventual discovery of the children's murders took place during what was already recognized as 'a decade of mounting alarm about violence threatening the citizen' (ibid.: 24).

Over the years, the ghosts of the dead children have been represented as spectral figures calling for vengeance. The Smiths' song 'Suffer Little Children' took its title, and many of its lines, from Williams' book, rewriting the inconsolable grief of the bereaved parent through the ghostly presence of the child victims: 'A child cries: "Oh find me, find me, nothing more/We are on a sullen misty moor/We may be dead and we may be gone/But we will be . . . right by your side/Until the day you die.'[10] The song's lyrics and plaintive melody evoke the desolate and barren moors. They also write haunting as the vengeful promise of the dead children to haunt Hindley: 'You might sleep . . . /But you will never dream . . . /I'll haunt you when you laugh.' This trope of the barren moorland graves, melancholic remembrance and retribution continues today. Val McDermid's popular crime novel *A Place of Execution* (1999) depicts the distress, acute pain, and fear of both fictional and Moors mothers. The lead detective, who is depicted as kindly and efficient, is converted to the pleasures of vigilante fantasy, 'now he was himself about to become a father, he felt for the first time in his life the tug of vigilantism' (McDermid 1999: 307). This intertwining of melancholic remembrance with vengefulness continues with the prominence of relatives of the Moors children within the victim's rights movement. Lesley's mother published an autobiographical popular work *For the Love of Lesley* in 1989, a narrative mingling her suffering with her hatred for her child's killers as righteously maternal duty. She writes that her love for her lost child leads her to oppose parole for Hindley, and refers repeatedly to the agony of hearing Lesley's pleading and terrified voice on the tape:

> the tape is still running. Every day and night it runs. Every day and night I hear those contradictory voices. The voice of she whom in this world

I probably loved the most . . . my Lesley. The voice of she whom in this world and the next I will pursue for vengeance . . . Myra Hindley.

(West 1989: 90)

This uncanny, ghostly recording of the last terrible moments of the life of her child grounds the mother's vengeance in the loss of her child and the horror of her death. Defending the court's and the government's imposition of a whole life tariff upon Hindley, Viscount Bridgeman told the Lords:

There are alive at least one parent of a child to whose murder Hindley has either confessed or of which she has been convicted, whose body has never been found. . . . We have to consider not only the parents of those whose bodies have never been found, but also the brothers, sisters and wider families of the other victims who have suffered and continue to suffer. I fear that Hindley has not fully paid and will never fully pay for that suffering.

(*House of Lords Hansard*, 4 May 2000, col. 1,185)

Here, melancholic remembrance authorizes a punishment which will never be sufficient, writing into the legal logic of proportionality that which can have no measure.

The end was unaesthetic

In this chapter, I have argued that the aesthetics of punishment in contemporary culture require us to discard the narratives of penal leniency inherent in the notion of abolition. The replacement of capital punishment by a mandatory life sentence was not a matter of the abolition of death in penality. The Murder (Abolition of Death Penalty) Act of 1965 did not eradicate penal severity, neither from the criminal justice system, nor from the circles of fear and fantasy that work to such potent effect in the sphere of the political. When Johnson wrote of the Moors trial, 'something violent should have happened to put an end to violence. Throughout, we were missing the shadow of the rope', she added, 'the end was unaesthetic' (Johnson 1967: 89). This 'something violent', something missing, this 'shadow of the rope' has haunted British penality ever since. Jake Arnott's novel *He Kills Coppers* (2001) reflects on abolition and the question of the unaesthetic:

When they got rid of hanging, it was an end of an era in crime reporting. . . . You just don't get the sense of drama any more. . . . The sense of completed narrative was all gone. A conclusion, that's what gives it all some sort of shape, makes it a story. Can't have a story without an ending. The climax if you like . . . the End, that's the point. Life, well, it just doesn't have the same ring to it.

(Arnott 2001: 47)

In his novel, Arnott depicts the substitute yet comparatively disappointing satisfactions of regular tabloid calls to 'Bring Back the Rope', or that 'Life should mean Life.' This is not a dilemma for crime reporting alone, but also for the staging of the communicative work of punishment. It required the emergence of a new aesthetics, a new penal style if you will. In this chapter I have looked into the aesthetics of life imprisonment, and the drama of the whole life tariff. I have explored the kind of mediated spectacle that supports the injunction 'life means life'. I have also argued that the poetic justice of the logic of proportionality is destabilized by the display of severe 'just deserts' punishment. This display is only deployed by conservative agendas of punitive escalation as a logic which constitutively transgresses its own limits. The spectacular culture within which punishment is enacted today mediates an abject display, within which legal and extra-legal merge and co-mingle. The concluding chapter of this book reprises the principal arguments that have been made in the text about punishment, culture and communication. It emphasizes that while punitive displays may be dramatic and emotive, consumed avidly by fascinated viewers, they are also readily open to critique.

Conclusion
Addressing the contemporary

This text opens up a space for debate on the possibilities of justice in the media age. Relatedly, the book is an invitation to develop modes of research, of reading and of writing, that are apposite to the challenges of today. The very offering of such an invitation begs the following question, duly to be considered in this postscript: what does it mean for a text to be 'addressed to the contemporary?' This question is central to the legitimacy of studies in the humanities and social sciences, raising imperatives to which all must respond. Regrettably, reflection upon this issue is often limited to the narrow matter of relevance to the policymaker's agenda. Framed in this way, the properly open character of the question is forestalled. So, to restore the breadth of the question, it is asked, just what does it mean for a text to be addressed to the *contemporary*? The word 'contemporary' is of common parlance, and is typically used quite casually. Nevertheless, it is necessary to consider some definitions. The term 'contemporary' is derived from the Latin, its prefix stemming from *com-* and its suffix from *-tempus*. The word hence connects 'being with' and 'time'. An initial definition might describe the contemporary as 'that which belongs to the same times'. In this way, 'the contemporary' would specify that which lives or happens at the same time as another person or event, that which is coeval with somebody or something. In vernacular usage, the term strongly privileges notions of the present, and of being 'there' at the same time as others. Thus arises the understanding of 'my contemporary' as one who dwells with me in this present, one who is here with me now, at this current moment of history. Consequently, the idea of the contemporary is heavily laden with the sense of being together at present, and hence of *belonging in time*. There are two further meanings of the term. These are not alternative meanings, for each time one invokes 'the contemporary', they come into force. First of all then, the notion of the contemporary denotes that which is characteristic of the latest, the novel and the innovative. It is the sign under which is written both that which has just arrived, and that which is imminent, in this way projecting the promise of the new forward into an imagined future. The contemporary is on the cusp, one might say, of what is and of what is about to be. There is something of an unspoken promise about it. A third meaning is that the contemporary indexes what is relevant to its time, what is appropriate or apposite. It specifies what matters and what may be deemed immaterial at a certain time. It bears implicit notions of those who matter, those who count, and can be counted upon to adjudicate. Upon this notion depends the judgement of a text as timely, as apposite, and as well placed in its time. Placing these three levels of meaning together, one sees that the vernacular of the 'contemporary' combines notions of belonging in time, of the futural promise of the new, and of what strikes as salient. Together, these three apply a potent illocutionary force to any evocation of the contemporary.

Having considered the meanings that emerge when the notion of 'the contemporary' is called up, a postulate may now be advanced. This may be stated as a formal proposition: the resolutely contemporary text is that text which reflexively ponders the stakes of its own contemporaneity. To convey the full significance of this statement, it will be necessary to return to the question, if only to take it somewhat differently this time: what does it mean for a text to be '*addressed to* the contemporary'? That which is 'addressed to the contemporary' is an engagement with particular times. It is an intervention in the contemporary scene. At the same time, as 'addressed to one's contemporaries', the text engages with the work of others. This assertion lays emphasis upon the act of writing an academic text as presumptive of readers who will respond. It construes the academic work as an open letter, in search of correspondents. To invite correspondence is not to write an 'authoritative text'. Indeed, and to borrow some useful terms from Barthes (1970), the contemporary text would aspire to the writerly rather than the readerly. It would invite the reader to produce a meaning that is not authorized. Offered in this way, in good faith, this address would call for that ideal figure the responsible reader, who can respond with a reading that is not assured or guaranteed in advance by the cipher of the author. One can imagine a text as 'addressed to my contemporaries'. Nevertheless, it is also the case that the contemporary text exceeds both the present time and the relation with one's immediate fellows. It is addressed to, or to be more precise to the memory of, certain forbears, including those who do not survive in this present as possible readers. What's more, the text inherits a certain epistemological and conceptual heritage. As Derrida (2003) has said, this is a heritage to which one is indebted, and to which there is a duty to do the impossible, to be faithful to the text. Yet, at the same time, this is a heritage that does not establish a set of desiderata. It is a heritage from which the contemporary text must depart if it is to follow, to come after. This is also the case when a text is written in the awareness that it itself bequeaths a certain heritage, for which it must be responsible. Indeed, a text that is resolutely contemporary would be reflexively aware of the legacies after which, in memory of which, and in anticipation of which, it is written. In this sense a text might be recognized as untimely, as making visible in the present that which does not seem to belong to it. This too pertains to the futurity of the contemporary text. Because it is on the cusp of what is and of what is about to be, and opens up certain relations with the future, the contemporary text has a care for those who follow. Such a text would be ahead of its time.

The timely untimely text seeks not familiarity with its readers. Those who 'belong in time' feel 'at home together' in the encounter with the text. A contemporary text would therefore refuse those gestures that bring the reader 'close to home'. For instance, it would avoid the dead hand of nostalgia when theorizing time and change, a term the first element of which stems from the Greek *nostos*, a return home, and its second element from the word for pain. The contemporary text would beware this longing for lost things, persons and situations of the past, this homesickness that idealizes an imagined past, forever lost and hence unchanging. It would beware this melancholic wistfulness that reifies, even in mourning its loss, a conception of an originary home, singular and timeless. This deadly nostalgia haunts the sociologized concept of ontological insecurity, and the narratives of 'decivilizing' antimodern trends, posited sometimes as explanatory of the 'punitive turn'. Such nostalgia inadvertently commits blackmail against the future.

What remains of this postscript reflects upon the manner in which this text, unfolding here on my screen, to be held in your hands, answers to the call of the contemporary. Any such response is made in light of the multiple temporalities and obligations that arise within such an aspiration, a number of which have been indicated in the preceding paragraphs. In addition, this postscript indicates something of the manner in which my ongoing work continues to respond to the call of the contemporary. First of all it seems necessary today to affirm that the challenges of the contemporary require the development of a properly sophisticated conceptual register. Scholars may aspire to empirical validity, theoretical virtuosity, ethical and political critique, or to any combination of these three worthy pursuits. Whatever their persuasion, they must produce concepts and arguments that do not simply repeat older models of identity, solidarity, civility and community. This book has hence engaged in critique, reading closely and, to the extent to which it is possible, reading on their own terms, the work of others. As I have said, reflection upon its inheritance is a first basis from which the departure of any text might be envisaged. If there is to be a departure, the text must move away. While considering what is being moved away from, one also thinks of how this movement can be mobilized, and of how the text will move the reader. I have argued that the challenges of today require a nuanced theoretical vocabulary. It must be emphasized that this ought to be developed *integrally with* a renewed commitment to reflexivity. Scholars would hence reflexively question notions of contemporaneity, of *belonging in time*. They would suspend grounding notions of a self-evident contemporaneity, as *the* moment in which *we* are living. They would refuse arguments ultimately premised upon a singular and indivisible time of the present, lived and experienced collectively. Therefore, in assigning a certain specificity to the demands of today, this is merely as a provisional gesture through which debate can be opened up. What, then, is it about the present that calls for a particular sort of analysis? If belonging in time is at the heart of the thinking of contemporaneity, critical scholars must reconsider their understandings of the passions of punishment, and in particular the significance of the compassional. At the same time, this analysis must address the respects in which tele-presence gives justice to be thought anew. Putting these two together, the compassional and the teletechnologies, makes for an incisive critique of contemporaneity.

Teletechnologies

And so to the teletechnologies . . . Teletechnologies, simply put, are the technologies of the afar. They usher in a notion of tele-presence, that is, of being present at a distance, and in doing so suspend prior ontologies of time and space. Nevertheless, these have a tendency to creep back into the analysis. For instance, Paul Virilio asserts that the current teletechnologies, which are technologies of real time, kill present time. According to him the teletechnologies 'are killing "present time" by isolating it from its here and now, in favour of a commutative elsewhere that no longer has anything to do with our "concrete presence" in the world, but is the elsewhere of a "discreet telepresence" that remains a complete mystery' (Virilio 1997: 10–11). Note the opposition of the concrete and the tele-. One should beware the nostalgia resident in the thinking of tele-presence. One should notice this way of thinking the loss of physical and mental territories, and fixed, local groundings. There is a melancholy in Virilio's thinking of real time as opposed to real presence, in his complaint that the place of the 'there' gives way to an ever-present 'now'. And so it is wise to beware, to respond to the imperative of being aware of, the spectres of proximity and immediacy that may be summoned by the theorist.

This text has looked into how penal practices have been, and are, inflected by the teletechnological. This has been a reciprocal process. On the one hand, it is possible to speak of criminal justice as situated within the mediatic, and to think of them as 'moulded' in various ways by changing media forms. On the other hand, it should also be noted that criminal justice has played an integral part in the meanings of the mediatic. They have been central to the very experience of the tele-technological, and its different modalities. From the nineteenth century, with time–space compression, punitive spectacles were occasionally presented as international media events. Cases of this order included those figuring the Tichborne claimant, Oscar Wilde, Alfred Dreyfus, Sacco and Vanzetti, and Emmett Till. From the late twentieth century, one can speak of global punitive displays, communicated in what seems like the immediacy of real time. The book has engaged with the theses of McLuhan and Rheingold, who employed concepts of the 'global village' and 'virtual community' to depict communicational flows as compassional. Within their work, the teletopian promise of the contemporary arises through the evocation of a certain pastoral. In the several chapters of this text, questions have been raised about the imaginative movement from tele-presence to co-presence. That is, the book has questioned the imagination of contemporaneity that inheres in the thinking of being present at a distance as 'meeting with' others at a distance. For instance, thought has been given to the communities that teletechnologies produce through imaginative travel, and 'in' virtual spaces. In the course of the analysis it has been argued that teletechnologies are neither inherently conservative, nor cosmopolitizing in and of themselves. For instance, there is a powerful appeal of the electric chair in cyberspace as a popular symbol of the death penalty, as described by Mona Lynch (2000b). On the other hand, there are the alternative visions of justice and punishment promulgated by the Zapatistas. There are the mediatic practices of these 'postmodern revolutionaries' who employ various image and communication technologies, as shown by Ronnie Lippens (2003). And so the movements towards, and together with, others, these movements that are inherent to co-mmunication, become a matter for close interrogation. It no longer suffices to state that 'punishment communicates shared meaning'.

Tele-vision

The film director Oliver Stone once said that we inhabit a society 'bloated, not just with crime: but with the media coverage of it' (*Independent*, 27 October 1994: 31). Questions about visual culture are hence not a specialist area to be summarily passed over by those who construct theories of criminal justice. On the contrary, attending to the power of the image, as of the tele-communicational more generally, ought to be recognized as integral to the very possibility of addressing oneself to the contemporary. When they have talked about visual culture, theorists of criminal justice have for some time tended to remain focused on the notion of surveillance, eschewing study of the spectacular. At the same time, there has been an unfortunate tendency to envisage visual culture as a matter of social facts, rather than through the lens of interpretation, as well as to focus on the official. This will not do! As I showed in 'Looking daggers' (Valier 2000), studying the visual culture of penality one finds a passionate drama, in which both subjectivity and the ethical are at stake. In the encounter with images of crime and punishment, the viewer is drawn into the scene. The viewer is brought into recognition, or owning, of his or her complicity in the act of punishment, as a citizen of a state that punishes in his or her name. Here, the punitive subject comes into being through complex acts of looking. It is therefore necessary to critique the televisualities through which punitive cultures are both reproduced and contested.

It is now widely accepted that all arenas are thoroughly permeated by the logic of the spectacle. It is quite commonplace to state that mediated visibility is definitive of politics and culture. Nevertheless, such ideas can be professed for a number of different purposes, and to a variety of effects. This book has argued that during modernity, spectacle began increasingly to be performed within the arena of mass media and communication technologies, rather than in direct co-presence of the viewers and the watched. Furthermore, with interactivity, spectacle is a matter of the participatory rather than of the distanced onlooker. As concerns criminal justice, the spectacular pertains in footage of criminal acts in process, of detection and the search for the criminal, in the drama of criminal trials, in images of victimhood and injury, and in images of punishment. For instance, I have shown that detective technologies have mediated ambiguous images and narratives of vulnerability and injury. Furthermore, the analysis presented in several chapters showed how a mediated spectacle of degradation and suffering operates. Images and information about the punishment of Dreyfus, McVeigh and Hindley textualize the body of the convict, mediating a spectacle of the body in pain. Here notoriety draws the attentions of the punitive subject. It is through this theatre of cruelty that forms of state power are communicated, that is, that they incorporate punitive subjects. This is not only a matter of wrath and outrage, as in the Durkheimian tradition, but also, and more emotively still, of the appeal to the punitive subject as a fellow sufferer. Through iconic images the imaginative engagement is drawn of punitive subjects who feel that they 'suffer together', and who display mourning publicly. Novel kinds of collectivities emerge, convoked around the scenes of crimes and their aftermath, for instance through the virulent spectacularity of terrorist attacks. There is a sensory participation in the spectacular, a corporeal and imaginative engagement which is heightened with the development of the technologies of tele-action.

Emotive images

Emotive images are moving and poignant. They are palpably felt to shock, disgust, fascinate, and accuse, as well as to document, and to haunt. They seem to bring the suffering of distant others into one's present, right there into one's very home. Nevertheless, suspending received notions of the contemporary is to reject the idea of immediate eyewitnesses to an event. Images hence do not simply stand as evidence to atrocities, and viewers do not simply 'see' and 'know about' horrors, unproblematically 'seeing' and 'feeling for' those who suffer. Similarly, scholars cannot recruit images as straightforward evidence about historical events. The testimonial power of images thus becomes a matter for discussion. This book has asked some questions about what is at stake in 'showing', 'seeing' and responding to images and narratives of criminal injury, loss and suffering. It has explored questions around the uses, the meanings and the effects of images, and in particular the senses of justice to which the encounter with images gives rise. The images and narratives that circulate within the cultures of criminal justice are experienced as compelling, and the encounter with them should be recognized as emotive and demanding. Nevertheless, just what does their emotive force and appeal consist in? It is evident that certain forms of representation are privileged as those that make 'us' feel traumatized. As Emma Wilson (2003) reminds in her book *Cinema's Missing Children*, the missing and endangered child is an insistent subject in film of the last decade, and a key trope for the thinking of mourning. Images of the bereaved mothers of murdered children have a similarly poignant and haunting power, and there is no self-evidently just response to them (Valier and Lippens 2004). The ways in which emotive images mobilize specific demands for justice should be examined.

Commemoration

Casual evocation of the contemporary relies upon unexamined presumptions about commemoration. As mentioned above, the idea of the contemporary is heavily laden with the sense of belonging together in time. It is this heritage that permits one, unthinkingly, to say 'in our times'. The notion not only presumes certain notions of shared time, and of shared experience in time, but also of collective memory. This text has hence rigorously questioned Durkheimian evocations of the collective, the shared and the univocal. The imagination of contemporaneity in terms of the space and time of the nation has been addressed. The relations between punishment, culture and subjectivity involve a complex series of connections between criminal bodies and national bodies. Spectacles have been understood in this text as juridico-political forms of display. Over and above any response to a legal infraction, these performances communicate messages about who belongs and who is an alien. Penal displays dramatize deeply felt matters of who can be welcomed into the body of the nation, albeit at the cost of assimilation. The argument has detailed some of the combative, hostile and exclusionary aspects of penality, in contradistinction to the liberal notion of a penal modernity characterized by rational tolerance and compassionate correctionalism. The punitive passions were a continuing facet of penal modernity. Indeed, they gave rise to a number of eloquent treatments by scholars like Durkheim, Nietzsche, Mead, Glover, Balint and Hart. The violent and 'emotional' past of penality is not one that should be incidental to the concerns of theorists of crime and punishment. The book has outlined a number of ways in which penal practices and criminological discourses are linked to the contestation of national boundaries. Crimino-legal displays and discourses have been linked to the marking, repudiation, exclusion and elimination of the alien, the other, and the abnormal. Penal spectacles have been linked to the repudiation of that which challenges the mythical cultural homogeneity of the nation-state. I have shown how the punitive subject is called to recognize itself through changing public master-scripts of crime and punishment, within which national belonging is at stake. The text is mindful that in writing of 'penal modernity' one establishes a relation to the legacies of a violent past, and to the diasporic. Any evocation of this past, after Toni Morrison's *Beloved* (1987), must answer to a complex set of debates at the borders of historiography and literary criticism around time, narrative and fiction in the retelling of the living heritage of violent pasts.

Counterpoints

There is no singular and univocal punitive subject. The practices of penal marking, stigmatization and exclusion are hotly contested. Similarly, there is both a public master-script and an array of what might be called counter-aesthetics. In terms of punitive cultures, counter-aesthetics expose the forms of address, at once expansive and exclusionary, through which the spectacular is maintained. They challenge the televisualities of the forensic and the surveillant. They are counterpoints, counterposed to the aesthetics of those teletechnologies that have become a pervasive part of the cultural landscape. This is seen, for instance, in the performances of the New York-based group The Surveillance Camera Players. Here we see the enactment, in the street, of moments of the return of the gaze. They come about as the players point out hidden cameras to bystanders, hold up message boards and gesticulate to the invisible operators. These are telling moments which, as I have said, are disruptive of the panoptical (Valier 2000). Nevertheless, the 'counter' status of any particular image or narrative is a matter of debate and cannot be assured in advance. There are moments, there are gestures, both of the dominant and of the counter-aesthetic, in any text. In this way, a detailed reading of films like *The Laramie Project* (2002), *Bowling for Columbine* (2002) or *Boys Don't Cry* (1999) may be seen as 'relevant'. A reading of the novels of J.G. Ballard or the audio art of Gregory Whitehead may be admitted into the order of the apposite. Scholars have a duty to bring to light these counter-aesthetics as part of their mapping of penality. It is insufficient merely to note the existence of 'multiple audiences' to penal spectacles. Instead, counter-aesthetics should be studied, and given their due prominence. The 'moving' modes of address through which counter-aesthetics establish their own poignancy, as counterpoignant, should be detailed.

Just feelings

The resolutely contemporary text is that text which reflexively considers the stakes of its own contemporaneity. Addressing the contemporary, the text, at once timely and untimely, suspends received notions of belonging in time. In doing so one thinks, in a Kierkegaardian way, of *becoming contemporary*, rather than of being contemporary. To do so is to reflexively interrogate those acts of faith and of imagination through which one envisages the approach to the other. The term 'belonging' within this concept 'belonging in time' is fortuitous because of its dual emphasis on both subjectivity and ethics. Why is this important? It is possible to write today of the punitive subject, of the subject of surveillance and control, and of the vigilant subject. To do so within a critique of contemporaneity presupposes another concept however, namely that of the subject of justice. This is the subject that demands justice, and that responds to the appeal for justice made by, or in the name of, the suffering other. How ought one to move, compassionately, with others, to demand justice? The contemporary text integrally pursues an emotive theory of the ethical. This inquires closely into the evaluative terms and judgements inherent in readings of emotive images and narratives, as concerns their own capacity to engage readers affectively. An emotive theory of the ethical considers the illocutionary force of critical discourse. This discourse both commits the speaker and calls for more than mere assent in the hearer.

Notes

Introduction: punishment, culture and communication

1 See, for instance, Pratt (1998) and Garland (2001).

1 Murder will out

1 Chaucer's verse reads, 'Mordre wol out, certeyn, it wol nat faille' ('The Prioress's Tale', *Canterbury Tales*, line 576).
2 Foucault described his works as fictions on numerous occasions, and stated, 'I am well aware that I have never written anything but fictions. I do not mean to say, however, that truth is therefore absent. It seems to me that the possibility exists for fiction to function in truth, for a fictional discourse to induce effects of truth, and for bringing about that a true discourse engenders or "manufactures" something that does not as yet exist, that is, "fictions" it. One "fictions" history on the basis of a political reality that makes it true, one "fictions" a politics not yet in existence on the basis of a historical truth' (Foucault 1980a: 193).
3 In 'La poussière et le nuage', Foucault (1980b: 35) chided readers who had understood by what he had termed 'disciplin*ary* society' a disciplin*ed* entity. Yet the question is not simply how totalizing and effective disciplinary power was able to be. Rather, we must address whether the schematic discontinuities constructed by Foucault assist or hinder us in our understanding of modern, and in the terms of this book contemporary, penality.
4 Neither are criminal detection methods appropriately understood as panoptical techniques of surveillance, despite the efforts of a few scholars to characterize them in this way (Jones 1994, Hannant 1995, Thomas 1999, Cole 2001).
5 This phrase is from a Home Office Press Release, 239/99 and 299/99. Similarly exuberant claims are seen in the publicity disseminated by the Forensic Science Service.
6 The report of the investigation of the Road murder can be found in the Public Records Office (MEPO 3/61 and HO 144/20/49113).
7 The following discussion of reward notices is based in part on a study of numerous surviving notices in the Bodleian Library, Oxford, John Johnson Collection of Printed Ephemera (Crime, Box 9 and Public Services, Box 12).
8 The legal proceedings in the Smethurst case can be found in *Central Criminal Court Sessions Paper* 1858–9, 504–587.
9 My analysis of Bertillonage is based on study of the extensive collection in the Archives de la Préfecture de Police de Paris, which includes original artefacts like photographs and record cards, newspaper reporting, and Bertillon's unpublished professional memoir.
10 Missing bodies and concealed identities were a feature of many nineteenth-century

novels. To cite several texts from the 1860s alone, these included Braddon's *Lady Audley's Secret* (1862), Le Fanu's *Wylder's Hand* (1864), Payn's *Lost Sir Massingberd* (1864), Dickens' *Our Mutual Friend* (1865), Reade's *Griffith Gaunt* (1866), Harwood's *Lady Flavia* (1866), Speight's *Under Lock and Key* (1869), and Lytton's *The Disappearance of John Ackland* (1869).

11 An account of the case is presented in Kenealy (1913) and the full account of the legal proceedings is published in nine volumes (Kenealy 1875).

12 A representative collection of these artefacts can be found in the John Johnson Collection of Printed Ephemera at the Bodleian Library, Oxford (Tichborne, Boxes 1 and 2).

13 Public Records Office (HO 144/220/A49301B).

2 Punishment, print culture and the nation

1 Bertillon's increasingly 'bewildering' and 'insane' theories were ridiculed overseas, for instance by Blair (1901).

2 On the question of Durkheim's Jewishness, see also Pickering (1994).

3 Similarly, Poggi (2000: 13) criticizes Durkheim's political blind spots, writing that he had 'an inadequate appreciation of the extent to which historical societies are internally divided'.

4 *Le Procès Zola devant la Cour d'Assizes de la Seine et la Cour de Cassation* 1898 Paris.

5 The phrase is Doyle's (1927: 5). As well as studying the published material on the Slater case, my analysis is based on a reading of the extensive documents and newspaper cuttings collected at the Scottish Records Office in Edinburgh.

6 The issue of the relationship between the Dreyfus affair and changing Jewish identities has received a number of different answers. According to Marrus (1971), most Jews asserted their Frenchness and devotion to the Republic, and only a few rejected the assimilationist ideal. However, later studies have placed greater emphasis upon processes of questioning, diverse new expressions of Jewishness, and a newly emergent Zionist identity (Rodrigue 1996; Strenski 1997).

3 Travelling cultures

1 On early-twentieth-century literatures of passing and imposed identities, see Lively (1999).

4 Irony and the state of unitedness

1 Sixty cartoons on the McVeigh execution, and thirty on the death penalty, are archived at www.cagle.slate.msn.com. An annual selection of American editorial cartoons can be found in the book *Best Editorial Cartoons of the Year* (Brooks 1999).

2 *Entertainment Network Inc* v *Harley Lappin, Kathleen Hawk Sawyer and John Ashcroft*, TH01-0076-T/H.

3 Congress passed 18 U.S.C. § 3510(a) and 42 U.S.C. § 10608, and revisions were subsequently made to the Department of Justice *Guidelines for Victim and Witness Assistance*. Details of the transmission to Oklahoma City were outlined in 'Arrangements for Victim Viewing of McVeigh Execution', Attorney General's Statement, 19 April 2001, (202) 514–2007.

4 George W. Bush, 'Statement on Execution of Timothy McVeigh', White House Press Office, 11 June 2001.

5 ENI Press release (undated) 'The McVeigh Execution and Entertainment Network, Inc.'

6 Dismissing ENI's case for the execution webcast, the judge described it as, 'the logical extension of Marshall McLuhan's prophetic proposal from the 1960s that the 'medium is the message'.' The phrase, 'the medium is the message', was first used by McLuhan in 1957 according to Gordon (1997), later to supply the title for the first chapter of *Understanding Media* (1964). McLuhanesque ideas have been taken up by death penalty abolitionists who favour the broadcasting of executions. For instance, John Bessler's *Death In The Dark* emphasized a qualitative difference between printed material and film, stating, 'when Marshall McLuhan wrote that "the medium is the message" he was right' (Bessler 1997: 195).

7 *United States of America* v. *Timothy James McVeigh*. Brief of the United States Opposing Stay of Execution.

8 The text of this legislation is contained in the Death Sentence and Veterans Benefits Act 1997, 38 U.S.C. § 2411.

5 The internet, new collectivities and crime

1 These online polls can be located at http://www.ship-of-fools.com/Vote/Votes01/Vote82.html and http://cgi.pathfinder.com/cgi/cgi-bin/time/europe/gdml3/osform/generic

2 *R* v. *Bernardo* (1993) O.J. no. 2047, Action no. 125/93, Media Ban.

3 Rishab Ghosh 1994 'The wild west of cyberspace' Electric Dreams 19 http://dxm.org/dreams/dreams.cgi?number=19

4 Karla Homolka Plea Bargain Agreement. Presentation of Petition. The Senate of Canada, 19 October 1995.

5 This protest site is at www.tpg1.com/protest/ontario/homo/homolka.htm.

6 This site is at www.angelfire.com/ca4/BernardoHomolka/Karla5.html. The death pool site is at www.geocities.com/byebye/Karla

7 *Venables* v. *News Group Newspapers Ltd* [2001] 1 All ER 908.

8 Denise Fergus, cited in Sarah Lyell 'Bulger killers get court protection for life outside' *The Age*, 10 January 2001, page 8.

9 The two texts of the injunction are HQ0004737 and HQ0004986.

10 Internet Freedom, 'Amended Bulger Ruling Good News for ISPs But Bad News for Net Users' Media release, 12 July 2001 (this can be read at: http://www.netfreedom.org/news.asp?item=164); Index on Censorship, Natasha Schmidt, 'Reasoned Steps in a Coded World', 20 July 2001 (this can be read at: http://www.indexonline.org/news/archives/INTERNET200701.htm).

11 This petition can be found at: http://www.islingtongazette.co.uk/bulletin/reply.asp?ID=190&Reply=190. Another message-board can be found at http://survey central.org/survey/8526.html. There are also pages on the Charles Bronson site, at http://www.bronsonmania.com/jamesbulger.html.

12 http://www.petitiononline.com/Jamie91/petition.html

13 The ribbon campaign is at http://www.supportjamie.cjb.net/. It asks people who protest the release of the Bulger killers to place a blue ribbon graphic on their site.

14 The petition can be found at the URL address: http://hoaxinfo.com/bolger.htm

15 This site can be found at: http://www.jamesbulger.co.uk

16 http://library.lovingyou.com/poetry/37/37714.shtml

17 The site can be found at: http://godhearsyou.homestead.com/jamiebulger.html. See also www.geocities.com/cagney555UK/Jamesbulgermemorial.html and www.angelfire.com/vi/babyangels.

18 'Revealed: the Bulger killers as they are today. We found them on the net!' can be found at http://www.humdrum.demon.co.uk/bulger.html. See also http://www.martian.fm/bulger_killers.htm

19 These can be found at http://www.thedespondent.com/comment/archive/bulger.htm

and http://www.urbanreflex.com/bulger.html. See also http://lifeshouldmeanlife.
freeservers.com

20 http://newsvote.bbc.co.uk/hi/english/talking_point/newsid_1394000/1394456.stm
21 See, for example, http://clubs.yahoo.com/clubs/supportforbulgers and http://clubs.
yahoo.com/clubs/jamiebulgerdebate
22 'Editorial Opinion' *The Age*, 20 December 2000, page 10.
23 This online poll can be found at http://www.ivillage.co.uk/homepage/dilemmas
24 Andrew Probyn 'No haven for Bulger killers' *Herald Sun*, 19 December 2000, page
5.
25 'Canada shuts door to child killers' *The Age* 23 December 2000, page 9.
26 *Guardian*, 20 December 2000, at http://www.guardian.co.uk/bulger/article/
0,2763,413906,00.html
27 'EVIL PAIR COULD COME (and we would never know)' *Herald Sun*, 24 December
2000, page 9.
28 Brett Foley 'Bulger Petition' *The Age*, 24 January 2001.
29 'Editorial: No entry for child killers' *The Courier Mail*, 11 January 2001, page
16.
30 Hansard House of Representatives, 5 March 2001, page 24,930.
31 http://www.studentz.co.nz/news/general/article.asp?aid=569
32 http://news.ninemsn.com.au/voteresults.asp and http://poll.co.nz/results.cgi?number
=41
33 Tim Colebatch 'Ruddock assurance on Bulger Killers' *The Age*, 25 June 2001,
page 3; Megan Saunders 'No sanctuary for Bulger Killers' *The Australian*, 25 June
2001, page 8.

6 Punishment and the powers of horror

1 The relevant case law is reported as follows:

> Decision of the High Court in May 1996: *R* v. *Secretary of State for the Home
> Department ex parte Venables* [1996] NLJ 786. Decision of the Court of Appeal
> in July 1996: *R* v. *Secretary of State for the Home Department ex parte Venables*
> [1997] 2 WLR 67 and [1997] 1 All ER 327. Decision of the House of Lords in
> June 1997: *R* v. *Secretary of State for the Home Department ex parte Venables*
> [1997] 3 WLR 23 and [1997] 3 All ER 97. Decision of the European Court of
> Human Rights in December 1999: *T* v. *United Kingdom. V* v. *United Kingdom*
> [2000] 2 All ER 1024 and [2000] 30 EHRR 121. Lord Woolf's reduction of the
> tariff in October 2000: *Thompson and Venables (Tariff Recommendations)*
> [2001] 1 Cr. App. R. 25. Ralph Bulger's case for leave to appeal against this
> decision in February 2001: *R (on the application of Bulger)* v. *Secretary of State
> for the Home Department* [2001] 3 All ER 449. The anonymity order granted in
> January 2001 (amended in July 2001): *Venables* v. *News Group Newspapers Ltd*
> [2001] 2 WLR 1038 and [2001] 1 All ER 908.

2 Julia Kristeva was born in Bulgaria, and moved to France in 1965. She was a
prominent member of the influential Tel Quel group, which also included Roland
Barthes and Michel Foucault. Her corpus now spans three decades, and melds
together cultural, political and philosophical critique through rigorous scholarship,
reflexive speculations, interviews and novels. Her publications include reflections
on foreigners and nationalism, and a trilogy of books on horror, melancholia and
love.
3 See, for instance, Channel 4 *Dispatches, Unforgiven: The Boys Who Murdered
James Bulger*.
4 The Hindley case is addressed in the next chapter of this book. For excellent critical
readings of the Spanner case, see Moran (1995), Stychin (1995) and Weait (1996).

7 The shadow of the death penalty

1 The tariff is the minimum period which must be served in custody for purposes of retribution and deterrence. The tariff figures in the text of law, politicians' statements and popular discourse as a predominantly punitive measure rather than a deterrent, hence its description as the 'penal tariff'. The Sentencing Advisory Panel (2001) suggests replacement of the term 'tariff' by 'punitive term'.

2 Nor did the 1965 Act command outright abolition, retaining the death penalty in certain categories. The last of these was only removed in May 2002, when the UK signed Protocol 13 of the European Convention on Human Rights, which prohibits the use of the death penalty in time of war. The last free vote on capital punishment in the Commons was in 1998.

3 *R* v. *Secretary of State for the Home Department, ex parte Hindley* [1998] 2 WLR 505; Q.B. 751; *R* v. *Secretary of State for the Home Department, ex parte Hindley* [1998] AC 539.

4 The severe mental anguish brought by this indeterminate 'whole life' tariff may be sufficient to constitute inhuman and degrading treatment in violation of Article 3 of the European Convention of Human Rights (Foster 2000: 242).

5 'Myra's Turn To Feel Pain' *Sun*, 10 March 2001, pp. 4–5. In April 2001, solicitors for Hindley lodged a complaint with the Press Complaints Commission over an article 'Myra: Weeks to Live' in the *Mirror*. This had erroneously stated that she was suffering from terminal cancer. For similar actions brought by Ian Brady, see *Stewart-Brady* v. *Express Newspapers plc* [1997] E.M.L.R. and *R* v. *Press Complaints Commission, ex parte Stewart-Brady* [1997] E.M.L.R. 185. The spectacle of Brady's suffering was used to infotainmental effect when he fought for the right to die (*R* v. *Collins ex parte Brady* [2000] Lloyds Med Rep 355).

6 In 1976 Brian Clemens play *Our Kid* opened in London, starring Sue Holderness as Hindley and was bombarded with hate mail. In 1998 Diane Dubois' play *Myra and Me* was the subject of controversy at the Edinburgh Fringe Festival when venue-backers objected to its inclusion in the programme.

7 Fassbinder's play *Antitheatre. Pre-Paradise Sorry Now*, performed in New York in 1999, implicated its audience in the sadistic voyeurism surrounding the Moors murders. Other works have linked the sexualized commodification of Hindley to a cynical electoral politics. Chris Morris's satirical comedy *Brass Eye* (5 March 1997) depicted a pop group performing a controversial song to cash in on the voyeurism around Hindley, and related this fascination to both media hype and populism. The Manic Street Preachers' 'Archives of Pain' criticizes the celebrity status of notorious criminals, but calls for retribution. It begins with a Hindley voice speaking of her diabolical crimes. The further lyrics proclaim, 'Prisons must bring their pain . . . /There is never redemption/Any fool can regret yesterday . . . /A drained white body hangs from the gallows/Is more righteous than Hindley's crotchet lectures/Pain not penance, forget martyrs, remember victims/Kill . . . Hindley and Brady . . . /Give them the respect they deserve' (Manic Street Preachers, 1994, *The Holy Bible*, Sony).

8 These displays of vengeful populism were not limited to the Moors case. For instance, there were photographs in the press of the bereaved mothers of young girls killed in the Cannock Chase murders of the mid 1960s campaigning for the restoration of the rope (Molloy 1998: 155). The crowd in the town square chanted 'Hang him! Hang him!' when Raymond Morris was found guilty of one of these murders in 1969, and the press published a photograph of the car used by him to abduct his young victims being publicly burned (ibid.: 254 and 259).

9 The recognition of the epic quality was sometimes quite direct, 'When I was there the clouds seemed to weep over the scene, as if lamenting life's eternal tragedy.

The moor is desolate and denuded. It is wet and treacherous. A dank mist seems to shroud its secrets. It was a wonderful setting for the culmination of great evil' (Sparrow 1966: 59).

10 The Smiths, 'Suffer Little Children', *The Smiths*, 1984, Warner.

Bibliography

Adamson, C. (2000) 'Defensive localism in white and black: a comparative history of European-American and African-American youth gangs' *Ethnic and Racial Studies* 23 (2): 272–98.

Allain, M. and Souvestre, P. (1987) *Fantômas* London: Pan.

Anderson, B. (1989) *Imagined Communities* London: Verso.

Anderson, D.C. (1995) *Crime and the Politics of Hysteria: How the Willie Horton Story Changed American Justice* New York: Times Books.

Anderson, R. (1896) 'Professional crime' *Blackwood's Edinburgh Magazine* 159: 294–307.

Archer, T. (1863) *The Pauper, the Thief and the Convict* London: Groombridge.

Arendt, H. (1951) *The Origins of Totalitarianism* London: Allen & Unwin.

Arnott, J. (2001) *He Kills Coppers* London: Hodder and Stoughton.

Atwood, M. (1996) *Alias Grace* London: Bloomsbury.

Aycock, A. and Buchignani, N. (1995) 'The e-mail murders: reflections on "dead" letters' in Jones, S.G. (ed.), *Cybersociety: Computer-Mediated Communication and Community* Thousand Oaks: Sage.

Aylmer, A. (1897) 'Detective day at Holloway' *The Windsor Magazine* 6: 90–6.

Baker, T.B. (1889) *War With Crime* London: Longmans, Green & Co.

Baldick, C. (1992) 'Introduction' *The Oxford Book of Gothic Tales* Oxford: Oxford University Press.

Banks, I. (1984) *The Wasp Factory* London: Abacus.

Barker, P. (1998) *Another World* London: Penguin.

Barker, Pat (2001) *Border Crossing* London: Viking.

Barthes, R. (1957/1993) *Mythologies* London: Vintage.

Barthes, R. (1970) *S/Z* Paris: Seuil.

Barwell, G. and Bowles, K. (2000) 'Border crossings: the internet and the dislocation of citizenship' in Bell, D. and Kennedy, B.M. (eds), *The Cybercultures Reader* London and New York: Routledge.

Baudrillard, J. (1967/2001) 'Review of Marshall McLuhan's "Understanding Media"' in Genosko, G. (ed.), *The Uncollected Baudrillard* London: Sage.

Baudrillard, J. (1983) *In the Shadow of the Silent Majorities . . . Or the End of the Social, And Other Essays* New York: Semiotext(e).

Baudrillard, J. (1983/2001) 'Our theatre of cruelty' in Genosko, G. (ed.), *The Uncollected Baudrillard* London: Sage.

Baudrillard, J. (1990) *Fatal Strategies* New York: Semiotext(e).

Baudrillard, J. (1990/1993) *The Transparency of Evil: Essays On Extreme Phenomena* London: Verso.

Baudrillard, J. (2001) 'L'espirit du terrorisme' *Le Monde*, 2.11.2001, pp. 10–11.

Bauman, Z. (1998) *Globalization: The Human Consequences* Cambridge: Polity.

Bauman, Z. (2000) *Liquid Modernity* Cambridge: Polity.

BBC News Online (2001) 'Paper denies breach of Bulger order' 23.6.2001.

Beck, U. (1998) 'Politics of Risk Society' in Franklin, J. (ed.), *The Politics of Risk Society* Cambridge: Polity.

Bellah, R. (1973) *Emile Durkheim: On Morality and Society* Chicago: University of Chicago Press.

Bentham, J. (1789/1996) *An Introduction to the Principals of Morals and Legislation* Oxford: Clarendon.

Bentham, J. (1791/1995) 'Panopticon Plan' in *The Panopticon and Other Prison Writings* New York: Verso.

Berlant, L. (1997) *The Queen of America Goes to Washington City: Essays on Sex and Citizenship* Durham: Duke University Press.

Berlant, L. and Warner, M. (1998) 'Sex in public' *Critical Inquiry* 24: 547–66.

Bertillon, A. (1881) 'Une application pratique de l'anthropométrie' *Mémoires Anthropométriques de M. Alphonse Bertillon, 1879–1890*. Unpublished volume at the Archives de la Prefecture de Police de Paris.

Bertillon, A. (1883) 'Question des recidivistes' *Mémoires Anthropométriques de M. Alphonse Bertillon, 1879–1890*. Unpublished volume at the Archives de la Prefecture de Police de Paris.

Bessler, J.D. (1997) *Death In The Dark: Midnight Executions In America* Boston: Northeastern University Press.

Bhabha, H.K. (1998) 'Designer creations' in Merck, M. (ed.), *After Diana: Irreverent Elegies* London: Verso.

Birch, H. (1994) 'If looks could kill: Myra Hindley and the iconography of evil' in *Moving Targets: Women, Murder and Representation* Berkeley: University of California Press.

Blair, F.P. (1901) 'A review of Bertillon's testimony in the Dreyfus case' *American Law Review* 35: 389–91.

Bleackley, H. (1905/2000) 'The love philtre' in Wilkes, R. (ed.), *The Mammoth Book of Murder and Science* London: Robinson.

Bogard, W. (2000) 'Simmel in cyberspace: strangeness and distance in postmodern communications' *Space and Culture* 4 (5): 23–46.

Bonhomme (1892) 'La Service Anthropometriques' *Le Palais de Justice de Paris, ses Monde et ses Moeurs* Paris: Librairies-Imprimeries Réunies.

Botting, F. (1996) *Gothic* London: Routledge.

Bourne, R. S. (1916/1996) 'Trans-National America' in Sollors, W. (ed.), *Theories of Ethnicity: A Classical Reader* New York: New York University Press.

Brennan, J.F. (1998) *The Reflection of the Dreyfus Affair in the European Press 1897–1899* New York: Peter Lang.

Brontë, E. (1846/1992) 'Faith and despondency' in *Emily Brontë. The Complete Poems* London: Penguin.

Brontë, E. (1847/1995) *Wuthering Heights* London: Penguin.

Brooks, C. (1999) *Best Editorial Cartoons of the Year* Gretna, Louisiana: Pelican.

Burgess, E.W. (1925/1967a) 'The growth of the city' in Park, R.E. and Burgess, E.W. and McKenzie, R.D. (eds), *The City* Chicago: University of Chicago Press.

Burgess, E.W. (1925/1967b) 'Can neighbourhood work have a scientific basis?' in Park, R.E., and Burgess, E.W. and McKenzie, R.D. (eds), *The City* Chicago: University of Chicago Press.

Burgess, E.W. (1926/1971) 'The scope of human ecology' in *The Urban Community* Chicago: University of Chicago Press.

Burgess, E.W. (1929) 'Communication' *American Journal of Sociology* 34 (6): 1,072–80.

Burgess, E.W. and Bogue, D.J. (1964) 'Research in urban sociology: a long view' in Burgess and Bogue (eds), *Contributions to Urban Sociology* Chicago: University of Chicago Press.

Burn, G. (1991) *Alma Cogan* London: Minerva.

Burns, M. (1993) *Dreyfus. A Family Affair 1789–1945* London: Chatto & Windus.

Butler, J. (1997) *The Psychic Life of Power: Theories in Subjection* Stanford, CA: Stanford University Press.

Cahm, E. (1994) *The Dreyfus Affair in French Society and Politics* London: Longman.

Cahm, E. (2001) 'Moderate anti-Dreyfusism: the forgotten ideology of France's Republican elite in 1898' in Grossman, K.M., Lane, M.E., Monicat, B. and Silverman, W.Z. (eds), *Confrontations: Politics and Aesthetics in Nineteenth Century France* Amsterdam: Rodolpi.

Cain, Maureen (2000) 'Orientalism, occidentalism and the sociology of crime' *British Journal of Criminology* 40: 239–60.

Carpenter, E. (1905) *Prisons, Police and Punishment* London: Arthur C. Field.

Castells, M. (2001) *The Internet Galaxy* Oxford University Press.

Castles, S. and Davidson, A. (2000) *Citizenship and Migration: Globalization and the Politics of Belonging* London: Macmillan.

Cattell, W. (1895) 'Measurements of the accuracy of recollection' *Science* 2: 761–6.

Caussé, S. (1854) 'Des empreintes sanglantes des pieds et de leur mode de mensuration' *Archives D'Hygiene Publique et de Médecine Légale* 175–89.

Chaillé, S. (1876/1979) 'Origin and progress of medical jurisprudence' *Journal of Criminal Law and Criminology* 40 (4): 397–444.

Chicago Commission on Race Relations (1922/1968) *The Negro in Chicago* New York: Arno Press and the New York Times.

Claparède, E. (1907) 'What is the value of evidence' *The Strand Magazine* 31 (200): 143–9.

Clarkson, C.T. and Richardson, J.H. (1889) *Police!* London: Field and Tuer.

Clifford, J. (1997) *Routes: Travel and Translation in the Late Twentieth Century* Cambridge: Harvard University Press.

Cohen, R. (1997) *Global Diasporas: An Introduction* London: UCL Press.

Cohen, S. (1972/1980) *Folk Devils and Moral Panics: The Creation of the Mods and Rockers* Oxford: Martin Robertson.

Cohen, S. (2000) 'Some thoroughly modern monsters' *Index on Censorship* 5: 36–43.

Cole, S.A. (2001) *Suspect Identities: A History of Fingerprinting and Criminal Identification* Cambridge, MA: Harvard University Press.

Collins W. (1861/1994) *The Woman in White* Oxford: Oxford University Press.

Conybeare, F.C. (1898) *The Dreyfus Case* London: George Allen.

Cornick, M. (1996) 'The Impact of the Dreyfus affair in late-Victorian Britain' *Franco-British Studies* 22: 57–82.

Cotterell, R. (1999) *Emile Durkheim: Law in a Moral Domain* Edinburgh: Edinburgh University Press.

Cressey, P.G. (1932/1971) 'The taxi-dance hall as a social world' in Short, J.F. (ed.), *The Social Fabric of the Metropolis: Contributions of the Chicago School of Urban Sociology* Chicago and London: University of Chicago Press.

Cross, A. (1998) 'Neither either nor or: the perils of reflexive irony' in Hannay, A. and Marino, G.D. (eds), *The Cambridge Companion to Kierkegaard* Cambridge: Cambridge University Press.

Datta, V. (1995) 'The Dreyfus Affair and anti-Semitism: Jewish identity at La Revue Blanche' *Historical Reflections* 21 (1): 113–29.

Department of Justice (2000) *Responding to Terrorism Victims Oklahoma City and Beyond* Washington, DC: United States Department of Justice.

Debord, G. (1967) *La Société du Spectacle* Paris: Editions Buchet-Chastel.

De Man, P. (1969/1983) 'The rhetoric of temporality' in *Blindness and Insight: Essays in the Rhetoric of Contemporary Criticism, Second Edition* London: Methuen.

De Man, P. (1977/1996) 'The concept of irony' in *Aesthetic Ideology* Minneapolis: University of Minnesota Press.

Derrida, J. (2003) 'Following theory' in Payne, M. and Schad, J. (eds), *Life. After. Theory* London: Continuum.

De Ryckere (1893) 'Le signalement anthropométrique' *Actes du Troisième Congrés International D'Anthropologie Criminelle* Bruxelles: F. Hayez.

Dickens, C. (1851) 'On duty with Inspector Field' *Household Words* 64: 485–90.

Dickens, C. (1868) 'Eye-Memory' *All The Year Round* 473: 545–8.

Diken, B. (1998) *Strangers, Ambivalence and Social Theory* Aldershot: Ashgate.

Dixon, H. (1850) *The London Prisons* London: Jackson and Walford.

Doyle, A.C. (1907/1985) *The Story of Mr George Edalji* London: Grey House Books.

Doyle, A.C. (1912) *The Case of Oscar Slater* London: Hodder and Stoughton.

Doyle, A.C. (1927) 'Introduction' in Park, W. *The Truth About Oscar Slater* London: The Psychic Press.

Dreyfus, A. (1977) *Five Years of My Life: The Diary of Captain Alfred Dreyfus* New York: Peebles Press.

Du Bois, W.E.B. (1903/1989) *The Souls of Black Folk* London: Penguin.

Duffy, C.A. (1999) *The World's Wife* London: Faber and Faber.

Duggan, L. (2000) *Sapphic Slashers: Sex, Violence and American Modernity* Durham, NC: Duke University Press.

Durkheim, E. (1901/1992) 'Two laws of penal evolution' in Gane, M. (ed.), *The Radical Sociology of Durkheim and Mauss* London: Routledge.

Durkheim, E. (1893/1933) *The Division of Labour in Society* New York: Bobbs-Merrill.

Durkheim, E. (1898/1969) 'Individualism and the intellectuals' *Political Studies* 17 (1): 19–30.

Durkheim, E. (1899) 'Contribution' in Dagan, H. (ed.), *Enquête sur l'antisémitisme* Paris: P.V. Stock.

Edalji report (1907) *Home Office Papers Relating to the Case of George Edalji, British Parliamentary Papers 67*, Cd 3503.

Ehrmann, H.B. (1970) *The Case That Will Not Die: Commonwealth vs. Sacco & Vanzetti* London: W.H. Allen.

Ellman, M. (1990) 'Eliot's abjection' in Fletcher, J. and Benjamin, A. (eds), *Abjection, Melancholia and Love: The Work of Julia Kristeva* London: Routledge.

Eribon, D. (1992) *Michel Foucault* London: Faber.

Essig, M. (2002) 'Poison murder and expert testimony: doubting the physician in late nineteenth century America' *Yale Journal of Law and the Humanities* 14 (1): 171–210.

Fanon, F. (1961/1990) *The Wretched of the Earth* London: Penguin.

Faris, E. (1926/1971) 'The nature of human nature' in Burgess, E.W. (ed.), *The Urban Community* Chicago: University of Chicago Press.

Faris, R.E.L. (1938/1971) 'Demography of urban psychotics with special reference to schizophrenia' in Short, J.F. (ed.), *The Social Fabric of the Metropolis: Contributions of the Chicago School of Urban Sociology* Chicago and London: University of Chicago Press.

Feldman, E. (1981) *The Dreyfus Affair and the American Conscience 1895–1906* Detroit: Wayne State University Press.

Fielding, H. (1752) *Examples of the Interposition of Providence in the Detection and Punishment of Murder* Dublin: James Hoey.

Fiske, J. (1998) 'Surveilling the city: whiteness, the black man and democratic totalitarianism' *Theory Culture & Society* 15 (2): 67–88.

Fleming, A. (1859) 'Blood stains' *American Journal of the Medical Sciences* 37: 84–119.

Foster, H. (1996) 'Death in America' *October* 75: 37–59.

Foster, S. (2000) 'R v. Secretary of State for the Home Department ex parte Hindley' *Journal of Civil Liberties* 5(2): 231–43.

Foucault, M. (1975/1991) *Discipline and Punish: The Birth of the Prison* London: Penguin.

Foucault, M. (1980a) *Power/Knowledge: Selected Interviews and Other Writings* Brighton: Harvester.

Foucault, M. (1980b) 'La poussière et le nuage' in Perrot, M. (ed.), *L'Impossible Prison* Paris: Seuil.

Foucault, M. (1984) *The Foucault Reader* London: Penguin.

Foucault, M. (1984/1990) 'On power' in Kritzman, L.D. (ed.), *Michel Foucault, Politics, Philosophy, Culture. Interviews and other Writings, 1977–1984* New York and London: Routledge.

Foucault, M. (1996) *Foucault Live* New York: Semiotext(e).

Foucault, M. (1997) *Michel Foucault, Ethics, Subjectivity and Truth* London: Allen Lane.

Fox, R.L. and Van Sickel, R.W. (2001) *Tabloid Criminal Justice in an Age of Media Frenzy* Boulder, CO: Rienner.

Freeland, C.A. (1995) 'Realist horror' in Freeland, C.A. and Wartenberg, T.E. (eds), *Philosophy and Film* New York and London: Routledge.

Frye, Northrop (1957) *The Anatomy of Criticism* Princeton, NJ: Princeton University Press.

Garland, D. (2001) *The Culture of Control: Crime and Social Order in Contemporary Society* Oxford: Oxford University Press.

Garson, J.G. (1906) 'untitled' *Transactions of the Medico-Legal Society* 2: 115.

Gatrell, V.A.C. (1994) *The Hanging Tree: Execution and the English People 1770–1868* Oxford: Oxford University Press.

Giddens, A. (1972) *Emile Durkheim: Selected Writings* Cambridge: Cambridge University Press.

Gilligan, P. (1996) *Report to the Attorney-General on Certain Matters Relating to Karla Homolka* Ontario.

Gilman, S.L. (1990) '"I'm down on whores": race and gender in Victorian London' in Goldberg, D.T. (ed.), *Anatomy of Racism* Minneapolis: University of Minnesota Press.

Gilman, S. (1991) *The Jew's Body* New York and London: Routledge.

Gilman, S. (1995) *Franz Kafka, the Jewish Patient* New York and London: Routledge.

Goldberg, V. (1998) 'Death takes a holiday, sort of' in Goldstein, J., (ed.), *Why We Watch: The Attractions of Violent Entertainment* New York: Oxford University Press.

Goodrich, P. (2001) 'Europe in America: grammatology, legal studies, and the politics of transmission' *Columbia Law Review* 101(8): 2,033–84.

Gordon, W.T. (1997) *Marshall McLuhan: Escape Into Understanding* Toronto: Stoddart.

Graham, P. and Clarke, J. (1995) 'Dangerous places: crime and the city' in Muncie, J. and McLaughlin, M. (eds), *The Problem of Crime* London: Sage.

Gross, H. (1911) *Criminal Psychology* London: Heinemann.

Guarnieri, P. (1991) 'Alienists on trial: conflict and convergence between psychiatry and law (1876–1913)' *History of Science* 29: 393–410.

Halberstam, J. (1995) *Skin Shows: Gothic Horror and the Technology of Monsters* Durham, NC: Duke University Press.

Hall, S., Critcher, C., Jefferson, T., Clarke, J. and Roberts, B. (1978) *Policing the Crisis: Mugging, the State and Law and Order* London: Macmillan.

Hall, S. (1996) 'Introduction: who needs identity' in Hall, S. and du Gay, P. (eds), *Questions of Cultural Identity* London: Sage.

Halttunen, K. (1998) *Murder Most Foul: The American Killer and the Gothic Imagination* Harvard: Harvard University Press.

Hamm, M.S. (1997) *Apocalypse in Oklahoma: Waco and Ruby Ridge Revenged* Boston, MA: Northeastern University Press.

Hanna, M. (1998) 'Laying siege to the Sorbonne: the Action Française's attack upon the Dreyfusard university' *Historical Reflections* 24 (1): 155–77.

Hannant, L. (1995) *The Infernal Machine: Investigating the Loyalty of Canada's Citizens* Toronto: University of Toronto Press.

Heinzelmann, S.S. (1994) 'Guilty in law, implausible in fiction: jurisprudential and literary narratives in the case of Mary Blandy, parricide 1752' in Heinzelmann, S.S. and Wiseman, Z.B. (eds), *Representing Women: Law, Literature and Feminism* Durham, NC: Duke University Press.

Herbert, S. (2000) 'Zoning cyberspace' in Sarat, A. and Ewick, P. (eds), *Studies in Law, Politics and Society* Stamford, CN: Jai Press.

Hetherington, K. (1998) *Expressions of Identity: Space, Performance, Politics* London: Sage.

Higham, J. (1974) *Strangers in the Land: Patterns of American Nativism, 1860–1925* New York: Athaeneum.

Hine, C. (2000) *Virtual Ethnography* London: Sage.

Hutchings, P. (2001) *The Criminal Spectre in Law, Literature and Aesthetics* London: Routledge.

Hyde, A. (1997) *Bodies of Law* Princeton, NJ: Princeton University Press.

Ingebretson, E. (1998) 'The monster in the home: true crime and the traffic in body parts' *Journal of American Culture* 21(1): 27–34.

Jacobs, R. (1996) 'Civil society and crisis: culture, discourse and the Rodney King beating' *American Journal of Sociology* 101 (5): 1,238–72.

Johnson, D. (1966) *France and the Dreyfus Affair* London: Blandford.

Johnson, P.H. (1967) *On Iniquity: Some Personal Reflections Arising out of the Moors Murders Trial* London: Macmillan.

Johnson, V.E. (1999) 'Fertility among the ruins: the "heartland", maternity and the Oklahoma City bombing' *Continuum* 13(1): 57–75.

Jones, C. (1994) *Expert Witnesses: Science, Medicine and the Practice of Law* Oxford: Clarendon Press.

Jones, H. (1965) *Crime in a Changing Society* Harmondsworth: Penguin.

Joseph, A. and Winter, A. (1996) 'Making the match: human traces, forensic experts and the public imagination' in Spufford, F. and Uglow, J. (eds), *Cultural Babbage: Technology, Time and Invention* London: Faber.

Justice (2000) *Intervention to the House of Lords in the case of R v. Secretary of State for the Home Department, ex parte Hindley.*

Kallen, H. M. (1915/1996) 'Democracy versus the melting-pot: a study of American nationality' in Sollors, W. (ed.), *Theories of Ethnicity: A Classical Reader* New York: New York University Press.

Kellner, D. (1989) *Jean Baudrillard: From Marxism to Postmodernism and Beyond* Cambridge: Polity.

Kember, S. (1995) 'Surveillance, technology and crime: the James Bulger Case' in Lister, M. (ed.), *The Photographic Image in Digital Culture* London: Routledge.

Kenealy, E.V.H. (1875) *The Trial at Bar of Sir Roger C.D. Tichborne* London.

Kenealy, M.E. (1913) *The Tichborne Tragedy* London.

Kierkegaard, S. (1846/1992) *The Present Age* New York: Harper and Row.

Kivisto, P. (1990) 'The transplanted then and now: the reorientation of immigration studies from the Chicago School to the new social history' *Ethnic and Racial Studies* 13 (4): 455–81.

Knelman, J. (1998) *Twisting In The Wind: The Murderess and the English Press* Toronto: University of Buffalo Press.

Kristeva, J. (1980) 'Feminism and psychoanalysis' in Guberman, R.M. (ed.), *Julia Kristeva Interviews* New York: Columbia University Press.

Kristeva, J. (1982) *Powers of Horror: An Essay on Abjection* New York: Columbia University Press.

Lahiri, S. (1998) 'Uncovering Britain's South Asian past: the case of George Edalji *Immigrants and Minorities* 17 (3): 22–33.

Lash, S. (2002) *Critique of Information* London: Sage.

Lehmann, J. (1994) *Durkheim and Women* Lincoln: University of Nebraska Press.

Leroux, G. (1985) *The Phantom of the Opera* London: W.H. Allen.

Lesser, W. (1994) *Pictures At An Execution* Cambridge, MA: Harvard Press.

Levinson, P. (1999) *Digital McLuhan: A Guide to the Information Millennium* London: Routledge.

Liberty (2002) *Liberty Response-Tariffs in Murder Cases* 03.01.02.

Life (1996) 'Oklahoma City' *Life* January 1996: 42–6.

Lindemann, A. (1993) *The Jew Accused: Three Anti-Semitic Affairs, Dreyfus, Beilis, Frank, 1894–1915* Cambridge: Cambridge University Press.

Lindner, R. (1996) *The Reportage of Urban Culture: Robert Park and the Chicago School* Cambridge: Cambridge University Press.

Linenthal, E. (2001) *The Unfinished Bombing: Oklahoma City in American Memory* Oxford: Oxford University Press.

Lippens, R. (2003) 'The imaginary of Zapatista punishment and justice. Speculations on the "First Postmodern Revolution"' *Punishment & Society* 5(2)

Lively, Adam (1999) *Masks: Blackness, Race and the Imagination* London: Vintage.

Lukes, S. (1969) 'Durkheim's "Individualism and the Intellectuals"' *Political Studies* 17 (1): 14–19.

Lynch, M. (2000a) 'The disposal of inmate #85271' in Sarat, A. and Ewick, P. (eds), *Studies in Law, Politics and Society* Stamford, CN: Jai Press.

Lynch, M. (2000b) 'On-line executions. The symbolic use of the electric chair in cyberspace' *POLAR. Political and Legal Anthropology Review* 23

Lynch, M. (2002) 'Capital punishment as moral imperative: pro-death penalty discourse on the Internet' *Punishment & Society* 4(2): 213–36.

Lyons, E. (1927/1970) *The Life and Death of Sacco and Vanzetti* New York: Dacapo Press.

Macaulay, T. (1849) *The History of England From The Accession of James I* London: Longman.

McConville, S. (1995) *English Local Prisons 1860–1900 Next Only To Death* London: Routledge.

McDermid, V. (1999) *A Place of Execution* London: HarperCollins.

McEwan, I. (1975/1997) 'Butterflies' in *First Love, Last Rites* London: Vintage.

McGrath, P. (1997) 'Transgression and decay' in Christoph Grunenberg (ed.), *Transmutations of Horror in Late Twentieth Century Art* Boston, MA: MIT Press.

McLuhan, M. (1964/2002) *Understanding Media. The Extensions of Man* London: Routledge.

McLuhan, M. and Fiore, Q. (1968) *The Medium is the Massage* New York: Random House.

McLuhan, M. and Fiore, Q. (1968b) *War and Peace in the Global Village* New York: Bantam.

McLuhan, M. and Powers, B.R. (1989) *The Global Village: Transformations in World Life and Media in the 21st Century* New York: Oxford University Press.

McMaster, D. (2001) *Asylum Seekers: Australia's Response to Refugees* Melbourne: Melbourne University Press.

Magraw, R. (1987) *France 1815–1914: The Bourgeois Century* London: Collins.

Mainwaring, G.B. (1821) *Observations on the Present State of the Police of the Metropolis* London: John Murray.

Man de, P (1969/1983) 'The rhetoric of temporality' in *Blindness and Insight: Essays in the Rhetoric of Contemporary Criticism, Second Edition* London: Methuen.

Marchbanks, D. (1966) *The Moor Murders* London: Leslie Frewin.

Mares, P. (2001) *Borderline: Australia's Treatment of Refugees and Asylum Seekers* Sydney: University of New South Wales Press.

Marrus, M. (1971) *The Politics of Assimilation: The French Jewish Community at the Time of the Dreyfus Affair* Oxford: Clarendon Press.

Mathiesen, T. (1997) 'The viewer society: Michel Foucault's "Panopticon" revisited' *Theoretical Criminology* 1 (2): 215–34.

Matthews, F. H. (1977) *Quest for an American Sociology: Robert Park and the Chicago School* Montreal and London: McGill-Queen's University Press.

Merle, I. (1996) 'Colonial experiments, colonial experiences: the theory and practice of penal colonisation in New Caledonia' in Merle, I. and Aldrich, R. (eds), *France Abroad: Indochina, New Caledonia, Wallis and Futuna, Mayotte* Sydney: University of Sydney Press.

Michel, L. and Herbeck, M. (2001) *American Terrorist: Timothy McVeigh and the Oklahoma City Bombing* New York: HarperCollins.

Miller, J. (1971) *McLuhan* London: Fontana.

Miller, W.W. (1996) *Durkheim, Morals and Modernity* London: UCL Press.

Mitchell, C.A. (1911) *Science and the Criminal* London: Pitman.

Molloy, P. (1988) *Not the Moors Murders* Llandysul: Gomer.

Moore, M.T. (1997) 'The hazards of using powerful images from real life in editorial cartoons' *USA Today* June 20, 1997.

Moran, L.J. (1995) 'Violence and the law: the case of sado-masochism' *Social & Legal Studies* 4: 225–51.

Moran, L.J. (1996) *The Homosexual(ity) of Law* London: Routledge.

Morris, D. (1999) *Vote.com* Los Angeles: Renaissance Books.

Morrison, B. (1997) *As If* London: Granta.

Morrison, T. (1987) *Beloved* New York: Chatto & Windus.

Munsterberg, H. (1909) 'Nothing but the truth' *McClure's Magazine* 614–21.

Nead. L. (2002) 'Visual cultures of the courtroom: reflections on history, law and the image' *Visual Culture in Britain* 3 (2)

Nelli, H. S. (1970) *Italians in Chicago, 1880–1930. A Study in Ethnic Mobility* New York: Oxford University Press.

Noveck, B.S. (2000) 'Paradoxical partners: electronic communication and electronic democracy' in Ferdinand, P. (ed.), *The Internet, Democracy and Democratization* London: Cass.

Nussbaum, M.C. (1999) '"Secret sewers of vice": disgust, bodies and the law' in Bandes, S.A. (ed.), *The Passions of Law* New York: New York University Press.

Paley, W. (1785) *The Principles of Moral and Political Philosophy* London: R. Fauldner.

Park, R.E. (1914) 'Racial assimilation in secondary groups with particular reference to the negro' *American Journal of Sociology* 19 (5): 606–23.

Park, R.E. (1917/1950) 'Race prejudice and Japanese-American relations' in *Race and Culture* Glencoe, IL: Free Press.

Park, R.E. (1922) *The Immigrant Press and Its Control* New York and London: Harper.

Park, R.E. (1922/1968) *The Negro in Chicago* Chicago: University of Chicago Press.

Park, R.E. (1925/1950) 'Culture and cultural trends' in *Race and Culture* Glencoe, IL: Free Press.

Park, R.E. (1925/1952a) 'The urban community as a spatial pattern and a moral order' in *Human Communities* New York: Free Press.

Park, R.E. (1925/1952b) 'Community organization and the Romantic temper' in *Human Communities* New York: Free Press.

Park, R.E. (1925/1967a) 'The city', in Park, R.E. and Burgess, E.W. and McKenzie, R.D. (eds), *The City* Chicago: University of Chicago Press.

Park, R.E. (1925/1967b) 'Community organization and juvenile delinquency' in Park, R.E. and Burgess, E.W. and McKenzie, R.D. (eds), *The City* Chicago: University of Chicago Press.

Park, R.E. (1925/1967c) 'The mind of the hobo: reflections upon the relation between mentality and locomotion' in Park, R.E. and Burgess, E.W. and McKenzie, R.D. (eds), *The City* Chicago: University of Chicago Press.

Park, R.E. (1926/1950a) 'Our racial frontier on the Pacific' in *Race and Culture* Glencoe, IL: Free Press.

Park, R.E. (1926/1950b) 'Behind our masks' in *Race and Culture* Glencoe, IL: Free Press.

Park, R.E. (1926/1971) 'The urban community as a spatial pattern and a moral order' in Burgess, E.W. (ed.), *The Urban Community* Chicago: University of Chicago Press.

Park, R.E. (1928) 'Human migration and the marginal man' *American Journal of Sociology* 33 (6): 881–93.

Park, R.E. (1930/1950) 'Personality and cultural conflict' in *Race and Culture* Glencoe, IL: Free Press.

Park, R.E. (1931/1950) 'The problem of cultural differences' in *Race and Culture* Glencoe, IL: Free Press.

Park, R.E. (1934) 'Industrial fatigue and group morale' *American Journal of Sociology* 40: 349–56.

Park, R.E. (1938/1950) 'Reflections on communication and culture' in *Race and Culture* Glencoe, IL: Free Press.

Park, R.E. (1939/1950) 'The nature of race relations' in *Race and Culture* Glencoe, IL: Free Press.

Park, R.E. and Burgess, E.W. (1921) *Introduction to the Science of Sociology* Chicago: University of Chicago Press.

Park, R.E. and Miller, H.A. (1921/1969) *Old World Traits Transplanted* New York: Arno Press and the New York Times.

Philpott, T. L. (1978) *The Slum and the Ghetto: Neighbourhood Deterioration and Middle-Class Reform, Chicago 1880–1930* New York: Oxford University Press.

Pickering, W.S.F. (1994) 'The enigma of Durkheim's Jewishness' in Pickering, W.S.F. and Martins, H. (eds), *Debating Durkheim* New York: Routledge.

Poe, E.A. (1840/1984) 'The man of the crowd' in *The Complete Edgar Allen Poe* London: Penguin.

Poggi, G. (2000) *Durkheim* Oxford: Oxford University Press.

Potter, J.D. (1966) *The Monsters of the Moors* London: Elek.

Pratt, J. (1998) 'Towards the "decivilising of punishment"' *Social & Legal Studies* 7(4): 487–515.

Pugliese, J. (1999) 'Identity in question: a grammatology of DNA and forensic genetics' *International Journal for the Semiotics of Law* 12: 419–44.

Radzinowicz, L. (1956) *A History of English Criminal Law and Its Administration from 1750, Volume 3* London: Stevens.

Rajchman, J. (1988) 'Foucault's art of seeing' *October* 44: 88–117.

Reckless, W. (1926/1971) 'Commercialized vice areas' in *The Urban Community* Chicago: University of Chicago Press.

Reiner, R. *et al.* (2000) 'No more happy endings? The media and popular concern about crime since the Second World War' in Sparks, R. and Hope, T. (eds), *Crime, Risk and Insecurity: Law and Order in Everyday Life and Political Discourse* London: Routledge.

Rheingold, L. (1994) *The Virtual Community: Finding Connection in a Computerized World* London: Minerva.

Robbins, B. (1993) *The Phantom Public Sphere* Minneapolis: University of Minnesota Press.

Rodrigue, A. (1996) 'Rearticulations of French Jewish identities after the Dreyfus Affair' *Jewish Social Studies* 2(3): 1–24.

Rohmer, S. (1913) *The Mystery of Dr. Fu-Manchu* London: Methuen.

Rorty, R. (1989) *Contingency, Irony and Solidarity* Cambridge: Cambridge University Press.

Rose, J. (1993) 'Margaret Thatcher and Ruth Ellis' in *Why War? Psychoanalysis, Politics and the Return to Melanie Klein* Oxford: Blackwell.

Roughead, W. (1910) *Trial of Oscar Slater* Edinburgh: William Hodge.

San Juan, E. (1994) 'Configuring the Filipino diaspora in the United States' *Diaspora* 3 (2): 117–33.

Sarup, M. (1996) *Identity, Culture and the Postmodern World* Edinburgh: Edinburgh University Press.

Sassen, S. (1998) *Globalization and Its Discontents* New York: Free Press.

Scheuer, J. (2001) *The Sound Bite Society* New York: Routledge.

Schone, J.M. (2000) 'The hardest case of all: Myra Hindley, life sentences and the rule of law' *International Journal of the Sociology of Law* 28 (4): 273–89.

Sekula, A. (1986) 'The body and the archive' *October* 39.

Seltzer, M. (1997) *Serial Killers: Death and Life in America's Wound Culture* New York: Routledge.

Sentencing Advisory Panel (2001) *Tariffs in Murder Cases: Consultation Paper* 13.11.2001.

Serrano, R. 1998. *One of Ours: Timothy McVeigh and the Oklahoma City Bombing* New York: W.W. Norton.

Shakespeare, S. (1998) 'Books about nothing? Kierkegaard's liberating rhetoric' in *Kierkegaard and Freedom* Basingstoke: Macmillan.

Shade, L.R (1996) 'Is there free speech on the net? Censorship in the global information infrastructure' in Shields, R. (ed.), *Cultures of Internet: Virtual Spaces, Real Histories, Living Bodies* London: Sage.

Shaw, C.R. (1930/1968) *The Jack-Roller: A Delinquent Boy's Own Story* Chicago: University of Chicago Press.

Shields, R. (1996) *Cultures of Internet. Virtual Spaces, Real Histories, Living Bodies* London: Sage.

Sibley, D. (1995) *Geographies of Exclusion: Society and Difference in the West* New York: Routledge.

Silverman, M. (1992) *Deconstructing the Nation: Immigration, Racism and Citizenship in Modern France* London: Routledge.

Slayden, D. and Whillock, R.K. (1999) *Soundbite Culture: The Death of Discourse in a Wired World* Thousand Oaks, CA: Sage.

Smith, A. (1996) *Julia Kristeva: Readings of Exile and Estrangement* Basingstoke: Macmillan.

Snyder, L.L. (1973) *The Dreyfus Case. A Documentary History* New Brunswick, NJ: Rutgers University Press.

Solzhenitsyn, A. (1974) *The Gulag Archipelago 1918–1956* Glasgow: Collins/Fontana.

Sparrow, G. (1966) *Satan's Children* London: Oghams.

Spearman, E. (1890) 'Mistaken identification and police anthropometry' *The Fortnightly Review* 279: 361–76.

Spearman, E. (1893) 'Criminals and their detection' *The New Review* 9: 65–84.

Spiegel, L. (1992) *Make Room for TV: Television and the Family Ideal in Postwar America* Chicago: University of Chicago Press.

Stapleton, J.W. (1861) *The Great Crime of 1860* London: Marlborough.

Steiker, J. (2001) 'Did the Oklahoma bombers succeed?' *Annals of the American Academy of Political and Social Science* 574: 185–94.

Stern, W. (1902) 'Zur psychologie der Aussage: experimentelle Untersuchungen ueber Erinnerungstreue' *Zeitschrift fuer die Gesamte Strafrecht Swissenschaft* 22: 315–35.

Stevenson, N. (1996) *Understanding Media Cultures: Social Theory and Mass Communication* London: Sage.

Stevenson, R.L. (1886/1979) *Dr Jekyll and Mr Hyde* London: Penguin.

Stonequist, E.V. (1937) 'The problem of the marginal man' *American Journal of Sociology* 41 (1): 1–12.

Streck, J. (1998) 'Pulling the plug in electronic town meetings: participatory democracy and the reality of the usenet' in Toulouse, C. and Luke, T.W. (eds), *The Politics of Cyberspace* New York: Routledge.

Strenski, I. (1997) *Durkheim and the Jews of France* Chicago: University of Chicago Press.

Stychin, C. (1995) 'Unmanly diversions: the construction of the homosexual body (politic) in law' in *Law's Desire: Sexuality and the Limits of Justice* London: Routledge.

Sumner, C.S. (1991) 'Ideology and law: Some reflections on postmodernist-sociology and the ideological character of criminal justice' in Bergalli, R. (ed.), *Sociology of Penal Control Within the Framework of the Sociology of Law* Oñati: Oñati International Institute for the Sociology of Law.

Sumner, W.G. (1906) *Folkways* Boston: Ginn & Co.

Surette, R. (1998) *Media, Crime and Criminal Justice: Images and Realities* Belmont, CA: Wadsworth.

Tagg, J. (1988) *The Burden of Representation: Essays on Photographies and their Histories* Basingstoke and London: Macmillan.

Taylor, A.S. (1873) *Principles and Practice of Medical Jurisprudence* Philadelphia: Henry C. Lea.

Taylor, I. (1999) *Crime in Context: A Critical Criminology of Market Societies* Cambridge: Polity.

Thomas, R.R. (1999) *Detective Fiction and the Rise of Forensic Science* Cambridge: Cambridge University Press.

Thomas, W.I. and Znaniecki, F. (1958) *The Polish Peasant in Europe and America, Volume II* New York: Alfred A. Knopf.

Thompson, J.B. (2000) *Political Scandal: Power and Visibility in the Media Age* Cambridge: Polity.

Thompson, K. (1982) *Emile Durkheim* London: Tavistock.

Thrasher, F.M. (1927/1936) *The Gang: A Study of 1,313 Gangs in Chicago* Chicago: University of Chicago Press.

Tilley, N. and Ford, A. (1996) *Forensic Science and Crime Investigation* Police Research Group, Crime Detection and Prevention Series, Paper 73.

Tole, L.A. (1993) 'Durkheim on religion and moral community in modernity' *Sociological Inquiry* 63 (1): 1–29.

Tombs, R. (1998) '"Lesser breeds without the law": the British Establishment and the Dreyfus Affair' *The Historical Journal* 41 (2): 495–510.

Tomlinson, J. (1999) *Globalization and Culture* Cambridge: Polity.

Troup (1894) *Report of a Committee Appointed by the Secretary of State to Inquire into the Best Means Available for Identifying Habitual Criminals* London: HMSO.

Tuttle, W.M. (1974) *Race Riot: Chicago in the Red Summer of 1919* New York: Atheneum.

Twain, M. (1894/1969) *Puddn'head Wilson* Harmondsworth: Penguin.

Ungar, S. (2001) 'Moral panic versus the risk society: the implications of the changing sites of social anxiety' *British Journal of Sociology* 52 (2): 271–91.

Valier, C. (2000) 'Looking daggers: reading the scene of punishment' *Punishment & Society* 2(4): 379–94.

Valier, C. (2001) *Theories of Crime and Punishment* London: Longman.

Valier, C. and Lippens, R. (forthcoming) 'The weeping mother and the demand for justice', *Theory, Culture and Society*.

Virilio, P (1997) *Open Sky* London: Verso.

Wacquant, L. (2001) 'Deadly symbiosis: when ghetto and prison mesh and meet' *Punishment & Society* 3 (1): 95–134.

Walkowitz, J. (1992) *City of Dreadful Delight: Narratives of Sexual Danger in London* London: Virago.

Wallace, P. (1999) *The Psychology of the Internet* Cambridge: Cambridge University Press.

Warner, M. (1994) *Managing Monsters The 1994 Reith Lectures* London: Virago.

Weait, M. (1996) 'Fleshing it out' in Bently, L. and Flynn, L. (eds), *Law and the Senses: Sensational Jurisprudence* London: Pluto.

Webster, D. (1851) 'The murder of Captain Joseph White' in *The Works of Daniel Webster, Volume VI* Boston: Little & Brown.

Welsh, A. (1992) *Strong Representations: Narrative and Circumstantial Evidence in England* Baltimore and London: Johns Hopkins University Press.

West, A. 1989 *For the Love of Lesley* London: W.H. Allen.

Wilkinson, L.R. 1992 'The art of distinction: Proust and the Dreyfus Affair' *Modern Language Notes* 107 (5): 976–99.

Williams, E. (1967/1968) *Beyond Belief: A Chronicle of Murder and Its Detection* London: World Books.

Wilson, E. (1991) *The Sphinx in the City: Urban Life, the Control of Disorder, and Women* London: Virago.

Wilson, E. (2003) *Cinema's Missing Children* London: Wallflower Press.

Wilson, R. (1986) *Devil's Disciples* London: Express Newspapers.

Wilson, R. (1988) *Return to Hell* London: Javelin.

Wilson, S. (1973) 'The anti-semitic riots of 1898 in France' *Historical Journal* 16 (4): 789–806.

Wirth, L. (1927) 'The ghetto' *American Journal of Sociology* 33(1): 57–71.

Wirth, L. (1931) 'Culture conflict and misconduct' *Social Forces* 6: 484–91.

Wirth, L. (1938) 'Urbanism as a way of life' *American Journal of Sociology* 44(1): 1–24.

Young, A. (1996) 'The Bulger case and the trauma of the visible' in *Imagining Crime: Textual Outlaws and Criminal Conversations* London: Sage.

Young, A. (2000) 'Aesthetic vertigo and the jurisprudence of disgust' *Law and Critique* 11: 241–65.

Zangwill, Israel (1892) *Children of the Ghetto. A Study of a Peculiar People* Detroit, MI: Wayne State University Press.

Zola, E. (1898/1996) 'Letter to M. Félix Fauré, President of the Republic' in Pagès, A. (ed.), *The Dreyfus Affair. 'J'Accuse' and Other Writings* New Haven, CT: Yale University Press.

Zorbaugh, H. (1926/1971) 'The rooming house population' in *The Urban Community* Chicago: University of Chicago Press.

Zorbaugh, Harvey W. (1929) *The Gold Coast and the Slum: A Sociological Study of Chicago's Near North Side* Chicago: University of Chicago Press.

Index

eBooks – at www.eBookstore.tandf.co.uk

A library at your fingertips!

eBooks are electronic versions of printed books. You can store them on your PC/laptop or browse them online.

They have advantages for anyone needing rapid access to a wide variety of published, copyright information.

eBooks can help your research by enabling you to bookmark chapters, annotate text and use instant searches to find specific words or phrases. Several eBook files would fit on even a small laptop or PDA.

NEW: Save money by eSubscribing: cheap, online access to any eBook for as long as you need it.

Annual subscription packages

We now offer special low-cost bulk subscriptions to packages of eBooks in certain subject areas. These are available to libraries or to individuals.

For more information please contact webmaster.ebooks@tandf.co.uk

We're continually developing the eBook concept, so keep up to date by visiting the website.

www.eBookstore.tandf.co.uk